THE HEALING OF LIA

THE HEALING OF LIA

Winfred O. Ward, M.D.
& Lia Farrelli

Macmillan Publishing Co., Inc.
New York

TO G.

Lia

TO ANNE M.

W.O.W.

*Macmillan Publishing Co., Inc.
866 Third Avenue, New York, N.Y. 10022
Collier Macmillan Canada, Ltd.*

*Library of Congress Cataloging in Publication Data
Ward, Winfred O.
  The healing of Lia.
    1. Farrelli, Lia. 2. Mentally ill—United
States—Biography. 3. Hypnotism—Therapeutic use
—Case studies. I. Farrelli, Lia. II. Title.
RC464.F37W37   616.89′09   81-14264
ISBN 0-02-623880-2   AACR2*

Designed by Jack Meserole

10 9 8 7 6 5 4 3 2 1

Printed in the United States of America

Acknowledgments

During the past four years while we have worked on this book, many people have offered their encouragement and at times their sympathies. We wish to thank all of our friends who helped in less obvious ways but let us know they cared. Betty Jenkins is an efficient secretary-assistant who typed and retyped the manuscript, seemingly always with a deadline on the horizon, always smiling and only rarely saying, "Oh, God, here we go again." We are grateful to Nanci Crookshanks and Robin Reynolds, who typed and extended their workloads to cover the needs of the project. Anne Ward provided a sense of patience, encouragement, sharp criticism, constructive suggestions; typed the original manuscript; and served innumerable pots of tea during the work sessions. We owe a debt of gratitude to Patricia Williams, an objective, knowledgeable lady, who read the manuscript and made valuable suggestions. George Turner aided us repeatedly with copy production. Our editor, Ilka Shore Cooper, made our work a pleasure. We could never sufficiently thank Mel Berger, our agent, who was willing to persist and never lost faith in us or in the project.

Prologue

I have been told that this book could not be written. People who should know have told me this, and at one time I would have listened. But not now, not anymore. The day I found the journal, everything changed.

I have always kept a journal of the happenings in my life and my thoughts about them. But this journal had been carefully hidden, and it contained the thoughts of a Lia Farrelli I hadn't known existed.

When I found the journal, I had only shortly before begun to undergo new psychotherapy under the care of Dr. Winfred O. Ward, a physician and hypnoanalyst. After a lifetime of emotional illness I had begun to hope. I had heard of Dr. Ward and his unusual approach to analysis through the use of hypnosis, and even though he was located in Richmond, and that meant a drive of several hours, I had an inner faith that in his care I would be helped.

I found the hidden journal on one of my "well" days and although some of the dates were as recent as only the week before, I had no memory whatever of writing it. It was my journal, as the contents proved, but the writer was a Lia Farrelli I knew nothing of, and the reading of it explained many things.

Twelve years before I had voluntarily committed myself to a mental hospital for the first time and had been diagnosed as a depressive. At the time I felt this was the end of everything for me. In a way it was, but not in the way one might think. Reading the journal in a random way, I could see that it spanned many years and had no orderly composition. Because of missing dates on many of the papers, I judged that it had been begun sometime during the period when I suffered my first breakdown and had severe memory lapses because of electroconvulsive shock treatments. I had been assured that the memory loss would be temporary (six weeks to a few months) and that the effects of the treatments were not damaging in any way. That had been fully twelve years ago and my memory was (and still is) full of holes. Now, since I have found the journal I have learned much about those years and what took place before and since.

The found journal was not in book form. There were only loose pages, over one hundred of them, some written in neat, precise script, others in erratic, bold scrawls. No one would have thought that the same hand had written it all. A number of the entries were incoherent and unclear; many were cruel; almost all were introspective. It seemed at first simply a compendium of thoughts, each page signed Lia, the writer telling in graphic detail a story—the story of my life, my illness, my torment. But she told it in strange words that I did not remember writing. Clearly she felt pain, too, and she was not afraid to tell much of what I should never have recorded. I began to understand that somewhere within me existed another Lia. So I hid the journal from everyone—even Dr. Ward.

The writing of this book has been extremely hard for me, for in order to tell of the illness I must relive it. At times I have had to walk away from the work, so strong has been my fear of remembering. And the further I come away from the illness, the harder it is for me to reenter the aura in which I lived, which I *must* do in order to tell of it. A year from now I most probably would not attempt to begin the book. It must be done now, for to me it is unconscionable to hide an experience from which others may learn and benefit. I do not mind in the least my therapy records, my weaknesses, my private writings, being made public. I *do* mind that there are wards and hospitals full of suffering people who, because of public ignorance, apathy, or shame, are kept drugged and stunned while their caretakers argue about which method is best (or worst). Each of these humans, living on the outer fringe of sanity, is myself, save for the grace of God. Perhaps we are not very attractive people during this time, and certainly not very lovable. But we deserve better than to be hidden, shamed, drugged, and shunted about like pieces on a chessboard. I spent forty-four years seeking the one

Prologue

person who would heal me. I find this a sad testimony in such an enlightened day.

This book is a personal one which touches many lives. As I do not want to hurt those whose lives touched mine, I have chosen to use a pseudonym for myself and also for everyone mentioned in this book (with the exception of Dr. Ward) and have altered all places and events or details that might identify anything or anyone, whether living or dead. In preparing the book Dr. Ward and I decided to occasionally let the journal entries speak for us. We present them just as we found them, believing that cleaning them up would destroy the integrity of the meanings.

One prime concern we had in presenting the book was the fear that the nature of the material might mistakenly be thought of by some as depressing. But long ago we came to the conclusion that first, this is not a "story" at all, it is an accounting, and second, rather than depressing, it is actually a very hopeful accounting. But to reach any sort of ending one must first endure the telling. This is an accounting of a human being no one really saw or listened to. Not family, friends, doctors, priests. No one. That is why the telling is so very important to us. They must be told; they must *know*, so that a thing like this may be unlikely to happen again.

It has occurred to me during this writing that if they do read it, the family, the friends, the doctors, the priests, that they may not agree with it. They may say: "Now, Lia! Surely such-and-such was not that bad!" And if so, this will happen because they don't want it to be true. There is a phrase, *vera pro gratis* (loosely translated to mean "True things instead of pleasant things"), which fits the way the journal saw it all. In the light of truth; not truth prettied up by gossamer camouflage, but truth laid bare as we humans seldom like to see it.

This book is not written as an indictment or as a criticism of the medical community. Admittedly, at the inception of this work I wanted to strike out at my medical caretakers and many others. I wanted nothing more than to hurt those who had hurt me. I no longer feel this way; I have learned much in Dr. Ward's hands. It is not our intent to make judgments, and while my opinions may shock many and my medical history may be doubted, fact is fact and truth remains the greatest weapon when coupled with the written word.

Much of this truth is not pleasant, and many times I have been tempted to turn away from it myself. Following my therapy, it would have been far easier for me to have just left behind me the very words "mental illness." To have put it all behind me, forgotten about it, and gone on with the rebuilding of my life. It would have been easy enough—except for the lantern-slide images of those I left behind, those not lucky enough to have found Dr. Ward.

I am not a brave woman, and the job I have undertaken frightens me. There is always the fear that the world-out-there will laugh at me and ask, "Just who does she think she is to try to tell us these things?" I am willing to take that chance because there are things I know that the world-out-there doesn't.

I know what it is to feel fear each time I fill out an application for a job or a license of any kind and must answer the question: "Have you ever at any time suffered from any kind of mental illness?" I know my chances of getting the job or the license are slim, no matter how qualified I am.

I know the necessity of having to fake a medical history in order even to be listened to by a new doctor, the look to expect, the subtle change in attitude if there is a fleeting whiff of history of emotional illness. I know what it is to sit in terrible pain and be considered, not a patient with a probable herniated disc (it was!), but rather a hysterical woman with imagined pain. Why? Because the referral to this doctor came from Dr. Ward and Dr. Ward is a psychiatrist. I have seen the mincemeat made of dedicated people when any past history of psychiatric care is brought forth by the media.

I know that unless there is a complete turnaround in the attitudes of both society and the medical community, no former mental patient will ever walk in this society as a full, completely free member. Almost as though we have not yet had our slave collars hammered from our necks, we drag the links that chained us behind the wall. Our society will accept back into itself anyone who has lost a part of himself—an arm, leg, eye, or more—with one exception: the mind. Ironically, this happens to be the one part that can be restored fully!

Prologue

There is in me still a great deal of anger, which I continue to fight, and angry, cutting words, which I hope to blunt. I believe that there is purpose in everything and, if God intended my illness for the purpose of this telling, it must not be abased. As with many other things, Dr. Ward is probably the only one who knows the terrible guilt I feel, even now, concerning this anger. If it is a sign that I sometimes have the human failing of judging, I pray that time will soften and heal this weakness. Anger is a perfectly normal emotion when held within limits, but with me it was not. During my illness often it was the *only* emotion I felt. Strangely, it was this negative emotion that frequently saved me from an act of self-destruction. Reaching a nadir, and having no positive strengths in my life, I countered, fighting back with the only strength available to me: anger. It was, as Dr. Ward later said, the flame that kept me alive.

This he and only he recognized. He is, in my mind, right up there on a level with God and the angels. The voice from the other room—teaching, directing, suggesting, cutting out the sickness. Hurting, healing. I gave my mind to him when I had lost my direction. He took it, with all its atavistic properties (how many of his patients, I wonder, have beaten themselves with lead weights?) and returned it to me gently, with the healing begun. What I gave him was sick, distorted, ugly. What he has given me is a beginning, a chance to pick myself up out of the dust of despair, and make a new life. The process was painful, as are all birth processes, and at times I felt I hated him. But I know now that sometime between now and tomorrow, when I discover just who this new "me" is, all will be forgotten.

If there is magic in this thing called hypnosis, it was wrought by his caring warm interest, his firm knowledge and skill. *Nothing* was left to chance. I never knew the whys of what he did, and often the therapy sessions were like being caught in a cage of tigers—without a whip, a chair, or a gun. I was stripped of all the protective ploys I had used so successfully to fool everyone. I don't believe I fooled him for an instant.

Each week after my therapy session I left his office ill, angry, and in tears. I would drive off cursing him with disease, pestilence, death! But each week found me again in the dim, quiet room, listening and learning under hypnosis. And finally after three months came the day that I consider my own personal incarnation. This day a part of me was born and a part of me died. This is really what the book is about: why there was an illness, and why there was a hidden journal, the journal of the other Lias. Suddenly what Dr. Ward had learned during the long weeks of analysis, and what he discovered this day, fused, merged, and became the source for which he had been seeking. The journal held the clues that had for over forty years been hidden behind a wall bonded with the mortar of terror. The weapon he used to break through this wall was hypnosis and the outcome is the reason for this book.

After my breakthrough in therapy, my feet were firmly set on a good path to recovery. Had it not been for an unforeseen happening, I might never have known what Dr. Ward was really like. As it happened I wasn't conscious of him as a "person," as opposed to being a doctor, until some months later when I was told by a surgeon that I faced possible cancer and that he would not perform the surgery until I had talked with Dr. Ward.

The man I finally "met" and really "saw" was not the enemy from the therapy room, but a warm listener with a roguish sense of humor and a mischievous look in his eyes when he laughed. That day I was not angry, not even frightened. But I did need to talk with someone because I was not foolish enough to consider myself fully "healed," though a full six months had passed since my therapy ended.

Indeed, I knew that what I faced then, coupled with the past months of stress, therapy, and physical pain, would have been reason enough to just give in, give up, and let the world go on without me. I could easily have done this! Except for this niggling, nagging doctor who gave hoots of derision when I showed signs of weakness or cowardice. And later, after the surgery, when I wanted to sink tearfully into the sheets and give up the fight, he would have none of it.

"Bullshit, Lia! Don't hand me that stuff!" he chided. "I didn't bring you this far just to give up and lose you to cancer—if it *is* cancer! And we don't know that yet!"

I found that it was not easy to give up the fight with him pushing, pulling, ignoring me when I sniveled that I could not face more surgery, more pain, or more anything. "Oh, yes you *can!*" he said again and again until I began to believe it, too.

When the time came to face this surgery, it was he who implanted in me whatever will I had to fight the unknown thing in me. For twelve years I had been "cared" for by another doctor who had watched me endure one surgery after another, year after year, and that is *all* he did—watch. But on the morning of this surgery, and unknown to me, Dr. Ward took the time and trouble to come into the operating room and stand by me to witness exactly what was being cut from me.

Beyond all else I believe this one act speaks of the caring and attention he gave to me as his patient and as a person. He cared, and it showed in very positive results exactly what such caring can do. It was at this time, during my recovery, that I knew I wanted him to become a part of this book. God knows that without him there might have been no book; even more to the point, without him there might have been no me.

Looking back, I don't know how I came this far. I'm high on the mountain of my years and from here I can see many valleys, rifts, depressions. Few ups, many downs. For a long while I looked for an intellectual answer to why such things as mental illness are permitted to happen. There was none. A deep faith was needed and in my illness I had lost or misplaced mine. I do have two things now that I never before had: first, hope, and secondly, a future. They did not come cheaply. The price I paid was dear. I could never have found them by myself. I was led to them by a wise man, a good man, who knew that pity was no substitute for fulfillment.

Perhaps for a physician, this is the greatest wisdom of all.

Lia

PART ONE

1

It is morning of another day. For a moment I hold my breath and lie very still as I listen for them. The house is quiet except for the dog's tail wagging, making drumming sounds against the washing machine downstairs. Drum, drum, drum.

I know the house is empty because I heard the door slam shut earlier. I had lain very still, listening to the morning sounds of Paul making breakfast for the girls. The clinking of spoons and forks, the whispers of words about me.

"When does she see the new doctor, Dad? Will she be able to get up today?" and the reply, "Tomorrow. And I don't know."

He did not tell them what happened or why.

They never knew that I was awake and listening to them because I had been very quiet, not moving, hardly breathing, hoping they would not open the door and look in. Hoping they would all just eat and collect their books and leave me alone.

They all did just that, even Paul. Not even he looked in to see if I was all right. Or living. Or anything at all. This does not shock me. It merely reaffirms what I have known all along: that I am so much a Nothing to them that whether I am all right or not makes little difference to them. There is no room in their lives, no place in their hearts for, no understanding of the Thing I have become.

Knowing this and thinking about it makes the little jackhammer begin in my head. If only it would stay night, stay dark, then I would be all right. But the noise of the jackhammer wakes up the world and they all join arms and begin to march in a phalanx through my mind. All of my enemies here to chant their words, to jab and jeer, to play their games in my head.

3

. . . Mama is shouting, "Crazy! Crazy just like your Aunt Ava and all the rest of your father's family!"

. . . Paul's mother is sitting close to Paul, patting him gently on the leg and chanting on her rosary beads, "My son, my Paul, my boy, my, *mine*," and then she looks at me and smiles her sweet smile. She knows that I and only I see the look in her eyes. And I look away because it hurts me to breathe.

. . . Uncle Albie is saying to me, "Look at the *size* of those peaches! Planted that tree special for Gina the day she was born!" And I ask, "But where is *my* tree, Albie? Where is the tree for Lia?" But he is so old now and he doesn't hear, and then he is just gone.

. . . Papa doesn't speak. He can't; he is crawling in the dirt in agony. Papa is busy dying.

. . . Joy is bouncing up and down, laughing and singing a clever tune she made up in her own head: "Lia puts out! Lia puts out!" And Aunt Addie claps her hands and begins to sing along in tune.

. . . Aunt Nettie looks with stern disapproval on the lot of them. She tells them all to be still, for she has an important announcement to make. She says imperiously, "I am taking Gina on a trip! I am sending Gina to college! I am giving Gina the world!" and everyone joins in the applause.

. . . Paul is not visible at first. He is behind the bathroom door, which now has a crack in it where the lamp smashed through the wood. He pokes his head out and says to me, "You're nothing but a crazy woman! Just plain crazy!" And then Mama says, "No, she's no woman! She's crawling on the floor like an animal. She's not a woman at all!"

Enemies! My head expands and makes room for all of them to march through and tear at the lining of my brain. When their voices and laughing and hurting begin to spread over my body, I look to the Calm One who sits across the room in a chair and I ask, "Is it all right to do it now?" She replies, "Yes, go ahead, Lia," and begins to rock back and forth in the chair.

As always she is dressed in the clothes that, although they are not mine, hang in my closet behind my own clothes. Bright gypsy colors, dangling earrings that flash in my eyes. I blink and look away.

The Healing of Lia

I get out of the bed slowly because of the purpled bruises and knots of raised tissue on my head. Very, very slowly I crawl across the floor to the small door leading under the eaves of the roof. Opening this, I crawl under into the hot closeness and then shut the door behind me. Safe.

I make my way halfway across the distance of the house and, choosing a supporting beam near where Paul stores the Christmas ornaments, I kneel and rhythmically begin to pound my head against the wood. My hair catches in the splinters and this tears some of my hair out, but it doesn't seem to matter because I can't feel it.

Downstairs the dog is drumming his tail against the washing machine; up under the eaves Lia is pounding her head against a welcoming piece of wood. Drum, drum, *drum*. Pound, pound, *pound*.

And slowly they, all of my enemies, lock arms in a phalanx and march out of my head. As I lie there in the dark secret place, away from the outside world, feeling the warm sweat run down my body and face, the quiet in my mind is the first peace I have known since the last time I had to drive them out.

Was it only last night?

Last night, last week, last year—time is beginning to mean less than nothing because I lose so much of it. For over a year I have been finding myself walking down strange streets or driving in strange sections of town. People seem to know me when I don't know them. And they always seem to be men.

My brain seems sectioned off in some way. The part that says "Cook dinner, wash the clothes, vacuum the carpets" seems to function. The house is running along for the most part, normally. But there is another part directing me in unknown passages and then denying me the knowledge of what has happened to me. I seem to be always running. Running and hiding. But from what, from whom? And sometimes it seems that the Thing I am running from is trapped right here in my own brain. At times I catch glimpses of—what? Then a veil drops again.

The most important part of my brain is the part that tells me all is not well, I *must* get help, see someone, tell someone. The problem is that this knowledge is available only to one part of me. The other part—the part that says, "Don't be a fool! They'll lock you away just as they did me"—is guiding me into the other passages and away from help.

I know I must act quickly and not listen to this voice and a few days ago I did what I never thought I could. A few days ago I lifted the phone, dialed long distance, the area code, and then the number of a new doctor in Richmond. A doctor whose name is Ward. I made the decision quite alone, not telling anyone, even Paul, until the appointment was set firm. But the day I made the call I felt myself strong enough to fight the twisting in my mind. I had not counted on that other section of my mind —the part that knows the dangers of a new doctor, or a new therapy, or a new anything—being stronger still. I lost the battle again last night and knew that I might have lost more than that. I might have lost Paul, too.

The Healing of Lia

2

I met Paul, who was to become my husband, in the early fifties when I was twenty-
one years old and was recovering from the
painful reality of a broken engagement. A friend called and asked
me to double date with her on a Saturday evening. I had been
sick with a case of flu, looked like the wrath of God, and had ten
good reasons for refusing. I didn't, mainly because I have never
been able to say no firmly to anyone.

My date was Paul Farrelli, who stood well over six feet tall,
slim, handsome, darkly Italian, and who possessed the most
beautiful hands I have yet to see on a man. Grandmother would
have loved the hands ("Only peasants have stubby fingers. Long
fingers are a sign of breeding!") I remember being quite en-
thralled by his long, tapering fingers.

Even though I was Catholic myself, I had never before dated
a Catholic, nor was I familiar with the social clubs they fre-
quented. We went to the Knights of Columbus center and there
I met many young people who were very friendly, warm, and
who all had a great affection for Paul. Some of the girls were
familiar to me, having been schoolmates of mine at St. Martha's.
Surprisingly, they were friendly and quite different than they
had seemed only a few years back. With Paul, I seemed somehow
to be acceptable.

I have never been a stranger in any crowd, and as the evening
went on I found that I was having a wonderful time. Paul was
very, very quiet, stunned, perhaps, by this stranger who chat-
tered constantly (with anybody, it never mattered to me) and
who wore a flaming red velvet dress and enormous dangling
rhinestones in her ears. Compared with the other, more conser-

vatively (and expensively) dressed girls at the club that night, I stood out like Sadie Thompson. This didn't seem to matter to Paul, and we danced, drank beer, and had a pleasant discussion with a young priest who shared a table with us for a while.

Whatever else that might be said about our courtship, it can never be said that we were in bad company. Each weekend we shared our table with this affable priest who loved everyone in our crowd, which numbered about twenty young people. I remember vividly how impressed I was that they all seemed so relaxed with this gentle man. He laughed and shared our pitchers of beer, sometimes told (slightly) risqué jokes, and gave helpful advice when needed. He loved them all, they loved him—in fact, there was such an ambience of affection that I had a difficult time adjusting at first. After a while I relaxed and tried very hard to fit in with this new setting. And that was exactly it, having to "fit" myself in. I never really felt one *of* them, even though I, too, was a Catholic. There was some subtle difference and, as if I played a part on the stage, I said all the right things, did all the right things, in order to become the person they thought I was.

I wonder now just what would have happened to our relationship if I had told Paul then how recalcitrant I was to the church he loved. And he does love it.

I must accept the full responsibility for presenting a false image of myself to Paul in the very beginning. The truth is that I desperately wanted and tried to fit into the mold of the good Catholic girl/woman/wife. I wanted him badly enough to nearly destroy myself in the doing.

There was from the beginning a powerful physical pulling between the two of us. On my part I can see why: Paul has a classic physique and was a quiet, serious lover. I, on the other hand, had the body of an underdeveloped twelve-year-old and had angles and bones where there should have been curves and soft places. But he did not seem to notice this. I made him laugh, I amused him, and my verbosity did not bother him then as it does now.

Once or twice during the year we courted, I asked Paul to take me to a gathering or a party with my friends. He did, but was quite miserable and did not enjoy himself at all. They were different types from the young people he knew at the center, but to me they were not "weird," as he later described them in anger during an argument; they were simply different. Some of them were admittedly homosexual, some of them overaged perennial students, and some just eggheads. They also did not care for him and cruelly told me so after they met him.

"Marry him, Lia, and you'll dry up. We'll never see you again!"

Now so very much in love with "him," I stormed out of their lives, taking his hand with the belief of never more needing anything or anyone else.

Paul and I never discussed our homes—it somehow didn't seem important. The innocence of youth! I had never felt that I had a family, so there was little to discuss. In Paul's case his family was not a family in the usual sense; it was a matriarchy in the fullest sense of the word. (How often in our marriage I have tearfully screamed, "Your family is not a family! It puts the Mafia to shame!") I soon discovered that one never marries a person, one marries a family, a clan. If you don't jolly well get on with the clan, you are going to have a hard time indeed!

For months Paul had told me about his poor, old, sick mother. The day he finally took me to meet her, I was elated, hoping fervently that she would learn to love me. I had often dreamed of the meeting in which she would draw me close to her and impart a sense of warmth and peace to me. In reality, when the door opened she stood like a stern guardian of her portal, offering no warmth, no embrace, not even a handshake. I was shocked to see that, still in her early fifties, so unlike Paul's description, she was far from being "old."

Through the years I have watched her, first in a hope of being accepted and loved, later with interest and horror in the way she controlled her progeny. My fears of her grew to destructive proportions.

The day of our first meeting I realized that she was uncomfortable in my presence. I, in turn, was disappointed in the way I was received. She referred to all her children using the preface *my*.

"My Greg, my Mara, my Lois, my Paul. . . ." And "my Paul" would ring in my ears forevermore.

I was to discover an atmosphere of familial closeness bonding them, melding them firmly into a unit that was strong beyond belief. But no matter what Paul's family was like, I would have loved him, married him. I thought of him as a saint and felt an unpleasant humility in knowing that I would never be as good as he; never good enough, never good enough. . . .

At home, Mama, not pleased that Paul and I were planning a life together, lay awake each night that we dated, meeting me at the head of the stairs with vitriolic accusations.

"Either marry him and get out or I'll put you out!"

Paul and I would often park in the driveway and smoke a last cigarette while we planned our wedding. Inevitably the porch light would begin flicking on and off—a warning that I must come in.

During this time, a year before my marriage, my health rapidly got worse. I went weekly for hormone therapy which played havoc with my reproductive system. Well below my usual ninety-eight-pound level, I was barely eating. This, because of a very good reason: my mealtimes were the times Mama chose to drill and drum at me, snarling remarks about my thinness.

"*Eat, for heaven's sake!* What man in his right mind would want you, looking like that?"

Like a bête noire, bad health plagued me and six months before my wedding I was told by a surgeon that my "problem" was a fallen uterus. Seeing no way out, I made plans to have the surgery well before the wedding. I had every faith that this surgery was going to solve my troubles. Anything would have been better than the half-life I was living.

Paul and I had taken part in a Cana Retreat for engaged couples and I had been forced to leave the services. He had been very understanding when I told him I must sit in the back of the church on the last pew nearest the exit. He was kind enough not to question my reason. What would I have answered? ("I feel smothered, ill. I have to get *out of here!*")

I would have never admitted my true feelings about the church, knowing that Paul wanted a good Catholic wife. I intended for that wife to be me.

Taking an extended sick leave from my job, I had the surgery. Paul took his vacation, staying with me every minute he was

The Healing of Lia

allowed to do so. It was, for both of us, a happy time. I don't believe he thought of me as sickly then. Little did he (or I) realize the many, many hours he would spend in hospital rooms after our marriage, waiting for me to get "well."

The damage I feel we have suffered could have (and again, *should* have) been avoided if we had made other choices. Religion and the birth control question played havoc with our marriage. We both might well have acted—or reacted—quite differently for the good of our union.

I acted as I did from pure fear of damnation. No other reason would have driven me to accept near destruction. I feel I did fail in one thing concerning this, and that is, I failed to communicate my disgust and rejection to Paul—not disgust or rejection of *him*, but of the rules I felt we should not have followed when the results were so very damaging to my physical well-being.

My choice was to choke back my anger and rigidly follow the dictates of a religion I did not believe in. I did this for two reasons: first, since childhood I had been obedient and docile, consciously trying to please authority figures in the matter of religion; second, I was afraid that if I left the church, Paul would stop loving me or would leave me, thinking that I was not a good person. Obedience had been one of my marriage vows and I suppose I was willing to give up not only my health, but my life, for love of Paul. I very nearly did—many times.

I shall always believe that if we had left this place (and both families and in-laws) that we would have lived life quite differently. I begged for this and Paul refused over and over. He has seen me live in pain and near insanity, witnessed me wanting to take my own life, and still he has said no to this request. He calls it "running away from your problems."

In the end, of course, I did leave the religion that caused so much pain and damage to the one beautiful and good thing in my life, my marriage. If good does come out of all things, it remains for me to find it in this. I do not deny that the good may be there, but I cannot see it yet. I cannot accept the premise that it could *ever* be the will of a loving God for a pregnancy to occur that is, without doubt, medically speaking, an impossibility for the woman to endure. Not in this enlightened day. Perhaps today for some there is a choice. Twenty-three years ago we had

11

no choice. And for the staunch advocates of the rhythm method, my medical advisers could find no way possible for me to use it in my state of malfunction. For me there was no choice.

Paul accepted this with a deep faith. But, and I do not mean this to sound flip or crass, it was *my* body enduring the damage and *my* mind that was affected. He cared deeply and took very good care of me as he does to this day—but it, none of it, should have happened. If I had not been ill, it would *not* have happened, for I should have fought back.

I did eventually leave the church, and none of the terrible things I feared happened. Paul did not leave me (but, and I believe I am correct, he does pray earnestly that I shall one day return), and the world did not end. Perhaps because it was the first definitive decision I ever made without asking permission, I think of it as the beginning of something, not the ending.

I forced, pushed, drove myself to do what people felt was "the right thing," refusing to listen to the warning voice within me that said, "Stop!" What would they all think if I did stop? I was so afraid of "they" and "them" that I broke the commandment that directs, "Thou shalt not kill," because I was committing slow suicide both physically and mentally. I was unable to see that my anger was a healthy symptom of growth. A growth that was to take me forcibly out of the snug harbor of complacency and into the maelstrom of discovery.

After leaving the church I felt like a pilgrim and wondered where the journey would end. I am still alone in this and that is hard, but it is better than being the outcast in the back of the temple.

Paul and I set a summer day as our wedding date. He gave me a lovely pearl set in antique, twisted gold for my finger and we began making plans for the wedding. Well, not actually. I began being *told* what plans we should make, is more to the point.

Still home on my work leave, I wanted only a brief, quiet ceremony, not an "affair," for many reasons. Physically I was not very strong following the surgery. My medical bills had taken most of my meager savings and I did not want to spend what was left on a wedding I obviously couldn't afford. Neither Mama nor

Aunt Nettie offered any financial help for the wedding, no one did, but this did not keep people from telling me what I must have and do in order to be "proper."

I begged Paul to just take me away to some small place, find a priest to quietly marry us (we had all the necessary papers), and begin our life making our own decisions. But this was not to happen.

Paul's sister Mara came to the house one evening and told me how I would always regret not having a white wedding, a reception, lots of people, and both loving families. The more I explained to her how I felt, the more adamant she became.

"There *must* be a mass, Lia! And if you have a mass, you might as well have everything else, too!" (And just who was to pay for this, I wondered?)

That night as we sat there, Mama, Paul, his sister, and I, it became quite clear to me that Paul was saying nothing to help me, and so my hopes for a quiet, small wedding slid into oblivion.

I settled on an early morning wedding because it allowed more informality than a later hour would have. We were married at nine o'clock on a June day, and I wore white organdy and orange blossoms. The church was decorated with myriads of early summer flowers from Aunt Belle's gardens. There was no air conditioning, but cool morning breezes drifted in and stirred the candle flames. Father Jon wore new vestments, and the altar dripped with handmade lace; it was, in truth, a very lovely wedding. Little old neighbor ladies cried, and instead of running to the reception, we stayed a while at church and had an old-fashioned get together. It was altogether lovely.

Paul and I had discussed our future and decided that I should return to work and that he would work part-time and go to college part-time. I wanted so much for him to have the advantage of a fuller education. It would mean living at home for a while, but I believed that now, since I was married, Mama's attitude might change. The house was large and empty, as only my younger sister Dorrie and Mama were home. Gina had been gone since she finished college and Evan had fled at sixteen. Paul and I settled into two rooms and began our marriage.

I see married love as being much like the wings of the butterfly; strong enough to let you soar to unimagined heights, beautiful enough to bring tears to your eyes, and yet so fragile as to fall prey to damage that is irreparable. Paul and I had a deep love in which I immersed my whole being. For twenty-two years I had been crawling around in an emotional desert, now he was my source of life, my oasis. For the first time in my existence, I really wanted to live! I wanted to live to be five years older than the mountains themselves!

Paul did marvelously in college. Mathematically he astonished me. He brought home excellent grades and we both looked forward to his continuing on to obtain his degree. Rather unrealistically, the one thing neither one of us planned on was pregnancy. At the end of his first year I was pregnant and we found that the reins of our lives rather slipped from our grip.

I continued working until, too cumbersome to climb up and down from the high stool at my drawing board, I took maternity leave. Paul called me one day at work and said, "Don't worry, honey, I've just gotten a good job so you can come home and be a mama. We'll worry about college later."

I knew how disappointed he was, but there was no use in discussing it or grieving over it. We began living for "later" at that moment. Today, in our forties, we are still living for it. Perhaps I have a greater share of guilt in this attitude. I made a monolith of education for Paul and later for our children, and daily worshipped it. It is needless to dissemble concerning this point; Paul would have been happy to accept our life as it was given to us, but I was not. I anguished for him to have what became more unattainable as each year passed. The disparity between what we had and what I felt we *should* have had became a barbed sword which went deeper as circumstances developed beyond our control.

The Healing of Lia

3

Our first child, Katie, was born without difficulty by natural childbirth. Paul and I moved into a tiny cottage on Aunt Belle's land and began, for the first time, to feel like real married folks. Katie was a bundle of pink, with unusually dark mysterious eyes and jet black curls, a truly beautiful baby.

Whatever my ignorance of sex, it was diminished by my ignorance of childcare, childbirth, or child anything. I had postpartum depression without understanding what it was, and my doctor was of the opinion that after ten days of languishing, a woman should swing back into the routine of living. Each day I sat by a window in a rocking chair, clutching at my baby and weeping bitterly for hours. I could not have given a reason why, except that my spirit was somehow in pain.

When Paul came home from his job, I would play a pretend game, hiding what my days were beginning to become. If I had understood that what I suffered was something I should have shared with Paul, perhaps life would have been very different. Instead, I felt terrible guilt. I had a handsome, loving husband and a beautiful child—and I was simply unable to function because of a black torment which I felt no one would understand because I did not understand it myself.

When this child of my heart was twelve weeks old I was pregnant again. Why not? What else could we expect? I had been nursing Katie and had had only one scant menstrual period since her birth; finding my fertile time was an impossibility. Paul was a healthy, normal man; life had to be lived, and married love was a part of life.

Without knowing why or when, an intruder came into our

lives at this time and lingered to nearly destroy both of us. Its name was Anger, and like most negative emotions it disguised its ugly face and appeared as something else.

I dismissed my stomach pains, violent headaches, vomiting, and fear, spending hours each day in black moods. Tending Katie and doing my housework became a frantic rush between spasms of pain that butchered my days into periods of disassociation from reality. I was extremely clever about hiding it. No one, least of all Paul, knew how I was living. Emotional illness was something I dared not contemplate. Remembering my Aunt Ava, the insane one, whose blood ran in my veins, I knew that I must *never, never* act differently from others.

I did not do well during this pregnancy and lost weight instead of gaining it—almost as if by staying thin, I could deny the fact that I was pregnant at all.

There was happiness in our little cottage; Paul was devoted to his family and Katie was growing into a healthy, lovely child. Our lives centered on our family. We had by this time stopped seeing most of our friends, and our only outings were walks with the baby or Sundays spent at Paul's mother's house.

Each Sunday Paul's mother had a large spaghetti dinner for all her children and their families, and everyone came bringing playpens, diaper bags, dozens of bottles of baby food, and huge appetites.

Paul's sisters were prolific, healthy, and unperturbed by yearly pregnancies. Babies seemed to drop like manna from heaven every nine months or so. Christening parties, excited midnight phone calls, godchildren! Everyone was happy, family oriented, unquestioning, and dutiful. Everyone except Lia, who was dutiful, full of questions, becoming more and more ill, and very, very angry.

These Sunday visits were terribly painful for me. Seeing Paul's sisters sitting, bellies distended, happily chatting about diaper rashes, the most efficient detergents, more (or less) spice in the spaghetti sauce, Father So-and-So's recent sermon, and how *lucky* they were to have all these children, I felt selfish, guilty, inhuman, and a bad wife to Paul, whom I worshipped. I desperately wanted some beauty in my life, some diversion. No one was in the least interested in the books I was reading, in

The Healing of Lia

discussing anything other than potty training, the changes in the church, or paying the most recent hospital bills. They all seemed to have ceased existing as persons and to have merged into some sort of community breeding society.

Church, Children, Contentment. They had it all. So did I, but I wanted *one more thing* which would have shocked them all (including Paul) and that was Choice. I wanted to have some sort of choice in saying where my life was to take me and that choice was not allowed, was unreachable.

Paul was, I believe, happy. He adored Katie, loved me, and relished being with the burgeoning family group. I melded in with the family but never really became a part of it. In over twenty years of our marriage, I have never been asked by Paul's mother to call her "mother." To solve this I simply never address her directly as anything. This is merely a minor, interesting point, but it is quite embarrassing not to know how to address your mother-in-law.

Paul's feelings for his mother run deep, as they do for his whole family. He never saw in the beginning, just as he has difficulty in seeing now, the subtle ways of putting me in my place that this very strong woman uses.

Not long after Katie was born, we spent a holiday having a picnic with the family. Wanting both Paul and Katie to be presentable, I busied myself starching and pressing outfits for them the day before. Paul had several nicely pressed sport shirts in his closet, but his favorite shirt was still in the basket unironed. The day of the picnic was hurried and it was not until we were in Paul's mother's backyard and I was putting Katie in her playpen that I noticed the favorite (still unpressed) shirt which Paul had draped over a lawn chair.

Slightly miffed that he would bring a rumpled shirt on an outing when he had clothes that were more presentable, I gave no more thought to it until about an hour later when my mother-in-law disappeared with the offending shirt and reappeared some time later, with the shirt expertly pressed by Mother Farrelli! I felt humiliated that she would make an issue of such a thing, that what she was telling me, and the whole family present, was "If *you* won't see that Paul's shirts are properly pressed, *mother* will!"

I was hurt by her cruelty, and angry with Paul for putting me in such a vulnerable position. As not a word transpired during the incident, I could not bring myself to draw the subject out into the open, and so I just took the slap silently (a thing I have done for twenty years), keeping the hurt to myself. When, later at home, I tried to tell Paul that he had made me appear an inept and neglectful wife, he merely laughed and said I was imagining things.

This rather set the pattern for my relationship with Mrs. Farrelli, she jabbing cleverly when no one was looking and no one ever noticing the jabs except me.

In truth, Paul worked hard to be a good husband and father, just as I did to be a good wife and mother. Had there been a better element of communication between us, our life would have been quite different. He did not understand my feelings about our marriage, about my troubled anger in following the dictates of a church from which I felt alienated, about my questions concerning the rightness of pregnancies I felt unready for. But how was I to discuss or question subjects that he accepted as God's will?

To force these issues, as I tried to do in later years with disastrous results, only separated us further. He felt all along, as he still does, that sooner or later I would "see the light," that my problems would go away.

They did not, and the issue of religion and the damage that it has done to us is still very alive. We do not discuss it, but nevertheless it lies like a slimy monster beneath the surface of clear waters. Attempts to put the issue to rest merely stir up the waters, getting us nowhere. Our convictions are diametrically opposed.

Kara, our second child, a gift with golden curls, was born with great difficulty and we brought her home, very sick and thin. Because my milk would not flow as easily and abundantly as it had with Katie, Kara was bottle-fed. But she did not adjust to this artificial method and was a nervous, fitful sleeper who cried night and day as if she had not been welcomed.

I grieved over this, felt it my fault (as I still do) and imposed still more guilt on myself.

There never seemed to be enough time to sit and rock this child as I had Katie. She was born before Katie's first birthday

The Healing of Lia

and it was all I could do to keep up with an energetic toddler and a sickly infant. The symptoms of depression remained, growing gradually worse until they controlled my life. I began to have a fear of leaving the house, never knowing when I would be bent double in pain.

Our tiny cottage, with its one bedroom, became ridiculously crowded with the two cribs we had not planned on fitted into a corner. While most of our friends lived in comfortable apartments, we had made the choice to live Spartanly in order to save for a future without mortgages and debts. The choice was clearly ours, made mutually with good intentions. But these intentions suffered as my health failed, children were born, and troubles we had not expected entered our lives.

Fear became a leading factor in my life. It could happen anytime, anywhere; often, pushing my grocery cart down the aisle, my vision would black out. Sweat would pour down my arms, legs, and body. My clothes would stick to me, soaked through, and still the sweat would pour. Violently nauseated, my only impulse would be to get home. The safety of home.

Doctor after doctor told me the same thing: it was perfectly normal to be a little depressed after childbirth. Each X ray showed a fine, healthy stomach, a stomach that caused me to retch all day, rejected all but the simplest food, and caused me pain I cannot describe. What little food I retained caused chronic diarrhea and my weight loss was severe. Headaches became frequent and I began to see images superimposed on images. Even without the pain I felt "one-sided" and a feeling of diminishing reality swam in my head.

These were the lean years most every couple experiences; there was no automatic washer, no drier, no vacuum cleaner, no telephone, and no one who seemed to give a damn.

Paul, concerned with making a living and saving for our future, was tired when he came home, and I don't think that he even noticed how ragged my edges had become—but then, I was very expert in playing my game of pretend. I didn't want him to know how bad I felt, as I thought it would show that I was failing in my job. His sisters flourished with their growing families and I was ashamed that I was not doing the same.

Then the day came. A normal day except for what I can only

describe as a blackness that shrouded my mind. It was deathly cold, nearly Christmas. The kerosene heater refused to work properly and though I had dressed the babies in layer after layer of clothing, their tiny feet were cold. Both children whined and cried, but the baby simply would not stop.

I checked and rechecked her, heated bottles, walked her, rocked her, and ran out of ideas. By three o'clock my head was pounding, my vision was distorted, and each scream pierced my head like a physical wound. Even in that cold room the sweat beaded between my breasts and ran in a stream to my waistband, which was soaked.

I put Kara on our bed, sat beside her, and talked to her like a demented person, begging her to stop crying. Still she screamed.

Day, night, all the same scream, scream, scream! A blackness covered my mind, and the pain, which was so much a part of me, joined with it. I reached out both hands for her with one comforting thought in mind: please, God *make* her be still! Make her be quiet!

I felt so tired, was so afraid, but there was nobody to talk to. I rocked Kara for what seemed so long, and still she screamed and screamed. Then I sat in the rocker and it was as though my body was paralyzed. I could not move at all, and I hurt all over.

They had taught us in the hospital nursery to gently run babies under a warm stream of water to quiet and comfort them, and as I sat there crying, I saw someone take the baby to the kitchen sink and begin to run the water. She's going to help me, I thought, but then I saw that instead of gently running a warm stream over Kara's little body, she was running it over her head . . . and then her face . . . and I couldn't move, couldn't even scream. I just sat there watching her choke my baby until she did stop crying.

I felt as if I were not sitting in the rocker, but that I was a part of the rocker, a part of the wood. I was wood! Just a dead, inanimate piece of wood. And then I heard a sound, not even like a human sound, and I grabbed my baby and hugged her, dripping and sobbing.

It was later. The cold December air in the cottage was rent with screams, my screams. I sat on the bed and writhed like a person possessed. My own vomit stained the front of my clothes

The Healing of Lia

and my baby lay on the counterpane cooing and playing with her fingers. I looked at the clock. Two hours. Somehow I had lost two hours in that black, sick hell of an afternoon. Frantically I ran to see if Katie was safe, and I cleaned myself, fed the children, but I could not fix supper for Paul when he came home.

I never told. I never told of the blackness that day or any other. I was so afraid that they would take me away from my home, from Paul and my children.

To keep a tight rein on my actions I wrote notes to myself, checklists, to be sure the children had been fed, diapered, bathed. I had to, as I could not remember doing these things sometimes. That horrible day, as I watched someone else try to hurt my baby I knew I must watch carefully and be sure she never again had that chance.

After that time I lived in a prison, a prison with walls of guilt. What had happened on that afternoon? Had I wanted to kill my own baby? Was it all just a horrible dream?

I loved Paul so, worshipped my children, but lived in horror of another pregnancy. Lord, give me just a year to get well, please, I prayed, as my universe began to creak and wobble.

It would be grossly unfair to imply that there was never a happy time in our home. With two chubby children playing on the floor and a healthy, cheerful husband, I had many things to lift my spirits. There were days when things seemed almost normal—happy days.

Paul was an excellent handyman and he worked hard to make the cottage attractive. By now we were totally family oriented and he seemed to have no desire for outside friends or interests. Our social life was limited to taking the children to play with their little cousins. Life was busy and we had a goal in sight which, if things went well, would be reached in a year or two. Our marriage was firm, our commitment to each other deep. Perhaps even more important, Paul and I had a powerful physical relationship.

Paul is, to my mind, all the things that make a person good: kind, gentle, devout. He has steadfastly retained these qualities during our marriage. The anomaly of the situation is that the last attribute is the one that has cost us more grief than is to be

21

imagined. Again, I must admit this is purely because the Lia I am and the Lia he thought me to be were never one and the same.

Paul loves his church and lives sternly by its rules without questions. He will suffer pain, poverty, illness, and, I believe, even martyrdom for his faith. But it was not my chosen faith, and I found that in a united situation I was doing things that harmed my body in order to comply with the rules of an unyielding Entity I had no belief in, and I was doing this because I loved my husband. In this, what I felt was right opposed what Paul felt was right.

During this time in my marriage, I was told that a girl who attended St. Martha's with me died. She was only in her thirties and she died giving birth to her eighth child.

Marta had been a fragile, thin girl in high school, and I wondered how she ever managed to have eight children. I was told that after the seventh child her doctor firmly told both Marta and John that she could bear no more children, that she must be operated on. He told them in words that could not be mistaken: "If Marta continues on like this, she will be dead within a year." But both Marta and John rebelled when told this.

"God would never permit us peace if we lived in mortal sin," they said.

Marta carried the baby full term and died while giving him life. And they all, John, Marta's family, everyone who spoke of it, seemed to think that Marta had sacrificed her young life willingly, and they thought it very beautiful. I didn't see anything beautiful in it. I saw only a great waste and eight motherless children.

I think what Marta did to herself, and what John did to her, is beyond my comprehension. It frightened me because I could see myself in Marta's place one day . . . and what would Paul say? What would he do? But more than that, what would I do?

After the day of fear, I have little recollection for a time. I do know that the children thrived and were cared for. I know that we lived very close to the bone in all respects.

This began the first of five long years when we saw no movies, attended no parties, and completely lost contact with every friend either of us had. Paul had his job and he worked himself to exhaustion to reach his goal.

I did my work, moved like an automaton in the blackness, and lived like a starving person. I felt starved—lonely, cut away, and starved. My books had been cut from the budget as an extravagance, so my mind moldered. The theater, ballet, my precious museum membership, were all gone. Everything that in the beginning had made me an interesting person to Paul was now expendable. He was thinking in terms of concrete, brick, lumber, while I ached for—what? Only all of it. Everything. Something crept into my being now that was a far more ugly curse than the sickness or the blackness or the pain. It was bitterness. I was only twenty-five years old and I carried this curse like a leper, hidden, unacceptable, and most certainly fatal to the spirit.

Over the years Paul and I have tried to talk this out. He says, and truthfully so, that I agreed to do without for a few years in order that we might accomplish our goal of a mortgageless, debtless future. And I did. But "doing without" meant one thing in our inexperienced young minds and quite another thing in the cruel realities of our passing years. We both had known that sooner or later we would have a family, but unplanned pregnancies destroy the best laid plans. And unless you do *something* about unplanned pregnancies, they are apt to continue. Of course, this subject was a stalemate, and a small wall of discord began to build in my mind concerning the intimate relationship we had enjoyed.

Again, I found myself keeping this to myself. I wanted nothing to interfere with the closeness Paul and I had in that respect.

I was naive enough to believe that if you denied an anger, pushed it away into the dark corners of your mind, that it would very likely go away. I know now how very young and wrong I was. It did not go away; it festered into a malignant sore that ate nearly to total destruction the lovely, blessed, and healing thing we had so long ago. In the beginning of our marriage it would have been impossible for us to comprehend the deep hurt and injury we would one day inflict on each other. It is merciful, indeed, that we humans are unable to foresee our futures.

Paul was a tender, gentle husband and lover. We were happy, there is no doubt of that in my mind—but my happiness was unlike his; it was a conscious happiness. Neither of us realized that old injuries, coupled with present confusions, were causing a lack of balance in my mind. I looked like everyone else, acted like everyone else, but I certainly did not *feel* like everyone else. As for thinking like everyone else, that again was something I kept deeply hidden.

I wanted only to please, only that. I devoted my existence to making myself into the wife Paul wanted, sublimating every wish or desire I might have. I began to lose parts of myself, to deny that Lia even was.

I had begged God for a year, but when eleven months were up I was pregnant. I didn't panic; I fought for acceptance of this new life, spending much time "counting my blessings," trying to shame myself out of the depression. There were days when this was possible. But there were other days when, as I stood washing the dishes, tears dripped into the pan, unbidden and frightening. We were a rather typical young Catholic family, quickly out-breeding our financial ability. Hope for college for Paul or for me began to become a distant dream. Hopes that had kept me going were slipping away and I could see no possible way to regain any sort of control at this time.

My cousin Joy would often remark that Paul and I did not need birth control but rather self-control. This was typical of the advice and understanding we received from family or our religious advisers. To a young couple marriage means sexual union. And this in turn means children if a pattern or rhythm for ovulation cannot be determined. My doctors shook their heads and offered condoms, jellies, sprays, diaphragms, pills, none of which could be used unless we wanted to condemn ourselves and our souls for eternity in the eyes of the church. Pray, we were told. And we did—but we were young, and we loved each other. . . .

This third pregnancy was a particularly demanding one and I was violently sick for four full months. My eyebrows dropped out until my face was a bald, expressionless mask, my normally thick curly hair suddenly hanging in straight strings and growing thinner each day. I looked at myself and realized fully the word

The Healing of Lia

to describe myself: ugly. I had eyes to see and what I saw was ugly.

Paul was wonderful. He laughed at ugly and called me beautiful; he loved me enough not to care what I looked like. But I cared, I cared very much. Mama had long ago instilled certain criteria in our minds for judging people and good looks were highly placed on that list.

Mama and Aunt Belle had a grand time laughing, wondering how a well-built, handsome boy like Paul could possibly see anything in me.

One day Paul and I took a walk, and as we passed Aunt Belle's house we heard them laughing in the parlor. Later, in cruel detail, I was told how impossible the two of us appeared: Paul, large and broad shouldered, deeply tanned, Lia, thin (skinny was the word used), fragile, pale.

"How I could ever have had a child like you is quite beyond me!" was Mama's standard comment, dispensed with shaking of her head and a small smile.

I had little confidence as a desirable, functioning woman. Mama and Aunt Belle had done their jobs well.

I have no memory whatever of ever being held, rocked, cuddled, or shown any display of love by my mother. She simply never, except of necessity, ever touched me. She sewed all our clothes and when she "fitted" me, she jerked and snatched at the material as if in disgust at being in contact with my body. Never smoothing the fabric or patting me—it was all jerk, pull, snatch.

Mama was born in 1898 and was two years older than Papa. If she had lived longer, she would probably have been an amusing, feisty old woman to some. To those of us who survived living with her, she was not so amusing. Mama would have been, if born another decade or two later, quite attractive; she was very small-boned and slender, almost thin. But in 1898 the beauties were all plump (fat, really), dimpled of knee and ample of bosom. Now, Addie, Mama's baby sister, was all of those things. Addie had a chubby face, chipmunk cheeks, a pug nose, and a happy disposition (indeed, why not?). She had everything the virile male found desirable, while Mama had the family nose (quite noble, but a beak, nonetheless), a thin body, no breasts at all, and a sour disposition (again, why not?). Mama despised her sister out of pure envy, and hurt. There is no doubt that she had her pain. Many years later, when I was nearly grown, Mama told me how very homely and unattractive she had felt next to her sister. Addie was the family cutie pie and all the local boys who courted Mama ended up as admirers of Addie.

After a period of driving all the locals loco, Addie decided to marry Norm, who had a flourishing business and who slipped on her fat fingers large diamonds he repossessed from unfortunate debtors. He bought, furnished, and paid cash for a cute bunga-

The Healing of Lia

low, and Addie settled down to the life of the city matron who had everything to start with and no way to go but up.

Mama married Papa, who was not well, had a limited education, came from a family of eccentrics, and worked "with his hands" (a point of shame in Mama's eyes). Her envy of Addie and of practically everyone else grew through the years.

Addie produced one son and a daughter, Joy, who later proved to be my nemesis, during the same years when Mama produced the four of us. "Us" being my older sister, Regina (Gina to everyone), who was destined to become the darling of the family, my brother Evan, and Dorrie, the baby . . . oh, yes, and me.

Gina looked for all the world like Mama, family nose and all. And here I came, three years later, bearing Aunt Addie's chipmunk cheeks, pug nose (and later, her strange ability for attracting beaux). Mama was not pleased.

From the very beginning of my life I was the typical second child. Secondhand toys, clothes, baby books, the works! Gina, who had a head full of tight little blond ringlets, took dancing from the age of four and was always dressed like Shirley Temple. My curls were longer, I sucked my thumb for comfort, and ended up with protruding front teeth. Gina tapped and sparkled her way through childhood, while I sat sucking my thumb in the sandbox and got worms.

Evan was perhaps the most beautiful baby brother anyone ever had. I have a picture of him at four, sitting on a pony, laughing. He had thick black lashes and dancing happy eyes.

Dorrie, the baby, seems a dim memory of a dimpled darling in ruffly little playsuits who smiled all the time and bothered no one.

Our happy family. . . .

Well, not quite. There was also Aunt Nettie, who believed that God wanted her to practice charity in the home, and did just that. Because she lived in our home, she chose one child, Gina, and gave her all the advantages that money could buy. Throughout our childhood Evan, Dorrie, and I somehow accepted this as quite right and natural.

There were Aunt Belle and Uncle Carley who legally managed to manipulate Grandmother's farmland out of everyone's hands and into their own, leaving us, as Papa's heirs, in virtual penury.

And Albie, the uncle who loved all of us children equally, but who found the time to plant a tree in special honor of only one: Gina.

There were many others, too. Relatives who touched our young lives in one way or another. But none who touched us in ways as painful as these.

My memories of Papa are so misted; it's almost as if he had never been at all. He worked himself quite literally to death for all of us. I have no memory of ever having a Christmas, Easter, or any other holiday with Papa home. He worked to get the double-time pay to give us the music and dancing lessons he insisted we have in order to be cultured. He loved us; of this I am sure.

I was not yet eighteen when Papa died and I have only a dim remembrance of him as a gentle, kindly, loving man. I only heard him raise his voice once in my lifetime; one winter morning before light, I heard him shout and sob to my mother, "For God's sake let me die in *peace! I* have never lived in it!"

I can remember vividly so many of Papa's "men" coming to the house after he died. Most of them large, burly laborers, all black men, and they stood in small groups with tears running down their faces . . . tears for Papa. It was not false sympathy; they were crying because they loved him. Everybody who knew him loved him. Except Mama. She never looked beneath the surface; she saw only his poor hands which were never to come completely clean, his thin body, and incorrect English. We were not very old before we knew that Mama was ashamed of Papa. We knew it, he knew it, and she let most of the world know it by humiliating him in public.

I remember clearly and with hatred the few Sundays in my life that Papa could attend mass with us. It was special, so wonderful, or could have been except for Mama. There was a ritual we had to follow: first she made him park our old car two blocks down and one block to the right—even in pouring rain or snow. This was because she was ashamed for Papa to drive where "people" could see us getting out of the old car. We walked the three blocks regardless of the weather and Papa never said anything.

The Healing of Lia

After we got into the church, Papa, who was really a deeply devout man, always knelt, folded his hands, and bowed his head. This further incensed Mama because try as he did to scrub away the embedded grime of years of labor, his hands would not come completely clean. It was in his pores forever, but she would not accept this and so she would elbow him sharply, give him a scathing, humiliating look, and indicate that he was to lower his hands to where "people" could not see them. He did. She diminished him as a person, a provider, and as a man, and he never gave an angry reply or an argument. What she did to me, I could forgive, but I believed Mama killed Papa, and for that I had hated her.

We lived for a while in the old gray farmhouse where Papa grew up with his brothers and sister. Papa's family, in retrospect, seem only a sad collection of people who should never have had to live together. Uncle Albie and Papa were the only ones who had the ability to love. All the others can be described by one word: haters. They hated each other and spent their entire lives venting this terrible emotion in unspeakable ways.

Tragedy and eccentricities seemed to blight them all. Aunt Ava, the only daughter, had been confined in the state mental hospital after her attempt to kill Grandmother with a butcher knife while she slept. Apart from Papa, who was a good and loving man, the rest of the family was cursed by an inability to adjust to the outside world. They left this world after each working day and came home to sit in dark seclusion and hatch their various plots against each other. The two years we lived in Grandmother's house were when I learned my earliest lessons in how to hate—and I learned well. In the evenings they all sat silently thinking, seldom speaking. I also was silent during this time, but for another reason. I could not speak without stuttering badly and it had been decided that the proper cure was to ignore whatever I said unless I could say it without stuttering. Of course, I couldn't, so I stopped speaking at all. I was only ten years old and I had no friends, only my books—and words. Words, written words, became my toys, my comfort, my joy.

Papa insisted that we all be educated in Catholic schools. I remember these years as being ones of misery and fear, and I recall being "expelled" twice during the third grade, both times for reasons I could not understand. That intelligent adults allowed normal childhood incidents to grow so outrageously out of proportion caused Dr. Ward to remark years later, "Lia, this was ridiculous! I'd laugh if I didn't feel sick just reading about it!" And I agreed. It had made me sick, too, but in a different way.

One amazing thing about the family was their ability to look past me, over me, or around me. But never *at* me.

At fourteen it was discovered that I had a blood disorder that, if I had been male, might have been termed hemophilia. This was found when I had my first wisdom tooth, which was impacted, cut out. Chiseled out, really; the dentist used mallet and chisel and the procedure took four hours to accomplish. I spent the next week at home hemorrhaging badly. Mama, who hated to bother the dentist, decided that if I hung my head over the side of the bed, I could bleed into a receptacle and not damage the bedding. After the week passed, I was taken, more dead than alive, to the hospital emergency room. I was in the operating room twice in the next few days and finally, because there was nothing left to sew but pulp, they gave up trying to close the wound. After twenty-two days of bleeding (I had transfusions in both arms for days at a time), my blood clotted and I was released. This ordeal was repeated for the remaining three wisdom teeth except that they were better prepared for it each time. At the end of it all, the physical and emotional drain on me was more than evident. I had the last operation the year I graduated from high school and by then I weighed 97 pounds after a full meal.

Teen years are notoriously bittersweet, and mine were without a doubt more bitter than sweet. I wore braces on my teeth, had eyeglasses, and was thin and angular, a far cry from the standard beauty in those days! I attended St. Martha's, a private convent school, with about seventy-five other girls, including my cousin Joy (the familiar nemesis). Because I was sick so often and missed much basic learning, I spent most of my time trying to catch up with my class—and with Joy. I did not excel in anything. Joy did, and Mama never ceased letting me know this.

Joy was devout, she made straight A's, she was healthy, pretty, a credit to her family, the nuns, the church, and the world. This familiar litany, recited to me for the better part of

The Healing of Lia

my life, let me know that I fell short of the mark in every way. I didn't understand why Mama was pitting me against my cousin. Perhaps it was because when she looked in my face she didn't see me at all. Perhaps because she saw instead the visage of her sister Addie.

During the terrible years at St. Martha's when I was fourteen and fifteen (and school became for me as Buchenwald later became to the Jews), I had a more limited social life at school than away because I did not have the advantage of attending the proper cotillions (little white gloves, organdy dresses, curtseys), as my classmates had. I did attend some of the dances, but clothes were most definitely a problem, so for the most part I was left out of St. Martha's happy happenings.

Outside of school was a different thing. Our community had a large center where each weekend all the neighbors, young and old, gathered for square dances. I was lucky enough to have one or two boyfriends and it was a rare weekend when I was not invited out. We had professional musicians and "figure callers" and on Friday and Saturday nights we dropped our Bach and Mozart and went country!

Clothes again were a problem, but with dogged determination I sat at Mama's old treadle machine and made the proper dirndl skirt, three petticoats with ruffles, and a peasant blouse. And off I went, feet a-tapping!

Papa tried to keep me in Catholic school, but I grew to hate St. Martha's so, that in my third year I simply shut my books and began to bring home failing marks on my report cards. Religion has played an inexorable part in this illness. I don't know why. But it is a simple fact that took me nearly into insanity before I realized how bitter I felt about being trapped in a religion that I had not chosen and did not believe in—not even from earliest childhood when I was, as every child is, expected to march in time. I did as I was told, but never, never without an inward fight and terrible damage to myself. I wanted to believe! But if faith is a gift, perhaps I was not given this particular gift for a reason only God understands.

Papa, seeing how unhappy I was, relented and enrolled me in the nearby county school. It was the loveliest gift he could have given me.

My first day in a public school! A day to remember!

That morning in homeroom the principal came into the room. I was on my feet in a flash (all students in Catholic schools stand and sometimes curtsey when a teacher enters a room), but no one else stood. I stood alone, with my face burning, while everyone laughed and snickered. Mr. Rhoan, seeing (and understanding), drew up his face in anger and shouted for quiet. Thereupon, he gave the class a lecture in manners, deportment, and courtesy to elders. He then asked me to come to his office with him. He was a very small man in stature, but very large in compassion, and we became fast friends that day. For a short while my name was anathema to my classmates, but in time the kids gave me a second chance to act like an "ordinary" kid and I was off and running! There were many poor children in county schools, so no one tried to outdress or outdo anyone. I relaxed and did better emotionally than I had ever before. This was my sixteenth year, and I remember it as being one of the happiest times of my young life. I was again an A student, president of my class, on the student government council, and official go-between for reaching Mr. Rhoan's private ear.

Without realizing why, I was living in a totally unbalanced world: at school I was bright, accomplished, given responsibility beyond most of the other students. But after three o'clock, like Cinderella, I returned to the ashes of being less than a human should ever be—I always had to go home.

The Healing of Lia

5

My last two years in high school were strange years of anomalies. It was through my friends that I met an unusual old gentleman who played an odd part in shaping my future. I was at this time dating the brother of a classmate, who, while being much too old for me, was also a professional musician. I found myself being thrown into a world I was not ready for, and the person who helped me maintain my stability was an Englishman named Quinten LeRoy. Quint was a surgeon who had been relieved of his license to practice medicine in his country. He came here and built an enormous Tudor home in the country. He was quite elderly when I first met him (at least I felt so then—he was in his late sixties), and he had the patience of Job where we young people were concerned. He opened his home to us, welcomed us at ungodly hours, waited up all night on the evenings of dances and proms for us to come and tell him all the lovely things we did and felt. He was the grandfather I never had.

Quint rather adopted my girl friend Alice and myself. He'd sit by his fireplace and listen to every dull, boring detail of what we had done each day in school and with endless patience he gave us the best and most thought-provoking advice I have had, either before or since. His inability to practice medicine was merely a flea on his back. He read widely, built homes for the rich (he was also an architect), and instilled in us a love of fine books, music, poetry, and ethics. Every teenager should have a Quint in his or her life. Mine certainly would have been lacking without him.

At this point in my life the thing I sought so desperately flowed into it: love. But I soon realized that the having of it could be equally as painful as the lacking of it. I embraced this new

33

sadness and all the beauty I almost experienced, gladly. There should be an anthem sung to the young who survive youth! Childhood *is* hell, make no mistake about it. It was so new to me, this simple, primordial emotion. The pain was awful, but faced with the choice of losing it (as inevitably I did), it was worth it! All of it!

I believe that Quint saw in me a child of enigmas, a curious, ragged, waiting little stone in the rough. Somehow, I think, it rather became a challenge to polish that stone a bit. Alice, my friend, and I used to sit in awe for hours while he discussed poetry, music, religion—and rebellion. (I was never very good at being a rebel and disappointed Quint, but for a certainty, Alice made up for my lack.)

In the face of propriety, Quint called on Mama, who had begun to have grave worries because I no longer came home after school each day but went directly to Quint's house with Alice. I need not have worried. Quint, effusive with the old country charm (his accent alone was enough to throw Mama completely off-balance), won her over and thereby gained a seventeen-year-old protégée.

It was under Quint's tutelage that I found, like a fortune in a shoe box, a wealth of capacity in myself. He impressed on me to look beneath the clothes I wore and use the lovely gifts that Papa had given me. Years of classical music lessons on the piano, lessons in ballroom dancing, and appreciation of the written word, training in forensics. From the time we had been old enough not to squirm in our seats Papa and Aunt Nettie had seen that Gina and I had season tickets to every ballet, concert, and recital at our local center. It was all there, all the beauty of refinement, but there had been no one to share it with, no one to guide me, and now this lovely old gentleman took my hand and led me into a world beyond belief! A world of the mind, where there was no one to laugh at me for being "different."

Without a doubt, eyebrows were raised about Quint's obsession with and power over Alice and me. Being quite wealthy, and liking to have things his own way, Quint made things worse by buying a car, which Alice drove home at the end of each day, simply because he got tired of us having a problem getting rides to his home. It was in a very secluded area, and he would sit

The Healing of Lia

impatiently waiting for us while we begged rides from anyone at school who would take us. Finally, one day he said "Enough!" and marched out, bought a new Ford, thrust the keys into Alice's eager little hand, and thereby solved his problem and ours. Papa was aghast with shock, but when he saw how very much it meant to me, he calmed down and never said anything more about the car. When, in later years after my marriage, I told Paul about the "Quinten years," he laughed and said, "Face it, Lia, you and Alice had a genuine old sugar daddy!" Perhaps he was right, in essence, but not in intent. Quinten certainly "sweetened" those years for me, but he was an honorable old gentleman, with the mind of Schweitzer and the soul of an anarchist. An evening with him, sitting beside his fire and listening to him, was the equivalent of an evening with Bernstein, Gandhi, and Karl Marx. Two years ago Paul and I went to Quinten's funeral, and his coffin was closed so that I could not see his face. But as I stood by the bier, I could hear his wicked little laughter, remember all the wonderful (and often forbidden adventures) we had together, and I found myself smiling as if we shared some enormous secret together, even after death. It was as if he were still saying, "Tell me, Lia! Tell me all that happened . . . about school, about your new poem, about that boy in Georgia—what was his name now? . . ."

After my graduation Quint was not very pleased with my unhappy attitude and so one day he called on Mama and told her he wanted to give Alice and me a gift from him: two glorious weeks in Miami Beach! The only terms Quint dictated were that Mama was to accompany us and that we were to call him every other day to tell him what we had seen and done. We had the most outlandishly extravagant trip for impoverished people; call him whatever, sugar daddy or old fool—he loved us and we loved him. It was that simple. Every other night Alice and I would sit on the bed in our grand old hotel on the beach and giggle uproariously into the phone with Quint on the other end patiently toting up the bill for everything, except Mama's expenses; she would accept nothing for her trouble which caused Quint to snort in anger.

The second day of our visit Alice and I met two boys from Emory University who lived in Atlanta. Both Alice and I were swiftly introduced to the fact that there was a sizable rift between dating boys of our age in high school and the elegant "sophistication" of these fraternity brothers, who spoke in the soft tones of an Ashley Wilkes and had seemingly bottomless pockets where money was concerned. With Marc Durand I experienced for the first time the budding feelings of womanhood, which were lovely and yet so very painful. But for this young, Georgia gentleman I might have missed one of the most stirring experiences of my life. For certain, his impact has never left me, and even now in my mid-forties, I can sit on a quintessential day and feel all the pain I felt at seventeen. Words flow into my mind: good, clean, wholesome, sincere; all are apt and fitting to describe him and yet none are really adequate. He had an open freshness that set him apart, then as now.

The night before the boys were to leave for home, Marc invited the three of us to be his guests in Atlanta for the following week. He had phoned ahead for parental permission and his mother had spoken with Mama who was by now in a total state of confusion. Before he left, Marc slipped on my finger an old family ring and asked me to "think about" being pinned until we saw each other again. I taped the ring onto my finger (literally; I did such a good job that it was an effort to cut the damned thing off again), and spent the rest of that week speaking in unfinished sentences and hearing only parts of conversations directed at me.

As the weekend drew near it was Mama who spoke in soft tones over the phone to Quint, who was not too sure he was happy with this new development. Together they decided to let things go ahead naturally, and so on the next Friday, the three of us, Mama, Alice (who had painted her finger and toenails a livid fuchsia for the visit), and I left Miami and headed straight for Atlanta and to the greatest heartbreak I had yet experienced.

Marc Durand is, of course, a pseudonym. His real name is a historical one; he was the descendant of a very famous personage. He had, I found to my dismay, a dragon for a mother and a tycoon for a father, and Marc was most decidedly a pawn of both. We were both too young to know what the cold eye of adults can do to young lovers. However late we were in finding out, I doubt that either of us forgot our lesson.

The Healing of Lia

When we arrived in the city of Atlanta, we went to the hotel where Marc had reserved a suite for us. Later, at dinnertime, a limousine called for us and we were driving to the "house" where we were expected for the meal.

But is was not a house, it was a mansion, a white, monstrous, pillared Georgia mansion, complete with portico under which we drove and were assisted out of the car by the liveried and dignified black man. Mama was, for perhaps the first time in her life, totally speechless. I was terrified. How should I act? What should I do? And then Marc ran out to greet us and suddenly the cloud of fright was gone; he was here, everything was going to be fine. I was, of course, quite mistaken, but the young have a way of looking around rather than at reality.

A young, black maid showed me up the stairs to a bathroom to freshen for dinner, and Marc and I spent the time to better advantage, holding each other close in a terrible, aching way, while downstairs the parents were plotting their cruel strategy.

Dinner was unspeakably awful. We sat at a table that was suitable for signing NATO treaties—it could have easily seated thirty—and were served by the maid and their "man." The platters were held in midair by the maid, and I was unsure how to serve myself properly without dropping the food in my lap. I began to feel oddly out of place. Marc chatted on, laughing, amusing both our mothers and his father until the dreadful meal was over and we could leave for the dance at the university, leaving the parents alone.

After the dance we drove to the top of a hill and sat holding each other in the time-honored way of all doomed lovers, and it was a wondrous feeling. We were both so good, so in love, and so very, very young.

We stayed in Atlanta a week and Marc grew more and more haggard each day as the time grew near for our departure. On our last evening he took me to the country club and while a band played and we danced by candle and starlight he asked me to wear his pin until he graduated in two years and we could marry. And I, never doubting, never fearing, sat smiling through tears while he pinned the little thing on my breast. I felt totally safe. Loved and safe.

We left for home the next morning, early, without seeing

either Marc or his family. When we arrived home, Quint was noticeably unhappy; Mama was strangely silent. Nothing for me was ever to be quite the same and I learned in one searing moment just how treacherous adults can be.

Marc wrote daily, as did I. Awful, hurting, longing, young love letters. And then he began asking, "Why don't you answer? Are you angry?" Frantic, I'd post a reply and receive another, "Please write! I love you!" Until it seeped into my mind that someone was keeping my letters from Marc. I told Mama I wanted to phone him. And then she told me of the deception.

Marc's father owned two cotton mills and a machine plant to run the mills. He was a millionaire many times over. They all knew, *decided* is a better word, that I would never "fit" into the Durand family. I was poor, uncultured, uneducated, and worse still—a Catholic. They quite plainly told my mama the very first night that they did not want to "hurt" me, they only wanted me out of Marc's life. Mama tried, I know now just how hard she tried, to discourage the affair from the beginning. But I didn't know why. And so, she—and they—let it go on until we left, but had no intention of it going further.

"Mrs. Alexandre, you see, of course, how we could never permit Marc to marry Lia! Not a Catholic! Surely you see that?" asked Mrs. Durand (withholding the implied, "poor, unacceptable nobody," for propriety's sake). Hearing Mama recount what had been said, I hated them all. Dear God! How I hated them all.

I never went to Quint's house again. I never saw my friend Alice again. I cut my whole life out in a big section, and since they were a part of it I cut them out, too. In the fall I began studies at City College with a determination to cultivate myself so that no human being could ever, ever look down on me again. That year in college I coldly cultivated friendships with wealthy boys. I went for a while with a deposed Latvian prince whose name was not only unpronounceable, it was unspellable. I just called him "Prince," and we went everywhere together—most of the time with my not knowing what the devil he was even talking about. It didn't seem to matter, not to him, certainly not to me. He had flaming red hair and the most ungodly accent I had ever

The Healing of Lia

heard, and best of all, he had the entrée into a society I was determined to crash with a white-hot anger.

I lived and breathed for my studies. Learning! Every pore of my body was open and waiting. Lia was learning all the lovely things Gina had learned! And the year sped by with impossible swiftness. And then it was June, and then July. And my poor, sick Papa died, taking with him a part of me, a part of my life.

The remembrance of Atlanta has been for me the most painful memory to stir up and dig out from the dark places. It is not that I still grieve for a too-young love that might have been, but because it was decided for us; that offends my sense of justice. Given the time and opportunity we, Marc and I, might have seen the implausibility of our position for ourselves. We were both intelligent young people, not in the least headstrong or wild. Probably, as with many youthful loves, the separation and distractions of college would have dimmed the relationship, and we might have ended just very good friends, not lovers at all. I would feel privileged to have been even a friend to Marc; he was an exemplary young person.

Marc has most probably forgotten long ago the tall, tanned, thin girl in the two-piece Jantzen; I will always remember him as something almost esoteric, nonpareil, and I cry, not for the loss of a great love, but for what I cannot put into words. Something I almost had, and lost forever.

I was not a rebel (this much I learned from the Quinten years), and neither was Marc. I always obeyed; he always obeyed. And we stayed true to the mold, obedient to authority. Like marionettes, we had our strings pulled into a position and firmly knotted to prevent our changing positions again. . . .

I seemed, after that, to change, paradoxically, from the wispy gypsy moth of a girl into a rather different creature. I dressed oddly, altered my appearance cosmetically as much as possible, and affected bizarre behavior in an even more bizarre group of people. I took that young face and painted it, put streaks of platinum through my long, dark hair, and for the next four years I ran, drove, pushed, that person from girlhood into womanhood, using all the guile, craft, and cold maneuvers possible, without deciphering in the least the outcome of what I was doing to her. The scales almost tipped out of balance many times, my only erotic zone seemed to be in my mind; from here I derived my pleasures, my releases. My mind was me; perhaps that is why it became my enemy.

I stepped up onto a berserk carousel that went Faster! Faster! while it played the nursery tune: *I'm nobody! Who are you? Are you nobody, too?*

Sometimes people stepped on the carousel and rode with me, but they soon got off, or I pushed them off. It was, after all, my carousel! It moved all the time and went all sorts of marvelous places. It twinkled with mirrors, all of them different; some concave, some convex, some tinted lovely colors, some crazed and cracked. Wherever you looked you saw a different face reflected. But, as with all things, it slowed, and finally stopped altogether, except in my mind, and once again *They* beat the cadence and I marched in time. This is where you will go. That is what you must do. March in time! And I always did as I was told.

Often when I cannot sleep at night, I can hear the tinkling tune tiptoeing through the darkness, see the lights, blinking, flashing on the mirrors in my mind. You can never be seventeen again, but in the mind is a door leading outward . . . and inward; you have but to find the warp and walk through.

I got a job for the summer after Papa's death, and even though no one had mentioned my future, I believed that Aunt Nettie surely would help me as she had helped Gina. I obtained a very interesting job working as an engineering draftsman and I loved every minute of each week. I translated the rough sketches and figures of field engineers into concise and usable schematics and worked on a drawing board in an office with ten other girls who were also working their way through college. In August I silently waited for someone to mention my return to school, and when I could wait no longer, I asked and was told that my salary was needed at home to help support Evan and Dorrie. Aunt Nettie said nothing.

At the end of each week I kept back only enough money for bus fare and milk at lunch—the rest went into the house. I bought no clothes to speak of and sewed what I needed for the times I went out. I never had but one presentable pair of shoes at a time; there simply was not the money to spare.

The Healing of Lia

Gina had left home and had an apartment in town and a good job, but to my knowledge she sent no money home at all. I am sure now that my small salary did not play a big part in keeping the family together, but nevertheless, since no one said they would help me return to school, I spent the next year holding my breath and waiting. And then, one day, Aunt Nettie and Mama had a terrible fight and Aunt Nettie left. Now, I knew. There was no way back to school until Evan and Dorrie were older and settled. I put school somewhere in the back of my mind and the terrible need to learn burned out any pleasure I might have had when I reached the age of eighteen.

I remember that year, and my social life, as a parade of young, bland faces, none of whom meant a thing to me. I worked like a mad person, determined to "better" myself. I joined discussion groups, reading seminars, and a course in public speaking. I finally got an artist's membership in our fine arts museum. I stuffed every grain, every husk of learning I could obtain into my head. And I waited, and I hoped.

No matter that I was now a working person and contributing to the household in my small way, Mama was still very much in control of my life. Surely she was very lonely now with Gina gone and Papa gone, but she did not turn to me for either company or comfort. I was at this time under the care of an internist who gave me drugs to soothe the pains in my stomach and violent headaches, but from whom I hid the nightmare existence I lived at home.

I remember how afraid I was of Mama. Even when I was almost grown I was so afraid of her anger. I remember a date I had with Corry, a young friend, who, even after two years of dating, had never once tried to kiss me. This night we had come home, parked in our driveway, and Corry was listening to a championship fight on the car radio. The fight was almost over but as I knew what was in store for me if I didn't immediately get out of the car (Aunt Belle watching on one side, Mama on the other), I suggested that we go in.

"In a minute, Lia, it's almost over," said Corry. I was too humiliated to tell him what would happen to me if we continued sitting in the dark car, even in my own driveway. I was nineteen, and Corry would have most probably laughed and thought I was joking had I said, "I'm afraid of my mother."

We sat until the fight ended and then Corry took me to the door.

It happened as it always happened, the screams of "You whore! Trash!" Words that echoed in my ears. And afterward as I lay in bed I felt that Mama also lay awake on the other side of the wall—hating me.

Afraid. Fear. These words are not wholly able to express what I felt then. Or later. I was never able, during childhood, adolescence, or later in maturity, to tell any physician or psychiatrist exactly *how* afraid I have always been. It is rather like going to a doctor and trying to describe a pain. They become impatient with you. "What sort of pain? Sharp? Dull? Intense? How does it hurt?" And you want to say "*All* of them! Sharp, yes! Dull, yes! Intense, yes!" and because there is no way possible to tell another being how this thing is affecting you, after a while, you do not try anymore. I gave up any hope of being understood quite early in my childhood and let my body tell the story for me; I just stayed sick, or half-sick, all the time. Each year I had a series of colds during the winter months, and eventually I would give up the fight and a simple infection would drift into pleurisy and pneumonia. Lying in bed, week after week, I'd sink into a cocoon of burning fevers and delirium which was my way of reaching into a dark, safe place, the peace of oblivion. Somehow when I was sick, all the pain and fear went away.

During one terrible siege our old family G.P. had diagnosed my illness as spinal meningitis, and I had lain, unable to move my legs, on burning sheets for six days and six nights, not knowing when the light of day became darkness, not caring. And then I awoke to find Papa kneeling beside my bed. I had not been lucid for an eternity, but I was then, and after that my fever broke and I always knew that Papa had made me well again. He was not the sort of person to whom God would say no.

Now it was the year of my maturation, the turning into a full-blown adult. My twenty-first year. Thanks to my museum membership, when my birthday arrived so did the beautifully engraved invitation to the governor's ball at our annual festival. My best friend, Lynn, and I would sew madly each time we

The Healing of Lia

needed a dress for such events. Aunt Nettie often let me borrow her fur cape, and with the determination of the young, Lynn and I would boldly walk into reception lines at the member's entrance along with all the splendidly garbed people who seemed not to notice just how out of place we looked. I can't imagine how we ever managed, as Lynn was as impoverished as I, but we did. In the five years I worked I drew more pleasure from these often outlandish events than anything else. We haunted thrift shops and the Salvation Army store for unusual (dear heaven, I'll say!) bargains, such as shawls with beaded fringes and grungy but sparkling bags to carry. We must have blinded the eyes of many a dignitary. What I lacked in social graces, I tried to compensate for in being a good listener and in keeping quiet and learning. I can remember standing in line to shake the hand of some notable while wearing disgracefully ragged evening slippers (cast off by a relative), the borrowed fur cape, and my most prized possessions, spanking white elbow-length gloves. Besides concealing cold, clammy, nervous hands, they always, I felt, gave me the look of a lady!

This year after the arrival of the invitation, Lynn and I began spending our lunch hours scrounging around for exactly the "right" gowns to wear. We had been chosen to act as hostesses for two young fraternity men from the state of Utah. For this event I put together an outfit with a gold lamé top from one gown and, from the bottom of another, a pale green skirt with bustle and a peekaboo of lace at the hem. Sprinkled lavishly over this were tiny pink rosebuds. That not being astonishing enough, I wore my waist-long hair sprinkled with sparkle dust, gold eye shadow (when no one else dared, I did), and carried a long gold cigarette holder for the "effect." I really presented quite a picture (a sight, actually!) but having no shame whatever about my appearance, I was ready to spend an enjoyable evening. My unsuspecting young date, Randy Weekes, was speechless. Literally.

The ball was a huge success and every day for the three weeks he spent in the city, Randy met me at work for lunch and again for dinner. I don't believe he had ever dated a girl who wore gold eye shadow before, and he spent a good deal of time looking quizzically at my eyes. The day before he was to leave for the

43

trip back to Utah, Randy hung his little heart-shaped pin on my blouse and promised to return at Christmas.

Randy did come back at Christmas, but he did not arrive alone; he carried in his pocket a lovely diamond engagement ring. I was totally unprepared for this, very embarrassed, and so not knowing what to do, I let him put it on my finger, thus becoming engaged to a boy I hardly knew. Mama was delighted. Probably because Randy's father owned one of the most prosperous cattle ranches in his area in Utah. He came from a Mormon family of hard workers; they all, including Randy, worked their ranch—and he had the hardened hands to show for it. Randy's rearing had been austere. Although his family was quite wealthy in cattle, he had had little pleasure to show for this wealth. I suppose, in a way, I appealed to him, all 98 pounds of me, because being thin and wispy (he spent a good deal of time trying to fatten me up before his mother caught sight of me), it brought out very strongly how very huge and masculine he was. Randy must have weighed 250 pounds before eating. But he was kind, and very gentle, and he stayed with us for over a week before he had to go back to classes at the university. When Randy did leave, I was quite fond of him. He had written me daily and promised to continue doing so. He also did one more thing. He brought up the subject of his being Mormon and my being Catholic. He assured me that he was willing and happy to be married before a priest and raise our family in the church. He did so without my ever mentioning it to him at all. He was really a lovely, generous person.

I thought I could learn to love him, and when the letter came each day, I found that he was working late into each night to earn money so we would not have to depend on his family or mine. (He didn't know how funny this last statement struck me.)

I felt that my troubles were over. Mama was, for the first time in my life, happy with me. I badly wanted to help her and make life easier for her, and in my mind, marrying Randy would be the best thing I could do. But, unknown to me, things were happening out in Utah. Randy's family, finding out that his intended was Catholic, did something totally unsuspected. His father and mother put him out of the house, out of the family business, out on the street. I believe it came about when they discovered the promise he had made to me. They caused him to withdraw from the university, cut off his support, and would not let him return until he had broken with "That *Catholic!*"

I learned of all this by way of a horrible and vitriolic letter from his mother, who accused me of everything except the sinking of the *Lusitania*. Randy left, went off on a drinking spree (Mormons don't drink, and he was ill), and he enlisted in the army and was sent away to training camp. He called me only once—cried his heart out long distance—and I never heard his voice again. His last words over the phone were "Lia, why did I have to be a Mormon . . . and you a Catholic?"

We might have had a good life, given a chance, but we weren't given it. The next day at 6:30 A.M. a florist delivered three dozen red roses which I dumped on my bed and sat in the midst of, and I cried, not because of a lost love, but because I had lost a chance to alter the course of my life because of a religion I had never believed in at all.

6

So little time had actually passed since
that broken engagement to Randy, the meeting of Paul, and our marriage to this point.
Now I was pregnant for the third time.

The waiting time passed and my health improved until I
really looked forward to the birth of our new child. The delivery
did not go well and I was eighteen hours in hard labor, finally
being given drugs to speed the contractions. It seemed that
though I consciously welcomed this child, my body did everything it could to delay and prevent the birth.

Our lives, following the birth of Lori, our third daughter,
seemed to begin a slow, constant downhill course.

The physical implications of maintaining a family of five persons in a three-room cottage, with only the bare rudiments of
necessities and few comforts, began to pull at me badly. There
was no breathing room, no way possible for Paul and me to have
a few quiet minutes alone at any time. Babies were everywhere!
Our marriage seemed hung in a time warp and we neglected to
remember that we, too, needed certain attentions. At this time
our physical closeness began (at least to me) to mean only a
danger of another pregnancy, and a certain attitude of fear
embedded itself. Not fear of Paul; fear that I was not capable of
coping with another pregnancy. I *knew* this at this point. He did
not, and again I avoided discussion of such an intimate thing for
fear of losing the love we had.

I know now that I was wrong, because what had begun as
only a symptom, gradually progressed into a full-fledged illness.
Even this, I refused to recognize.

One primary reason why this illness flourished was because

The Healing of Lia

my way of dealing with it was to seek spiritual advice from every source available—and they all seemed to agree: birth control was mortal sin, the practice of it showing a lack of proper faith in God's mercy and grace, the desire for it showing a selfishness in not wanting every gift of life that Paul and I might be blessed in creating through our married love.

I knew for a certainty after Lori's birth that something was very wrong. I also knew a few other things: first, that I did not want to be a Catholic anymore (if, indeed, I had ever been one). Second, that I was not happy with my life as it was because of this religion that ruled our lives and that Paul loved and believed in. Third, that I was now too ill to do anything about it.

I also knew that something was very wrong in the way Paul's mother was affecting our marriage. Paul did not, and refused to recognize trouble when it came in our door.

The trouble came and I didn't know how to fight it.

Paul's brother, Greg, bought a car which he could not afford. Indeed, it was a far better car than Paul drove.

Paul's mother contacted Paul asking for money to make a payment on Greg's car. Until this moment Paul and I discussed every cent that left our pockets, never spending money unknown to the other. In our desk we kept an orderly file of budget envelopes which assured us that we could meet our obligations. Neither ever removed a dollar unless it was absolutely necessary—until now.

Paul took the money from our envelopes labeled doctor, food, milkman, insurance, and gave it to his mother without any word to me.

Later he shouted, "Lia, why are you upset? It's only a loan! Why are you so unreasonable!"

"Unreasonable! Why in God's name couldn't one of you consider mentioning this to me? I live on our budget, too! Your mother might have had the decency to have asked me, too!"

I found it hard to believe that he had given the money without discussing it and this stung, not the amount or when it would be returned.

"It's *not* the money, Paul! It's that none of you considered my feelings as your wife!"

Later Paul's sister Mara remarked in a rebuff, "Lia, you have to learn that Paul works for the money. It's *his* money, not *yours*. And he has a right to give what he chooses to his family."

His family. Even with three children, I was not considered as part of his family in their eyes. After this episode Paul and I were never able to talk about things. We argued, but we could no longer talk.

Enemies began to queue up in my mind after the episode of the money. I never felt safe after this. Now I felt—*knew*—that if his family made demands on him he would respond, and he might do so again without talking it over with me.

I was terribly money conscious, obsessively so. It was not that I was fearful of neglect or of hunger, but I had lost the security of feeling that, as his wife, I was the most important person in his life. I felt that I should be (and he assured me that I was), but I never believed it after this point. Whatever security other wives have to sustain them in times of hardship was lost completely. We had gone without things together, deprived ourselves together, always together. Now I felt that I was not important enough to consider, that I really counted for nothing. I blamed his mother, yes, but I blamed Paul also, and hated myself for doing it.

That afternoon I sat wooden and ill in the rocker for hours. Then, packing a small bag, I took the children across the road to Mama, telling her only that I was going away for a few days. I had no idea where, but I took the remaining money from the envelopes without caring what happened when the bills came due, and I called a taxi. For two days I stayed in a motel outside the city, not eating, not sleeping, encased in some sort of covering of pure fear.

Paul, his mother—the eternal twosome. Not Paul and Lia, but Paul and his mother. I hated her because I felt she was destroying the only love and security I had ever known.

Finally I called home and told Mama where I was. Paul came to me, and sitting on the bed across from me (I did not want to be touched), he promised that if I would come home, he would "straighten out" his mother, his sisters, and his family as a whole. He promised and I believed him. But he never kept his promise.

The Healing of Lia

After Lori's coming, we knew we could not remain in the cottage much longer. Ready or not, Paul made plans to break ground and have the footings poured for our house.

For months we had planned our home, and using the kitchen table in lieu of a drawing board, I drew the plans between diaper changes and bottle feedings, using the T square and the angles while Katie and Kara hung on to my legs. On Thanksgiving Paul was working up to his knees in mud digging out the footings, while I waited for him to finish and come home to his celebration dinner. Waited. This word has a special meaning because it formed the basis for our existence for many years to come. We always seemed to be waiting, waiting. . . .

For over a year I had been losing parts of my days. Just that, losing hours and hours, coming "awake" again as if I came back from some distant place where no one else had ever been. I seemed to exist in an envelope of misery and fear. Something was happening to me and I could tell no one. If I did, they would send me away. I knew this beyond a doubt. So I lived, hid it, and let it grow.

Building a house alone is a job to make a giant quake, but Paul undertook it willingly. I helped where I could, carrying tools, moving brick, holding Sheetrock to be nailed in place. I measured and marked, cursing myself for not being stronger as I watched Paul hoisting beams on his shoulders which left behind raw flesh. He lifted, pushed, pulled, and alternately froze and scorched in the seasons that passed, as he drove himself building a home for us.

When Lori was a few months old, I felt exhausted and carried a constant low-grade temperature. Blood appeared when I voided. My face was now marred by the appearance of some disgusting-looking and painful pustules that would not heal and were multiplying. I cried, looking at my complexion in the mirror each day, as they spread, grew angrier, and began causing scars. Dr. Randolph, my family physician, seemed not at all concerned, diagnosed simply cystitis, prescribed drugs, and dismissed me. Dismissed me to begin a journey that would end eighteen years later in Dr. Ward's office.

We lived in close touch with both families, and Mama kept me abreast of the glorious happenings, particularly of my cousin

Joy's courtship and engagement. Mama's attitude about Joy's approaching wedding was one of excitement, interest, and romantic illusion. Joy had the wedding that I had wanted: in a tiny chapel at a private mass, with only the family present. There were no objections or comments that she must have a white dress, an expensive reception in order to be "proper."

Most certainly at this time there were many happy moments in our home. We spent our spare time poring over books of house interiors and booklets for do-it-yourselfers, and working hard on the house. We had happy holidays playing Santa and Easter bunny, and I began reserving at least one evening a week for Paul and myself.

After putting the children to sleep for the night we would have a special dinner on a card table in the living room, complete with my wedding linens, candlelight, and wine. This was our time for each other and provided a nutriment we needed in this time of hardship. Our joinings were based on a deep love and need of each other. It is to my discredit that I allowed fear and illness to erode this lovely unity. I knew that to fight would mean not only the church, not only Paul, but my own dogged inability to stand up to everyone and say, "No! *I do not accept this!*" I began to feel myself weak, hypocritical, and manipulated—and most assuredly alone. My rebellion was scandalous for a Catholic; even I was scandalized.

Some weeks after my visit to Dr. Randolph the infections grew worse. My temperature climbed and my face was now a mass of sores, large draining lesions. Each week Dr. Randolph liberally dosed me and chortled that an old married lady with three kids should be troubled by "bride's disorder."

With ribald humor he said, "Honey, direct him toward the *rear!* That's the whole trouble, *misdirection!*"

I tried. In fact I tried everything humanly possible and physically practical, "directing" Paul everywhere except out the back door. Concerning this advice, Dr. Ward remarked that in my entire medical history this was, perhaps, one of the few correct things ever told me. Still, it did not help.

The pain only got worse and the burning urge to void, coupled with the inability to do so, caused me to become irritable with the children, with Paul, and with everything else.

The Healing of Lia

More serious, on my next visit, Dr. Randolph sat facing me and said, "Lia, your womb has fallen. It's pressing on the bladder and it calls for surgery now." He hinted at some sort of complications I did not understand and then said, "It would be useless to lie to you, Lia. You just can't have any more pregnancies. I could not let this be done unless you also have a tubal ligation.

"Go home and talk it over with Paul. But I am sternly warning you, don't put this off. Do it now, tonight."

Paul took me to get the opinions of two other doctors, surgeons. Each agreed with Dr. Randolph's opinion and each stated that he would not allow his hands to be tied with my moral problems.

"You have my sympathy, Mrs. Farrelli, but you are a lady who should not have another baby. You are not well, not strongly built. And you must resolve this in your mind. Speak with your pastor; surely you will have no problem."

Paul was horrified. Sterilization was a worse sin than contraception. We ran from doctor to doctor, from priest to priest, hoping for some magic cure or permission for the surgery. But since none of the doctors had warned of impending death and the issue was not an immediate death threat, no priest would give permission.

"Lia, my dear child, doctors are not God! They may be incorrect in this! I cannot advise you to let them mutilate your body by this surgery. You may be capable of bearing many more little ones with no damage at all! Let them repair the womb . . . but I cannot give permission to sterilize you."

I looked to Paul to take command, make the decision, as I was now too ill to think. Each day I was losing ground and I wanted him to say, "The heck with rules. You need help and I am going to see that you get it!" When he suggested more opinions, I felt a small wedge of anger but did not express it.

During the next year I had two miscarriages.

The day I lay in our bed and lost our baby is a day that Paul and I have seldom discussed. Gentle, kind, frightened, he removed the small red blob of tissue, which seemed to be covered in a sort of membrane, and went into the bathroom, closing the door.

I lay, fearful because of the warmth of my own blood which

I felt oozing from me, and listened as he turned on the water tap and, taking a bit of water in his cupped palm, did what every devout Catholic would have done: he baptized the tiny, innocent, unformed body of our lost child.

Whether he named it or used a simple, "I baptize thee, . . ." I have never asked. But he made very sure that the immortal soul was not to wander in limbo, where we had been taught unbaptized babies spent eternity.

When I heard the flushing of the commode, I turned my face from everything because I felt as if a part of myself had been washed away down into dark and unspeakable places. A child; our child.

The second miscarriage could not have happened at a worse time. Paul was working exhausting hours, trying to help me, and holding down two jobs to make ends meet. The day I lost the second baby, he was building a closet.

By now it is easy to understand how he might simply have been sick and tired of having a wife who spent most of her time in doctors' offices, most of the money on medical expenses, and lots of time crying because she didn't know what else to do.

After the worst was over, and I was lying in bed on towels bleeding badly, I told Paul he had better take me to the doctor.

"Lia, I don't think Maggie would mind taking you. I'll keep the children. Go and see if she will drive you. There's really not much I could do, anyway."

I got up, stuffed some diapers in place, and walked the block to my neighbor's house. I felt weak and I was angry with Paul for staying behind hammering on the closet.

I walked the road to Maggie's and a part of my mind and soul entered a black tunnel of despair. The blood seeped down, despite the diapers, and each drip drained me of any hope at all. I had just lost another child and here I was, trudging the road alone, while Paul built a closet! It was almost funny, but the words in my mind were those of Aunt Belle and Mama: when you make your own bed you must lie in it. Don't whine and cry about it. People always get what they deserve!

After this the months dragged on. Finally, in a state of near hysteria and unable to function to do even my necessary work, I told Paul not to worry, that I would take the full responsibility

The Healing of Lia

for the surgery, and I made an appointment to talk with another priest.

Once more I was told that the operation, which again he described as mutilation of the body, was against God's will, against the dictates of the church, and that if I allowed it to happen, I would be living thereafter in mortal sin in the eyes of the church.

Any Catholic can understand my grief and confusion. I drove home weak, ill, and to the point where I could barely think. Doubts nibbled at me concerning the church into which I had been born and baptized and which Paul loved so dearly that he was willing to see me live in illness and pain rather than to disobey. Fair or not, I felt this deeply. Never having been in the least iconoclastic about any institution, from here on I felt revulsion for the church. And fear—I was swallowed up in fear.

I had the surgery which put my womb in place, repositioned the bladder, and sterilized me. I had it without the permission or sanction of the church. At the end Paul had agreed, but left the decision totally up to me. In my mind was a mixture of hope and despair, hope that I would now be healthy and well, despair from dark guilt because even though Paul had agreed, it still was *my* body being mutilated, *my* guilt to do penance for in the eyes of God. In not being able to carry the cross I had been given to carry, I felt that everyone thought I had sought the easy way out. Easy. What a nefarious use of a word.

Recovery was slow because the infections remained as stubborn as ever. The lesions on my face never healed and I hated leaving the house to be seen by others. At the market people glanced at me sideways, out of the corners of their eyes. Acquaintances I might encounter often greeted me with a shriek, "God, Lia, what have you done to your face?"

Done? Did they really believe that I had *done* this to myself? I looked like a leper—there is no other way to describe those running, angry sores.

I have a keen memory of a night I had stood in the bathroom trying to cleanse my face before going to bed. Taking little balls of cotton, I dipped them in alcohol and tried to remove as much of the encrusted infection as possible. The burning of the alcohol caused my eyes to smart and tears to come. But not just the alcohol: the sight of myself.

Paul came into the bathroom to brush his teeth, saw me with reddened eyes, and asked what was the matter.

Like a creature gone mad I screamed, "Look at me, for God's sake! How can you see me and ask what is the matter?"

My anger was shocking to him, as if I blamed him for the condition of my face. I did not. I had terrible guilt about my medical expenses and hesitated suggesting such a thing for myself, so instead of asking if I might see a specialist, I, perhaps unfairly, expected him to take the initiative.

Soon after this I did see someone. The specialist sat in his big office chair for a long while in silence before asking, "Mrs. Farrelli, why have you waited so long?"

Why? There was no way that I could tell this stranger what the past year or so had been like. It beggared description.

He put me on a regimen of X-ray treatments and weekly injections, and slowly the bills began to mount faster and larger than we could manage without scraping. For a while the lesions seemed to respond but when the treatments ceased the flare-up was violent. It had been over a year since it had begun; it would be another five years—and the near loss of my left eye—before the germ was isolated and I would receive an antitoxin. The scars were there, as they still are, and I hate them as much today in middle age when thoughts of beauty are behind me, as I did in my twenties when I hid away from people because I could not bear the look in their eyes.

Lori was two, Kara almost four, and Katie five. They were healthy, lovely children. Only Kara seemed to need assurance and an extra measure of affection. Because of me? I shall never know and that is my punishment. Our Katie, though shy, was happily independent, while baby Lori spent her days chortling in the tiny swing Paul had made for her. Paul and I were fighting time to finish building the house. One night in the cottage bedroom we looked up after making love to find three pairs of innocent eyes staring at us from behind the slats of their little cribs. We had, of course, thought them all sound asleep. We realized now that finished or not, we *had* to move; it was imperative.

The children were not all we were thinking of. We also had

thoughts that for the first time since our marriage we would be out from under the eyes of Aunt Belle and Mama. It rather scandalized both of them that we had had the three children in almost as many years and they spent a good deal of time scrutinizing Paul and me, with us not faring well in the process. There were certain things that were proper and correct and I seemed never to do them.

There was a proper time to get your washing hung (before 9 A.M.), and a proper time to take it down (before 3 P.M.). I tried to nap while the children were sleeping and would often be in a dead, exhausted sleep, awakening past the three o'clock deadline to find my basket of diapers and clothes on the porch. All folded, neatly sorted, and stamped with the silent, implied criticism that while I slept, others were doing my work. When I told my helpmates that I appreciated their help but would rather do my work as my schedule permitted, they were faintly amused. Citing the dangers of becoming lazy and indolent from habitual daytime sleeping—and a belief that after three o'clock some sort of deadly afternoon vapors permeated the baby clothes—they insisted I must not leave my laundry on the line past that time!

We moved into our new house before the heating was installed, with the floors unfinished, and while the insulation still showed in the ceiling joists.

Not long afterward, as Paul and I worked side by side, I noticed an odd ache within me and I began to bleed profusely. I was ashamed to tell Paul, but he noticed when it got more severe and I had trouble moving my right leg. Insisting I see someone, he made an appointment for me with a gynecologist who diagnosed only "dysfunctional bleeding" and began a pattern of popping me in and out of the hospital for D and C's. No sooner would I get on my feet but it would begin again: pain, bleeding.

Mama stayed with the children, indulging them as only a grandmother can, but I really never had any period of recuperation—just in and out of the hospital and back on my feet again.

Trying to ignore circumstances, I worked harder to be like "other people," other young wives who were assets to their husbands. Pleasing Paul became an obsession. He loved an orderly, immaculate home and for things to be done in the old-fashioned way, no hurry-up mixes! I tried to please, priding myself that I

55

did everything from scratch. But this meant a rigid work schedule for me, and often, as weakness pulled at me, I indulged in a pool of self-pity. Days when I should have said, "Sorry, Paul, but we're having frozen dinners tonight," I cooked for hours and then ate in angry silence. I never realized that selfishness is often a necessary part of survival. I should have said no and I didn't.

At times the bleeding would check itself but the pain did not, often staying dimly in the background, more often becoming so severe that I hung on to furniture and gasped. Looking back, I have a greater understanding of what these years were doing to Paul, a healthy, vibrant young man tied to a woman for whom even the natural sex act was becoming impossible.

The infection, years of it, had caused a buildup of scar tissue in the urethra, partially closing it. Dr. Russell, my internist, began weekly treatments to dilate the tube, but any sexual activity, however gentle, caused irritation and a situation where to be a wife to Paul meant only pain and another agonizing dilatation. Each week even the smallest instrument caused tearing of the area and Dr. Russell, the soul of kindness, would say, ". . . only two more to go, Lia. For heaven's sake cry, do something. Don't just hold it in!"

But as he withdrew each bloody instrument I would lie, feet in the stirrups, determined to make no outcry. Some terrible inner anger kept me silent, hating my life, knowing that I would go home and be a useless wife to Paul, or be a good wife and end up back on the table in a few days. My choices were not broad. Neither were Paul's as he lived with me, but knew that to express his love brought only pain.

Prayer became very important to both of us. When we moved into our home, Father Bertran blessed it, praying, dedicating our family to life in the light of the Holy Spirit. Earnestly believing that I could pray away my illnesses, I faced each day with emotional problems I did not recognize and physical problems that staggered me. In my ignorance, and agony, I began not to like God very much anymore.

In the passing months the number of physicians treating me grew from five to twenty-two. At one time in the near future we would be paying four hospital bills at once. Eighteen months passed with the bleeding never stopping, greeting me each morning with a small warm rush that defeated ordinary feminine protection and caused me to resort again to diapers folded in place. The drug prescribed caused nausea, edema, and later, thrombosis in one leg, but it never stopped the bleeding.

One day something else stopped. Knowing nothing of "nervous breakdowns," nerves never entering my thoughts, I stood in the bedroom and felt a slow drip, drip, down my legs and I started to scream like a madwoman. I reached for my prayer cards on the bed table and wildly tore them into little pieces. I tore my rosary from the bedpost, threw it down, grinding it under my heel. Anyone watching would have seen at that moment a person as nearly an animal as a person could be, as nearly mad as a person could be. Screaming, cursing my pain, my wretched body, and finally God himself, I felt the pustules break and the infection run down my face with the tears. Paul called my regular gynecologist and finding him away was referred to another. An hour later I was on the examining table in a strange office, unable to speak or think coherently. Mute with fear, I lay there one hour and forty-five minutes as this man worked to cauterize and stanch the bleeding. At the end of that time he gave up the effort. He, the table covering, the nurse, and I, were in a state beyond description. Reeking with the smell of my own burned flesh, the room was like a charnel house, like an artist's depiction of some early surgical demonstration. It was not, I believe, to his credit that he subjected a semicatatonic woman to such an insult. Recommending another surgeon, he dismissed us saying, "Call me if I can be of any help."

Paul took me home, cold, shaken, ashen. After making me comfortable, he closed the door and began to make muffled phone calls. And on this afternoon he found someone who had an answer.

Two days later I was examined by Dr. Graham who, following the exam, abruptly left the room slaming the door. Slamming it so hard that the latch didn't catch and it ebbed its way open again. I heard him speaking to someone angrily.

". . . Eighteen goddamn months! Those sons of bitches—I don't give a shit, *find* a bed somewhere—yes, now! Today!"

I closed my eyes and almost drifted off to sleep lying on that table, with my bones digging into the hardness and my legs still in that ridiculous position. I felt somehow at peace; out of the blue Paul had found this man who might help me. A godsend. Such an odd word for one who had lost faith in God.

Before seven o'clock the following morning, Dr. Graham removed my uterus which he found to be filled with bleeding tumors, taking away the pain for what I hoped would be forever. There is no way that I can answer for the other respected and highly paid doctors who had put me in and out of the hospitals to perform their little D and C procedures. How anyone could treat a womb filled with tumors and not realize it is beyond my comprehension.

Still the vicious, stubborn infection that had dwelt in my body so long defeated each doctor I consulted. A prominent urologist, following a cystoscopic examination one day, prescribed a new drug and sent me home. An hour after I took the drug I began to convulse. Frantically Paul called for help only to be told that the doctor was unavailable. As I lay on our sofa, semiconscious, he tried to explain the problem to another doctor whom I had never seen, and sometime later I vaguely remember rolling tables, the cold, bright operating room, and the sharp pricking of tubes entering my body. As the infection crept into my kidneys, I drifted, day after day, and it was lovely. I no longer had to worry that I couldn't void, or that it hurt; there were the lovely tubes and drugs. Never giving my children a thought, far removed from rational thinking, I lay on cool sheets and crawled into a secure womb of unconsciousness. I never, never wished to wake. I lay, not drinking, eating, or evacuating voluntarily. Feeling neither love nor hate, only nothingness. When the infection was done with my body, it left me weak beyond telling, with damaged kidneys, and a mind that receded further into the abyss of emotional illness.

I have looked diligently for notes that may have been written during this period. There are none. There was an old letter I must have written to a friend, concerning Paul's mother following my previous surgery. After reading it there was no doubt in my mind just why I pushed myself out of sickbeds.

Christy,
    They have taken out my womb so there won't be any more babies for Paul and me. I don't feel anything—except tired, so tired. I had

The Healing of Lia

bled so long that one day before the surgery I actually fell off the commode. It wasn't funny but I tried to make the children think it was because Katie cried to see me humped over on the floor.

Paul's mother is here to take care of me. Oh, Christy, I couldn't tell this to anyone but you. No one would believe me! My first day home, after Paul left for work, I lay in this damned bed thinking she would bring me something to eat. She fed the kids, sent them off, and went into Katie's room to say her rosary. She never brought me a bite. At noon she warmed up some food, ate, and peered in to me and said, "Lia, there is soup on the stove if you'd like some."

I did manage to feed my own self. When the children came home she sent them to study so that Gran could "Make your daddy something nice!" . . . and spent the afternoon baking her head off for Paul—so he was greeted by the smell of freshly baked coffee cake. He stuck his head in the door and said, "Are you getting spoiled from all this good food, honey?"

Lia

After that time I determined never to accept any offer of "help" from Paul's mother. Rather than help, when I got up I found only subtle, silent reminders from her that said in a language only women understand: "Lia is not much of a housekeeper."

Paul could never fathom my annoyance at his mother.

"She only means to help, Lia!"

"There was no need for her to root into our drawers and rearrange your underwear, Paul! That's personal! And instead of decrumbing my kitchen drawers, and for God's sake, polishing the inside of my tea strainer, she could have helped in other ways! That was humiliating for me, Paul, can't you see?"

But he couldn't. Perhaps no one could and what he was saying to me began to sink in: "You are not normal, Lia. You see things no one else does."

Did I?

Locating a better job with an old, established real estate firm, Paul began to make a dent in the bills. When we had to take Katie for delicate, expensive eye surgery, it was not a major financial calamity.

Katie's eyes had crossed suddenly and severely when she was seven, and during the weeks when we sought a diagnosis, she came home from school one day, went silently to her room, and would not come out even for me. Going in, I found her slumped at her desk, crying.

"Katie, can you tell Mama what's wrong?"

"I look funny! Mama, I don't look right anymore!"

"What happened at school, Katie?"

When she told me I went to the phone and made a call that probably went down in the history of the convent as being ominous, evil, blasphemous, and insane. But I felt a lot better for making it.

That day as the children had stood in a practice processional for her first Holy Communion, hands folded just so, feet lined just so, they were instructed to look devoutly at the tabernacle where Jesus lived. Sister, coming along inspecting the line, stopped at Katie and said, "Katie Farrelli, did I or did I not just tell you to look at the altar?"

"Mama, I *was* looking at the altar . . . only my eyes weren't."

Clearly, I remember going to the phone that day, asking for a certain person, and telling her in a normal, plain, everyday woman's fighting language exactly what I thought. I was in no way frightened or guilt-ridden, and nun or not I was not letting it pass. Judging perhaps too harshly, and remembering other nuns and other hurts, the old bogey of religious authority reared its head.

Despite my ill health our lives had happy moments and times of respite. Even the year that Kara, then in the second grade, came down with rheumatic fever, became one to look back on and say, "That was a happy time for us." The full year that she lay abed, Kara and I played and studied together. She began to develop a fine artistic talent, along with the wonderful patience that very sick children seem to have. As time passed and Kara recovered and returned to school, only the remnant of a painful arthritic condition reminded us that she would need a bit of extra tending.

The children provided many bright spots in our life. Paul and I discovered that we, indeed, had three very different and independent little people on our hands. In Lori's case this came through loud and clear when she was only four.

Paul was in the habit of taking Lori with him each week on

his trip to the public library. On this particular day Lori wandered about, chose four or five books for herself, and took them to the checkout desk. Tiptoeing to the top of the counter, Lori made it clear that she wanted these books on her own card, not on her father's as the librarian had suggested. The unsuspecting and stern lady then told Lori that no child under school age, in fact no one not able to sign his own name, was ever issued a card. Period. Now, positively indignant, Lori made it even more clear (to anyone within hearing distance) that not only could she read and write, but that she most certainly could sign her own name and then proceeded to do just that. Lori was brought home by a very red-faced Paul, but she had in her possession her books, her library card, and the dubious honor of being the youngest child ever to be issued an adult card in our town library.

Pleased with his new job, Paul was happy. He had done a beautiful job building our home and we were better off financially than ever in the past. He put the past from his mind, concentrating on a good future, as those with healthy spirits do. But I was like some wounded animal; as a woman I felt ravaged, my small claim to beauty gone forever in a face scarred and pitted beyond surgical repair. Once abundant and curly, my hair, in which Paul had taken such pride, was now thin and streaked with gray. The hands which once had such control at the piano now had constant tremors. I knew that I presented a not very pretty picture.

Someone told me later this was my "Paul says" phase. My life took on the aspects of a monstrous harlequinade. I played, more desperately than ever, the destructive game of pretend for other people.

For Mama I tried to be more like cousin Joy; for Paul I tried to be more like other men's wives. Gradually the game became my whole life, seeping out as I tried to assume the color and characteristics of what seemed to be the spurious aura they desired me to have. During the next years I lost touch with reality, and like a magnetized spirit, absorbed whatever character delineations were most acceptable to those I wanted to please.

I lost my self and became rather an unperson in my own eyes: I believed that the real Lia was not and had never been anyone.

After a while I didn't know *who* or *what* the real Lia was anymore. Nor did I care.

I do not know at what hour or minute the curtain dropped, only that it did. Those foolish enough to believe that nerves, like hearts, do not really "break" have much to learn. Nerves do break, and to accompany them so do hearts and spirits.

There was very little of Lia left in the empty rind that went into the hospital one day in the care of Dr. Ling, psychiatrist. The person they locked behind the steel door and rat-wired windows bore no resemblance to the laughing young girl in a red velvet dress who had gone on a blind date ten years before. Vividly I can recall pressing my cheek to the cold steel and feeling that it, like my soul, was cold and dead.

Memories of this period in my life are scant and broken. But I remember how it was, how it felt to be locked away in a mental ward.

I remember the upside-down beds.

Each day that I was scheduled to receive a shock treatment I would find that they had made up my bed in reverse order; the pillows at the foot, the sheet tucked in at the head. And the sides of the bed were always up.

After I was comfortably settled and the machine rolled into place (they somehow always managed to obscure my view of the machine and even today I have no idea of what it looks like), they prepared my arm for the injection of Pentothal. I would dimly hear the nurse say, "Bite on this, Lia," and would feel the horrid tasting rubber mouthpiece being slipped into my mouth. And I would be gone.

When I awakened there was always a tray of food on my bedside table. By now I was right side up. How they managed to move my supine body and remake the bed was a thing I never understood. I would eat the cold cereal and drink the juice and then get up with the usual throbbing headache.

Everything out in the hallway would seem to be so open, so unsafe, and I would stay in my room until someone forced me to leave and "mingle." I remember being very afraid at these times. Some of the patients sat and stared at visions only they could see. Some cried in corners. One very old man walked about completely nude until the day when he just wasn't there

The Healing of Lia

anymore. In a large, old-fashioned wicker wheelchair sat a woman of perhaps seventy. She was completely swathed in bandages, like a museum mummy. There was no place on her body that she had not sliced and slashed with a razor.

I had two special friends who took their meals with me and chatted happily about what had put them there. I did not know what had put me there. One of my new friends began to ask me for my clothes, as she thought they were prettier than her own. And so I proceeded to give her whatever she fancied until I had given her everything, even my shoes. When the nurses discovered that I had only my robe and slippers left in my locker (and this did not seem strange to me in any way), they brought back my things with strict orders that I was not to give anything away no matter how she pleaded. I remember feeling that this was very harsh and unkind.

We had craft therapy, movies, television, and an old upright piano. I remember longing to sit and play, but I couldn't remember any of my music. I used to stand, often for an hour or so, leaning on the piano thinking about my music teacher and how he had rapped me on the hands with his baton and shouted, "Mein Gott, Lia! Timing, timing, timing!" And so after a while I avoided even the piano.

A childlike attitude increased each day of my stay in the ward. I became more and more docile, compliant, and unquestioning. Whatever I was directed to do, I did.

My mind was a total void. I couldn't read with any comprehension. I couldn't write. Among my belongings I found a book that had written on the fly page: "This is my personal journal. If found please return it to Lia Farrelli." The book was completely blank and remained so.

I didn't know then that years would pass before I could again read and write. Nor did I realize how many night classes it would take to restore any of my lost knowledge and basic skills. My caretakers told me that the effects of the electric shock treatments would be temporary, but this was a lie. They took from me things that could never be fully restored. I may never have written The Great American Novel, but at that time I couldn't even write a grocery list.

In the ward our baths were carefully watched. All razors were kept locked in a cabinet and only with written permission from your doctor would they be dispensed. I resented having to beg for permission to do my necessary grooming each week. I, of course, realized the reasons for this, but somehow standing in a line with other towel-clad women to make such a request made me feel as if I had no rights at all as a human being.

Time itself became unreal. Days dwindled and became weeks, and it didn't matter at all. I saw no one except Paul, Mama, and Aunt Nettie. As I improved and was being prepared for the outside world again, Dr. Ling gave me permission for weekends at home. This seemed wonderful, but everyone had to wait on me as one would a very small child: the only thing I seemed capable of was to stand about smiling. I was totally unable to prepare even a simple meal or do simple tasks. So I would sit in a chair and watch, watch, watch.

During my home visits when Paul made love to me, I felt outside of everything, even my own body. Nothing at all was "real" to me. And when, on Sunday night, he returned me to the hospital, I'm sure it was a relief to him.

At the hospital everyone welcomed me and I felt that I was again safe where I belonged. I do remember that everyone at home and at the hospital was very kind to me. Whatever anyone might have done to me before, or might do to me later, no one hurt me then.

Gradually I relaxed, my fears seemed to diminish, and other than the night horrors which persisted, my symptoms vanished and Dr. Ling pronounced me well enough to go home. My nights were still very terrible. The waking, screaming, crying for . . . something.

My stay in the mental ward remains with me today in an enigmatic terror I have retained. Despite the kind treatment I received and the safe, warm, protective atmosphere of its halls, I still cringe at the few memories that linger. Perhaps this is because I knew full well that I was not healed, only stunned. And that no one (not even I) actually knew *why* I was sick and perhaps never would.

And so I returned home to stay, only to begin slipping down into the illness again, slowly, very slowly, as I tried to hide it from everyone.

The Healing of Lia

I have few memories of the years between my breakdowns, only spotty remembrances. The fears of Paul's family increased and they became more and more sinister to me. I was always polite to them and they to me, but there was no real closeness. One evening as Paul and I sat watching a movie the phone rang and I answered.

"Lia, could I speak to Paul, please?" It was Mara.

I said, of course, and called to him. He spoke softly for a short while and it was impossible to ascertain from his end if the call was a business matter, family trouble, or just a courtesy call. Paul hung the phone up, returned to his chair, never mentioning what had transpired. Hesitantly I asked, "How are Mara and the children? Is everything okay?"

"Fine. No problems. She just wanted to ask how much we paid for Katie's new coat and where we got it."

"She wanted—what? Then why didn't she ask me? I answered the phone! I know the price of the children's clothes! *Why won't they talk with me, Paul?*" I was very definitely getting upset and Paul crossly accused me of being silly about nothing.

Later in bed I tried talking with Paul to find out why these strange calls went on, hoping he might begin to see that I felt left out and frightened. He did not see and only became more angry with me for being too sensitive.

Thinking I might break the barrier, that Christmas I tried very hard to be kind to Mrs. Farrelli, as Paul had told me she made requests of him because no one else would take her places and do for her. So, in November I told her that I would be happy to take her shopping each week and we would devote the entire day to getting just what she would like. Picking her up early in the morning, I drove the entire day, making the circuit of every shopping mall within a ten-mile radius of the city. She was cordial and seemed to appreciate my doing this, but still the wall was very much there and she continued each time she called to merely ask for Paul. If I answered and he was not home, she would never tell me what she wanted or needed. She never told me anything.

Paul did not understand that my illness had not been cured, nor did I, fully. I knew only that I was more and more afraid of everything and everyone. Each day something caused upset in our home; we were never at rest, never at peace. A current of distrust concerning Paul ran wildly about in my head. Fearing his mother, I took her portrait, which Paul kept on my piano, wrapped it in a towel, and rammed it behind the linens in the closet. Even so, I felt the power of her and had nightmares of that sweet grandmotherly face that brought a primal, antediluvian terror to break my sleep.

We visited Lois, Paul's sister, one summer evening, during which an explosion occurred in my brain. Keeping a rein on my emotions, I sat outside myself and viewed the three of them as an outsider, a stranger—as truly I was. I sat for three hours listening to them using the family "tone" with each other, this tone that had very nearly destroyed my confidence and sanity, that I have begged Paul not to use with me. For no reason at all, in quite ordinary conversation, their voices take on a tone of ridicule and derision, becoming caustic and abusive. It comes quite naturally; they twist their faces, narrow their eyes, and out it comes! Paul has told me that it means nothing, merely an emphasis they want noted. (And why not just use a two-by-four piece of lumber?)

We sat in the coolness of the evening, I next to Lois, Paul next to his mother, and I watched with fascination as she traced circles with her hand on his back, lovingly. Round and round. As we carried on a pleasant conversation, she would reach to pat his bare knee or give his leg a squeeze, a caress. Finally I was no longer outside myself, an objective observer. I was fighting a knot of anger in my belly.

What I saw, if done by *anyone* else, would without a doubt have been interpreted as overt sexual advances: it is what I myself do to love his body. I could not sit watching his mother touch him in this way. It seemed intimate and he was *my* husband, not *hers*.

"For heaven's sake, Lia! You are jealous! You are actually jealous of my mother!" This, Paul hurled at me later in anger. Shamed that I felt such an emotion, I tried to quell it.

I had a recurring dream, a clear picture of Paul and his mother. The place and time were not important. What was important was that she was hugging and kissing him, calling him, "My Paul."

The Healing of Lia

My anger, hidden behind a frozen smile, boiled into hatred for both of them. Paul, too—yes!—for having the food of life when I was starving, and most of all, for eating it in front of me.

Paul might be a thief, a murderer, and it would not lessen her love for him. I could have been crowned queen of the world and my mother still would not have loved me.

Even in our most intimate moments I felt his mother between us.

Exactly a year after my release from the psychiatric ward we had a surprise visit from Gina and her family. Elated, I spent weeks cleaning, polishing the house, and trying to hide the mountain of fat that had been piling up on my body since Dr. Ling had put me on drug therapy. From the thin wraith of 98 pounds I had gained to a blubbery 160—and was still gaining. I felt miserable and disgusted by my own body. I didn't understand exactly what was happening to me, but as I was happy, cheerful, and "functioning," attributes that impressed him, the therapy continued. He never told me that this weight gain was one of the less serious of the side effects of the drugs. There were things in store for me that, even now, are hard to accept. Symptoms developed that were clearly outlined in the physician's handbook. (I know this. Dr. Ward read them to me one day.) It was not a matter that no one knew; it was a matter that no one really cared.

Marriage and three children had not changed Gina. She was still petite, relaxed, well in control of her world. Donald, her husband, was a brilliant mathematician who also was relaxed and well in control. They seemed to have a sort of mutually respectful, unemotional rapport that was foreign to the way Paul and I communicated. I envied this terribly.

The day Gina and Donald were to arrive from Indiana, I had spent hours preparing my table, baking fresh breads, and making special dishes. As the day went on and the arrival time came and went, I began to get a bit uneasy. Afternoon drifted into dusk, and the food needed either to be put away or served. Finally, as we sat down to a nervous supper without them, their car pulled into the driveway.

After a confused smattering of hugs, kisses, and greetings ("So this is Mark! How he looks like his daddy, Gina!"), it was jovially revealed to us that they had arrived in town early in the day but had decided to ramble through our larger department stores, and "You know how I hate to feel tied to a schedule, Lia!" was Gina's way of telling me that she knew I had held dinner, but really didn't care to be *expected* on time.

Paul sat through the meal in silence, and I knew he was angry at having all the efforts I put forth for them received so casually. Gina's children clearly did not adjust to eating foods that were not their favorites and were allowed by their parents to voice this plainly.

"What is *bouillabaisse?* Fish stew! Ugh!" and the delicate dish I had spent hours preparing found its way into the dog's bowl while Paul grew more and more quiet.

Donald and Gina seemed not to notice, and while she and I washed up the dishes, Donald spent much time explaining centrifugal force to his son, who discovered that if he really *tried*, he could spin my cut-glass lazy Susan until it flew off its base. All in all, when they left to visit Aunt Nettie and Mama, it was rather a relief. Before leaving, Gina asked if we might all gather at Aunt Nettie's to celebrate the new year, and I agreed that would be nice. Paul said nothing. As they drove away I was peculiarly torn between anger toward Gina for her thoughtlessness, although for some reason it seemed quite natural to me that Gina would act as she had, and anger toward Paul for showing his disgust.

Back in the house Paul poured the remains of his special cappuccino and then he spoke.

"Your sister and her husband spent *the entire day* shopping for a damned suit for him—after twelve *years* of not seeing you! I think it is ridiculous! Don't they sell suits in *Indiana?* For God's sake, Lia! You spent so much time getting everything ready—in a few days they'll be gone again!"

"Paul, this visit means too much to me to ruin it by saying anything to Gina!"

Angrily he told me that if I went to their "damned party" he would not. He would, instead, go to Mara's house and celebrate the new year with his family.

"Paul, you can be with Mara and your family *anytime* at all. Gina and Donald might not be back for years!" But by now Paul was on his way upstairs, and as I sat drinking dregs from my cup,

The Healing of Lia

he went to bed and was asleep when I closed the house and went to our room.

The next day neither of us spoke of what we might do that evening, New Year's Eve. I hung out my long gown and found my evening slippers. Early in the afternoon I cooked an easy dinner, took a leisurely bath, and prayed that Paul would change his mind. In all my life, this would have been the first such gathering of my family, and I desperately wanted it to be "right."

But things were not right.

At dinner Paul told me that he had meant what he said, and that he was going to Mara's and be with his family.

"You are free to take the girls and go to Aunt Nettie's to see Gina if you want, Lia."

It had been a full year since I had gotten out of the hospital, but I still had a deathly fear of driving, even in the daytime, and I knew that I would never be able to drive with only the children across the city on darkened streets. Never.

Humiliated, I called Gina and made some sort of excuse. When I hung the phone up, I sat as Paul showered, dressed, and left me on the eve of the new year.

For the first time in so long I felt a flooding of emotion, a terrible mixture of fear (I was alone, and I knew it) and anger that my husband would do such a thing in order to make a point to someone else. And the point was quite lost on Gina; she could not have cared less. Only I cared, and for some reason, I didn't matter.

I put the girls to bed, and then went into our room and carefully packed away my gown. I sat in the semidarkness and waited for Paul to come home from his party, waited until almost two o'clock in the morning, and when he did come in I attacked him with all the hurt, anger, disappointment, in my being.

Looking at me (Paul is not a man to argue), he said, "You lack self-control. You are still not normal."

7

I had been out of the psychiatric ward only one year, and already I was beginning to stumble. I had no idea of how a "normal" wife might have reacted. I felt like one of those roly-poly dolls that children smash in the head and it only pops back up again. Exactly *why* people smashed me, I didn't know. But it was getting harder and harder to pop back up again.

One evening some weeks later, as we were all watching television, the phone rang and Paul called to the girls, asking them to go to their room. They were strangely quiet, considering that he had taken them from the middle of a favorite program. In a few minutes he knelt by my chair, took my hand, and told me that Mama had died suddenly and without pain.

"You always think you will be happy, Paul, when someone who has hurt you dies. But I'm not happy at all." I could not cry. There was nothing except a strange numbness in my head. Gina was in Indiana, Evan was gone, Dorrie was gone. Aunt Nettie could not be expected to "handle" everything, so I asked Paul to drive me to her house.

The following morning we went to Mr. Blakely's funeral parlor and chose the casket, giving the attendant the gown that Mama would have chosen as her favorite. We discussed the time of the mass and after Mr. Blakely phoned in Mama's obituary we were free to go home. But before we went, Paul insisted that I go with him and buy a black dress "that fits." By now I was getting so very large that nothing I had fit. When the overenthusiastic saleswoman asked, "Does madame want a simple black frock to wear to a dinner?" I replied, "No. Madame wants a simple black frock to wear to her mother's funeral."

The Healing of Lia

In fifteen minutes flat we were on our way home.

Whether it was because I was doping myself to the hilt or for some other reason, I seemed to be the only calm one in the family. I put on my new black dress, met the guests at the door of the "viewing room," and sat as Mama's old friends told me how many generous and kindly acts she had performed and how they treasured knowing her. I floated in a dreamlike aura of this outpouring of love for my mother. On the two nights that Mama lay in state, over three hundred people from the old neighborhood came to say good-bye to her. I realized that there must have been two persons in Mama; one, a lovely, talented, gregarious woman and another, the cold, unreachable person that I knew and feared for my lifetime. I had no way of understanding this, but it was the cause of most of my grief. I would have given half a lifetime to have known Mama as others had.

Gina was on a very ragged edge, exactly how ragged I found out later. Aunt Nettie and I had made all the arrangements and there was nothing for the others to do except help each other get through the ordeal. For some reason Gina seemed to resent that I had "taken charge." I had not expected praise for what I had had to do, but neither had I expected what I finally got.

We sat in my living room and as the will was read I found myself appointed to handle Mama's small estate. The will contained a simple paragraph saying, "As Lia is the only child in the city, I am leaving her to dispose of my personal household effects, which are hers to keep if she wishes."

To my knowledge, Mama had few effects other than her clothing and a few aged boxes packed away in Aunt Nettie's attic. She had long ago sold her home and furnishings. Feeling weary and sad, I said my good-byes and Paul and I saw everyone to the door, knowing that they had early flights out.

Later, at Aunt Nettie's, Gina broke down crying that she had nothing of Mama's to take home with her. Aunt Nettie, in tears, said, "For goodness sake, child, take anything you like!" and rummaged about for Mama's old set of silver dessert forks.

Evan called me the next morning and described what must have been a hideous scene: Gina standing, screaming that she'd be damned if she would take anything that belonged to Lia! And Aunt Nettie asking whatever she meant? At which point Evan had spoken up, "For Christ's sake, Gina! Stop being stupid! If you would like a memento, call Lia and tell her what you'd like or just take the forks!"

Thinking she was helping, Aunt Nettie quietly wrapped the tiny silver forks and tucked them into Gina's flight bag—not telling anyone what she had done.

A week later as I stood preparing lunch, my front bell rang and a small, registered special-delivery package was handed me. Postmarked Indiana, there was no note included. Just a neatly wrapped, insured parcel containing Mama's set of silver dessert forks.

I had no idea of what had happened or of why Gina would do this. When I did find out that my sister would rather be "damned" than to ask me for something belonging to our mother, I sat and wept for the first time since the funeral. None of it meant anything to me. I wanted all of us to touch each other, to finally reach out and touch. For a long while I was afraid to write to Gina, for fear she would return my letters.

I remember moving to a new house that spring, but after that I remember little.

I know that I was still under the weekly care of Dr. Ling and that severe problems were returning at an exponential rate.

Food became my friend, my bosom buddy. And that is an apt description, for that is exactly where a lot of it ended. By now I was well into "fat ladies" fashions (I shudder at snapshots of this era), looking at life over a monumental cleavage.

I did not bother to tint my silver hair which had been graying since my late twenties, and altogether, I looked to be a jolly, happy, fat lady. I certainly must have given that impression, but my mind, like the storm petrel, flew over the surface of life without knowing where to land. While I must have "functioned" during the next two years, there are no memories whatever of specific happenings to help me recall. But there are pictures.

There are pictures of a trip we took to Indiana to see Gina, Donald, and their children. I am told that I spent most of the time ill and in bed. I remember nothing of the trip, of coming home, or of going soon after back into the hospital for psychiatric care under Dr. Ling. By this time, I didn't even know Dr. Ling.

The Healing of Lia

It was late November when Paul came to drive me home from the hospital. For nine weeks I had been confined, following the breakdown I could not remember having. After the long series of electroconvulsive treatments I had become so docile that whether I stayed or left the hospital was a matter of indifference to me. I had absolutely no longing to see either my home or my children. There was, in my mind, no emotional attachment to anyone except Paul.

The crisp autumn air felt strange after so many weeks of the insulated areas I had occupied. It was rather nice, I thought, to be outside once more, but I couldn't think of anything to say to Paul.

I had no recollection of coming to the hospital, or of the reasons that had compelled me to come. And I was unaware that this was my second, not my first stay in the ward. I might have been aware of this fact at times, but thoughts drifted in and out of my mind with such swiftness that any memory at all was just a wisp—and then it was gone.

I was not aware of exactly why I could not remember anything (and somehow, questioning about it was unimportant). The shock treatments had done their work. From day to day I could not remember who had visited me, what I had eaten, nor exactly *why* I couldn't leave through that locked steel door.

I remember waking one day, I don't know when, and seeing Paul sitting by my bed in the strange room. Looking around, I saw that both windows were completely covered with a strong steel mesh. There was a terrible aching in my head and I asked where I was. He replied, "You've been very ill, Lia, and you're in a hospital."

But I didn't *feel* ill at all! Despite the headache, I felt wonderfully relaxed and well. I couldn't seem to remember anything at all. A uniformed nurse came and told Paul that it was time for him to leave and even that did not affect me. I was completely alone in a strange hospital, I knew little else besides my own name, and yet I felt at peace. I felt totally at peace.

Briefly, I wondered where I was and then even that thought drifted away. I got up to investigate the room. The doors and drawers to my bedside table were locked. How strange, I thought. Even my eyeglasses were locked away. There were metal lockers in one wall of the room, which had two beds and little else in it. I found my old, familiar "good" robe, some gowns and other clothes that I did not recognize, and shoes that fit and were obviously mine in the locker marked B. Passing the mirror on the wall, I stopped to run my fingers through my short hair (they had also locked up my comb and toilet articles), and feeling weak and cold, I stared into the glass at that strange face. Please, God! Not my face!

Pitted with deep purplish scars, my face was enough to give nightmares to any woman who had to live with it. This was not the Dark Ages when people were cursed by pox scars, and slowly something stirred in my memory: a dark, cool church, myself sitting, pleading to be made well, long, long ago? How long ago? Weeks . . . months?

I became conscious of a hard knot of pain in my abdomen (familiar, familiar!). I fled into the bathroom and the sounds of my retching caused a nurse and a male attendant to come in.

Later, when it was dark, a strange psychiatrist visited with me. I was in my bed and my face had been bathed and I was quite comfortable. This unknown doctor with kindly, Oriental features told me that he was Dr. Ling and that he was *my* doctor, and had been for many years. He sat on the side of my bed and repeated again who he was, and I had the feeling he must have done so often, because his voice was familiar and comforting.

Patiently Dr. Ling explained that I had been in "the hospital" (still no one told me *which* hospital) for two weeks and was receiving a series of treatments for clinical depression and "nerves." My disorientation and loss of memory was, as he put it, "Quite normal, even desirable." And he told me that I had been living with my ruined face for years, had seen it go from a clear, unblemished young face to the one with which I now faced the world. (He, of course, did not add this last, but nevertheless it was the truth.)

As time went by I found that physically the infection that caused the damage to my face was only a minor incident in my health history. Damaged kidneys and a scar-filled urethra caused the doctors more concern and they displayed little interest (and a lack of understanding) when it came to a woman's feelings about her face. I chatted at length with one young doctor who

The Healing of Lia

was greatly interested in removing a thick, red rope of scar tissue that ran down the middle of my stomach; he was really troubled by this, and yet he never *once* mentioned the hard, purple knots of scars on my face!

The days blurred as I took the series of shock treatments and received tranquilizers and antidepressants. I lived in a snug, secure place where the only decisions I made were what I wore, when I bathed, and which foods I chose to eat daily. No one was there to hurt me. Or correct me, or criticize me; I was safe!

Each day I sat in craft-therapy and made little ceramic knick-knacks. (Months later at home I smashed them all because I could not bear the sight of them.) And I watched the other patients, those poor creatures who inhabited a world of their own and spoke to no one but themselves, and those whose problems were poured from bottles in the form of alcohol or drugs, and those who were simply "nervous." I did not know where I fit among all these people because no one would tell me.

I was still quite unaware, at the point of first memory, that this was my second experience with emotional breakdown. As the shock treatments had done their work, I had an inability to concentrate on anything for more than a very few minutes. This effect is the desired effect because whatever one cannot concentrate on certainly cannot be worried about! But this inability to concentrate also makes it next to impossible to function on any fringe of normalcy.

I could not read with any depth of perception, couldn't properly write sentences. I constantly lost my possessions—clothes, personal articles, eyeglasses. On the days I was given a treatment, I awakened and forgot who my "friends" in the ward were. People with whom I had eaten, chatted, shared confidences, were completely obliterated from my memory; the patients I was familiar with yesterday were strangers with no names and unremembered faces, and it was frightening to experience this emptiness of mind. It became important to think of myself as "different." I kept telling myself, "*You* are unlike the others. *You* are still in control of yourself." And when, in the aloneness of the nights, after the lockers, drawers, and cabinets had been locked, I realized how helpless I was, there were no descriptive phrases to tell of the prideless feelings evoked.

I knew that I was not "normal," and I cared deeply to find out why this was so, but no one, not Paul, not the doctor, not the nurses or attendants, would discuss any of the whys of my imprisonment. And, call it what you may, imprisonment is *exactly* the word in the mind of the patient. Many months later I found that I signed myself into the hospital both times; I was not committed by anyone. Nevertheless, once in, one cannot get out until the doctor feels you are ready.

Patients are soon quite aware that any small infraction, anything not "normal," can mean a month more in the ward. Something as small as a crying spell, a sign of temper, a desire to be alone (any desire for basic human privacy being interpreted as "withdrawal"), any change in attitude or demeanor, could mean a lengthened stay.

One incident has returned and rankled in my mind. This unpleasant memory survived when others have drifted away.

During the last half of my stay, I was moved from my room into another because of my roommate Charlotte. Charlotte became more and more ill and I would awaken at any hour during the night to find her hovering over my bed, staring at me silently. She never touched me, never made a move to harm me, but the nurses found out and reported her actions to Dr. Ling, who seemed to think it strange on my part that I had not done so. At this point, living in an atmosphere where I accepted the odd as normal, I had seen nothing frightening in having Charlotte stand and stare at me while I slept. Truthfully, I do not think I would have complained in any event, for fear of being kept longer.

Dr. Ling moved me into a large, sunny, and pleasant room with six beds and a long wall of lockers and cabinets. One woman, Rena, in my new room was not really "ill." She was a bundle of nerves, admittedly, but seemed to be there only because of an indulging doctor and husband. She had privileges reserved only for patients who were well enough to go home but preferred to stay and "rest" a while longer. Rena was a wealthy woman and used to having her own way. And she was, if not the most thoughtless person I have met, certainly in the top two!

Each morning Rena got up before 5:30 A.M. and instead of turning on her small bed lamp she padded across the floor and switched on all the ceiling fixtures, flooding the room with a shocking glare of several hundred watts and immediately waking everyone else. As the regular getting-up time was not until seven-thirty, this meant a loss of two hours of sleep for each of us each day. Everyone was afraid of Rena, afraid of their doctors, afraid of the nurses, and definitely afraid to complain. One day when I could no longer stand it, I took the grievance to Dr. Ling. Calmly enough, I explained how irritating the situation was and for some reason (to this day, I have no understanding why) Dr. Ling jumped right down my throat. He shouted that he had no intention of moving me again (I had not asked him to) and peering angrily at me he blasted away until my reserve of courage dissolved and I began to cry. An attendant was called to take me to my bed and I was given a double dose of the drug that kept me docile.

This was the moment that probably caused the feelings of trust and reliance I had in Dr. Ling to dissipate. Just why he lost control of himself over such a trivial incident was never explained to me. Thereafter, I felt a strange desire to hold back from him, as I no longer considered him as having any interest in me, in getting me "well" (whatever that meant), or in having a proper control over his own emotions. He slipped in my esteem, and yet I realized my complete dependence on him; I realized that it was *his* signature I would need in order ever to get out. I believe that this was the place where playing the game of pretend became most important to me. And play it I did.

I also realized one other thing: there are things the mental patient *must* accept without question that in any other hospitalization, for "normal" reasons, would not be accepted by any "normal" patient.

The incident of Rena and her thoughtless attitude toward the other patients, the fear of speaking out, and the devastating repercussions of speaking out could only have happened in a mental ward. Having had many routine hospitalizations through the years, I know that in general-medical or surgical wards care is taken to treat the patients with the utmost thoughtfulness. Such things as coming in at unusual hours and switching on bright ceiling lights unnecessarily are unthinkable. Night nurses may come and go taking vitals, giving treatments and medications, making patients comfortable, often doing so with only the aid of a flashlight or a dim night-light. I nursed all of my children for 2 A.M. feedings in a dim, night-lighted room, with my roommate (a non-nursing mother) sleeping soundly in the next bed. I have shared rooms with women dying of monstrous cancers, with all ages and all kinds of ill women, and never, never would any of us have put up with the shenanigans of a Rena—not in a *normal* situation. So why is it different for the mental patient?

My game of pretend was one at which I became so clever, so proficient, that Dr. Ling was completely taken in. It was my own cleverness in hiding the very fact of my illness (which began to grow worse and proliferate immediately after my release from the hospital) that caused it to become so ingrained in my mind and spirit. I *knew* the things they looked for in the patients, and so I became very, very careful in everything I did and said in his presence.

I was properly meek and humble when he voiced his displeasure. I took the complete blame, as I was sure this would please him. It did. I took particular pains in my appearance, carefully using makeup and keeping myself well-groomed, because I knew that depressives are notoriously uncaring about such things. (So are some other people—but then, they are not laboring to "prove" themselves.) Clever, clever, clever! Enough so to get released and sent back to the world in which I could not cope. And, still, no one had found the reason why.

During the last of my stay I grew to hate and to fear the hospital because I began to find out things. Things such as most of the patients there were there for the second, third, fourth time. None had been "cured," none "healed." Over half of them did not know why they were there and, as with me, no one would really discuss this with them. It was as if we had been dehumanized, as if we *deserved* no better. I do not mean this to be a critique or a judgment of all psychiatric wards, certainly they have their problems, as do the doctors. But from the point of view of the reasonably intelligent patient, one unfortunate enough to be *put* into such a ward, I see things from the underside rather than the topside.

In the first place, putting the very sick in with the merely "nervous" or not so sick is quite often horrifying to the latter. There was, in my ward, a teenaged girl who was literally terrified

The Healing of Lia

of her surroundings and the other patients. Ages of the patients ranged from this young girl to the senile, some suffering from serious illness and others only from housewifely jitters. Some were cheerfully ill, others totally withdrawn. All of us were thrown together in a sort of mad hodgepodge, wandering about the corridors, bumping into each other, and yet each, in his own way, alone. Most or all of us were kept on some drug (or drugs) to keep us quiet and calm. Certainly none of these drugs ever played more than a temporary part in my actual "healing," and yet I had been, in the opinion of more than one doctor, addicted, both physically and psychologically, for the eleven years I was *on* tranquilizers and antidepressants.

This addiction is a terrible admission on my part, especially since twice during this time I have endeavored alone to shake the habit, cold turkey. Never did I really know what addiction was. I could go without the pills for days, weeks. But I had to know that they were *there.* I had to know that the bottle was full or I did not feel safe. I may not have touched them, only looked at them. To me, this was as bad as having to swallow them! In my opinion it is bad to feel that you *have* to have even *one* pill a day, just as some alcoholics maintain themselves on "Just one! I only need one!" The end is all the same and the word is dependence. I have hated every pill, every prettily colored, poisonous little pill I have ever swallowed in the vain, futile hope of being made "well." But I did take them, I did make the proper impression on my caretakers, and then came the cold, November day when I was told that I might go home.

Home. Our new home was a strange place. When Paul took me into the house I could not remember it. This house that we had worked so long and hard to remodel was itself unfamiliar. The rough, antiqued brick of the kitchen wall, the huge, dark exposed beams running across the living room, the richly grained, dark cabinets in the kitchen—mine? Yes, mine, but it all seemed so open, so unsafe, and when suddenly the phone rang in the hall, a fine dew on my face told me that there were still unknown phantoms to fight, and no one had told me really what they were at all.

I felt like a guest in the house, examining the color of the sofa, discovering where the bed was placed in our room, and finally, at four o'clock in the afternoon, seeing Katie, Kara, and Lori (who were now reaching adolescence), as they ran into the house to see their "well" mother.

We all hugged and kissed, but I seemed to have lost my ability to feel emotions. Love, hate, anger, sadness, happiness, all blurred into a soft, gray void of blank, noncaring disinterest in everything about me. Like a cored apple, an empty husk, I seemed to have an exterior but no interior. There was no inner me at all. As the days of my homecoming passed and they all took less notice of me, I found I could not care less if they were hungry or wearing clean clothes; I didn't care if I ate or dressed, except to play the pretend game for Dr. Ling. I merely sat all day, and as I couldn't read, the newspapers came and lay untouched, as did all my beloved books, my papers, and my journal. My family's life rotated around me without really touching me, and I seemed to be in a plastic bubble of nowhere.

Recovery from a breakdown is unlike any other recovery. You become aware that people no longer really "listen" to you. Your opinions are no longer acceptable or respected, and for a person of relative intelligence this is humiliating. I realized full well that those close to me began to patronize me, as one would a sick child, in order not to upset me. If I ventured an opinion on any adult issue or something requiring some intellect, they would smile, pat my hand . . . but they would not listen with respect.

Neither insane nor stupid, I felt that I was being treated as if I were both. Anger and frustration began to build in me, but knowing that I must hide this in order to stay "well" (and out of that place!), I found survival meant playing the Game. *Stay out! Stay out!* And the Game became in actual fact my whole life.

I had again the night terrors of being chained in dark places, and would awaken night after night with Paul shushing me, wiping my wet face, trying to keep me from crying out and frightening the girls. Life quickly slipped again into dark torment, and I knew I must hide it from everyone, even Dr. Ling. Most of all, Dr. Ling!

The Healing of Lia

8

I tried very hard to take over the duties of
the house and the mothering of Katie, Kara,
and Lori, who had reached their early teens
and needed a happy, understanding guiding hand. Right now
they needed someone to drive them to tennis lessons, help
choose their clothing, and share their exhilaration with life.
Everyone seemed busier than ever, especially Paul, whose business was doing well and who had enough to concern him without
worrying about me, which he had done for the greater part of
our life together.

I wanted badly to begin to live as a normal person, but some
dim fear kept me bound to the past. Health problems still tor-
mented me, but the worse I felt, the harder I drove myself. It
was a sort of endurance test I set for myself; I drove myself on
days when anyone else would have said "The hell with it!" and
gone to bed. I began pushing myself to do the very things that
frightened me the most, and this could mean anything from just
answering the phone (phones meant trouble), driving to the market (strange people were there), or visiting with Aunt Addie and
Aunt Nettie. I marched in weekly for my own psychic crucifix-
ion.

Paul encouraged me to get out, to make friends with the
women on our block. The only bright point in my day was waiting for him to come home. I was more and more afraid to drive
anywhere and fearful of meeting anyone. Yet I had a terrible
need for people.

Paul grew tired of my begging him to take me "somewhere,"
and of being my baby-sitter. He was busy and had other interests.
At this time, I had nothing at all.

I tried inviting my neighbors in for a morning coffee klatch and was astounded by the variety of reasons why they could not "tie themselves down" to a definite yes. They all seemed to live on rigid, inflexible schedules that could not be disturbed.

I tried to give a new neighbor an afternoon tea to welcome her, but even she could not come.

"I'm so embarrassed, Lia, but the baby won't nap anywhere except his own little crib!"

I tried visiting informally in the afternoons, just to say hello, offered to exchange recipes, slips of my house plants, or books. I met with such disinterest and apathy that I finally accepted the fact that I was the most boorish and unlikable person on the face of God's earth. All healthy, active, normal women, my neighbors were very polite and kind, but also very, very busy. It is interesting to me that they were all ardent and faithful churchwomen who devoted hours taking meals to invalids, visiting strangers in hospitals, and doing good. Oddly enough to my viewpoint, not one of them heard the knock on the door when it came.

I felt as if I were caught in the middle of an old war movie: I sat frozen, bombarded by tracer bullets from all directions. Things came winging past and there was no place to run, nowhere to hide. Neighbors, my family, Paul's family, my children, people. People. But they are not *just* people; they were becoming enemies.

I tried again to begin reading, but there was no one with whom to share.

I began to sew, but never went anywhere to wear the clothes I made. And each evening I sat and watched television with Paul, but even he slept as I watched. And it was like being totally alone.

Only a month after I came home from the hospital, I had to prepare for Christmas Day. Paul's family came to celebrate on the holiday and I found myself in the kitchen with sixteen people to feed, their children running, shrieking through the house. My in-laws, as usual, ignored me for the most part after their initial greeting. No mention was made of my illness, nor inquiry as to my health. They all ate what I served, admired the girls' gifts, and chatted on about things that they cared about. I baked pan after pan of hot rolls and carved the Smithfield ham with trembling hands while the visit went on.

Paul is never happier than when in the midst of his family and while he found perfect comfort in the visit, I moved in an aura of dismay in the laughing, happy confusion. I wanted it only to be over. For the next five years I spent most of my waking time wishing that *it* would all be over. Everything. Most of all, my life itself.

Dr. Ling sat for many years dispensing his candy-coated chemicals from behind his fine desk in his fine office, dressed in his fine clothes. Paul and I helped to keep him there while denying ourselves all the nicer things in order to pay him for "helping" me. I have grown to hate him and all his kind, who keep confused and hurting people drugged rather than seeking to find the reason why they are confused and hurting. As the side effects of one drug became glaringly apparent, he switched to another and another.

I never knew that I was addicted until Paul and I went to a marriage counselor who asked me how many pills a day I "needed." My answer shocked him to know that such amounts were readily available to me, or to anyone, for that matter. I hotly denied any addiction. Dr. Ling assured and reassured me that my pills were nonaddictive and I believed him. But my nicely dressed, kindly doctor, who handed the Magic Papers to me regularly, lied. Oh, God, how he lied!

It was not until I had a total paralysis of my colon that I knew what he had done to me, and then it was almost too late.

For months I had known that something was wrong, but people don't discuss their bathroom problems openly. At first I began to skip days between bowel evacuations. Then I noticed that it began to be increasingly difficult to evacuate at all. I was not constipated, I was simply not able to function. I would wait until tomorrow, and another tomorrow, and all the while I would take mild laxatives, and then not-so-mild ones. I flooded myself with fluids, ate more bran, green foods, *anything!* By the fifth day or so I would be decidedly uncomfortable and so, gritting my teeth, I'd get out the old enema bottle. Often spending an agonizing morning fumbling with this relic and spilling water all over myself and the floor, I'd accomplish the deed and sit with relief on the commode—but only the warm, soapy water would be expelled, nothing more.

Usually, at this point I began to suspect that something was indeed wrong. Ah! Naturally, tension is the culprit! And I would take a pill to help me relax and think "Tomorrow will be better."

Another day. I would not feel very much like eating, in fact, I would be afraid to eat. And going out I would buy what is laughingly called a purge, and take the nasty stuff.

By now, my body was definitely telling me something: pain in the left side, hardness of the abdomen. Then, pain all over the inside of me. And so I would take more of my Magic Medicine to relax myself.

On about the sixth day or so, I would call the internist who would tell me, "Take as many enemas as you need! A little hot water never hurt anyone, Lia!"

Back to the leaky old bottle, more pain, no success. One. Two. Three enemas. Back to the phone, and this time I would be crying, "Dr. Russell, I am hurting badly. . . ."

"Well, Lia, you are just nervous. Didn't Dr. Ling give you something for that?" Yes, he did, and so I would swallow another pill. They will help! They all told me that the pills would help and so I took more, and more, and more. . . .

On the tenth day of such an episode Dr. Russell recommended that I see a proctologist. This man took what felt like an old straightened-out coat hanger to break up and drag out the impaction from a colon that would no longer work for me. The delicate procedure had a tendency to tear the tissues because of the size and density of the matter removed. But, no matter, it was all over.

When I inquired of the doctor just how and why this thing happened he reiterated exactly what Dr. Ling, Dr. Russell, and everyone else had told me: it happened because I was nervous. I didn't relax enough. He, too, advised me to go home and take my pills.

It did happen again. Eventually it was necessary to have a hemorrhoidectomy and a "repair job" by this highly recommended surgeon. You would have thought that he would have known something was wrong, would have questioned, but he did not.

I never healed from this surgery, as the same problem presented itself, and my life at home became an episode in horror. Impactions became a part of my life. (Can you imagine an impaction after rectal surgery that has not healed?) But now the internal tears and damage were becoming more serious. I had infection, high fevers, pain, abscesses.

Back to surgery, and the kindly proctologist, who had spoken with Dr. Ling, was very concerned about my "tenseness." Together they decided to "up the dosage" on the pretty pink pills to help me relax. I had not had a normal evacuation for almost one full year. I was not just nervous, I was frightened and hysterical.

Finally, after the second surgery (which had never healed) came a day of success! And with this success came severely torn passages and hemorrhaging. Not knowing what to do, I sat for a long while and lost blood until a dim weakness told me that it was not likely to stop.

Paul came home early this day, luckily for me, and finding me in the bathroom, white, shaking, and pouring blood, he called the doctor's exchange and got the name of a strange doctor neither of us had even known, but who agreed to see me immediately. It was, without doubt, one of the best things that ever happened to me.

Dr. James sat on the edge of my hospital bed and talked with me of my medical history. He spied the bottle of pink pills in my purse when the head nurse asked me to give her all my current medication. He held the bottle for a minute in his hand, and then he knew for a fact exactly what had happened and what was wrong.

I was surprised when he put my bottle in his pocket, but even more surprised when he spoke. He told me that he had constructed for me an "almost-new orifice," that he had never seen such a "damned mess," and then he said, "Lia, for a fact, you are going to die. *If you take any more of that stuff, you will die!*"

"But that's my medicine! I need it!" But by now the bottle was deep in his lab-coat pocket and gone. Well, I told myself, I probably don't need them until I get home anyway. But the following day, after the anesthetic and the pain drugs had worn off, I felt . . . uneasy. My head began to hurt and I didn't want any of my food. Later still, my head hurt worse than the surgical work, and I was not just uneasy, I was highly agitated, irritable. My hands were icy cold, clammy, shaking with tremors. My eyes began to water and I felt nauseated. I rang the bell and asked the nurse for "something" and was told that there were no orders for any medication except antibiotics. No orders meant no pills! I grabbed my handbag and began to rummage through, hoping to find an odd pill in the bottom with the lint and the gum wrappers —nothing!

Then I realized exactly what I must have looked like! Shaking, sweating, frantically fumbling for a drug! And it had only been a matter of *one day* off the pills! Words came back with cruel clarity: "Did it ever occur to you, Lia, that you couldn't stop, even if you wanted to?" It was then I knew what Dr. Ling's pills had done to me.

Often wisdom and illness do not go hand in hand, and later, even while fighting hard, I did return to both Dr. Ling and his "medications." I think it was because I felt that there was no other place to go.

It began to be very evident to Paul that I was not doing well and he suggested that I begin taking night college classes to help me begin reading and writing once more. He knew how deeply upset I was about feeling stupid because I could no longer write correct sentences, or spell.

But above that problem I began to have others; I grew awkward and clumsy, sometimes walking into doorjambs and furniture. I dropped everything I picked up and carried bruises on my body which we joked about: "That one is from the washing machine ('How can anybody not *see* a washing machine, Lia?'). This one is from the edge of the vanity."

What Paul didn't know was that I was "disappearing" during the day when he worked. Not disappearing to the world—there is no doubt that I was out there somewhere—but disappearing to my own self. I was losing hours and hours I could not account for.

I had looked forward to the night classes so much, and I needed the vocabulary expansion badly. But I hadn't counted on meeting Devon Blaine.

The Healing of Lia

I could not understand why a young, charming man would be attracted to me when there were twenty other women, all prettier and all younger than I, in the class. He sat behind me, tapped my shoulder and told jokes, bought me Coke on our breaks, walked me to and from class. Sometimes we would sit and share my thermos of coffee and enjoy pleasant thoughts and conversation. He never touched me, or tried to. Devon and I found joy in talking and sharing with each other. But educated in a strict doctrine that women and men can never safely be "friends," an element of guilt began to grow in me. I was aware that an attraction existed and because of this my guilt increased along with my illness.

The class itself was wonderful. Suddenly I could remember things! Latin roots, declensions that I'd thought were gone forever were all there! My brain came suddenly alive, and I with it. But so did the guilt. It also was alive. Alive and chewing at my body.

The last night that I could bear to go to class I crawled into bed with a virulent illness and did not get up until three months later, and then only because I could not seem to die. I lay there fighting some sort of inner battle of senseless guilt. I lost in the end but had no way of knowing this. I lost in this because I accepted finally that ugly doctrine that said, "Men and women can't be friends."

When I told Paul about Devon he thought the incident only an incident, unimportant. But I felt so cheap, so awful to see myself in the mirror, my eyes shining, standing more erectly. Paul began to make jokes and noticed a difference. I began to wear baggy blouses to hide my breasts. I dropped weight and inches weekly and pounded on my body because I hated it so.

My three-month illness put the family through an ordeal they still talk about. It is a winter we would rather not remember.

My girls, now in college, were all drifting, drifting, and I was too ill to realize how or where they were drifting. They were at ages where a cutting off from us was natural, but when they refused to discuss their lives, friends, or plans with me, I felt rejected and hurt and was beyond understanding what I believed was needless rebellion.

When I finally crawled out of the bed a few days before

Christmas, I did a strange thing. As ill as I had been, I planned a huge party to be held right after Christmas.

Tinting my silver hair back to its natural ash brown, I bought a new hostess gown (by now Paul was most definitely confused by this wife who had only a few weeks before been invalided) and wrote invitations to everyone in our neighborhood.

And everyone came. The whole, damn shebang! As I wandered about with trays of food, I caught snatches of conversation that, for some reason, amused me.

"And when I saw her at the market just a few days ago, she looked like death!"

". . . well, she doesn't look like death tonight! She doesn't look like herself at all!"

I don't know how I did it (I was weak beyond belief), or why I did it, but for that one night a light burned brightly in me before it went out and again I would shut my door to the world. Perhaps I did it to show that world that I was not dead. Far from it.

Since Mama's death I had made a ritual of calling Aunt Nettie daily to see if she was well, but after the calls, or the weekly visit to her house, I began to have serious spells of depression and crying jags. Aunt Nettie tended to harp on the past and finally I told her plainly that I could not bear it anymore. She and Aunt Addie were clearly concerned by the fact that I was refusing to attend mass. Most of our conversations were tirades directed at shaming me back into the church.

"I never heard of such, Lia! Saying that church can make you ill! *Aren't you ashamed?*"

After this I stopped calling and visiting. And when calls came, I had Paul or the girls say that I was not at home.

9

I looked to Paul as a sort of surrogate knight-errant to defend me when I could not defend myself, to understand me when I could not understand myself, to support me when my own strength failed. I began to feel that not only was I failing, but that Paul was failing me, too.

Arguments of the day began to carry over into the night and whatever bridges we had built in our marriage began to sag and deteriorate. Bridges we had formerly crossed freely, happily, were now toll bridges, and the tolls we paid were high.

The one to fall first was in our physical relationship. I began to have less and less desire to be touched and my response to Paul's attempts to make love to me were met with violent reactions.

As incongruous as it sounds, my need for evidence of Paul's love was greater than at any time in our marriage. But if he suggested making love, I would rail at him.

"*Again?* My God, aren't you ever satisfied? We just made love yesterday! You tell me in one breath to stop acting like a crazy woman and in the next to make love to you!"

And the voice within my head was laughing tauntingly: "You'll never satisfy a man! I don't know how I ever had a child like you! *Crazy! I'll show you crazy!*"

Knowing that perhaps it might hurt less to reject than to be rejected, I began having trouble achieving an orgasm, and finally just gave in to the anger and stopped even trying. Lovemaking was not lovemaking anymore; it was just sex, and I hated it as I hated every other thing in my life that I had needed so much but had been betrayed by in the end.

At this time Dr. Russell and Dr. Ling were both working to keep me on my feet. I was having serious sieges with pain that enveloped my entire inner body at times. On each weekly visit I was told the same thing.

"Lia, you are just a victim of tension. Get your house in order and the pains will go away!" They did not go away; they got worse until I would awaken at night screaming in tears with the feeling that vipers were wrapping my vitals, choking my life out. I wanted to believe that nothing was really wrong with me, but I didn't. For once, I was right. The problem was that people seldom listen to someone they think of as crazy.

Christmas came and with it the annual visit of my in-laws. Determined to make the visit bearable, I felt my reserve slipping as I sat listening to Paul's mother speak of her "poor Greg." For the first time in twenty years I spoke my feelings to his family, as Paul withered in his chair.

"Your poor Greg! He is the only scum I know who has the nerve to charge visits to a massage parlor to his MasterCharge and then let the bill come to his house for Ellie to see!"

Seething with anger, I realize how I must have looked and sounded. I couldn't seem to stop. All those righteous, self-composed people, benignly digesting their Communion bread and sitting in judgment.

As we sat in the living room Paul and his mother drifted into the kitchen where, with about ten feet of space separating us, she made plans with him for the following day, ignoring any pretense or courtesy of asking if I had plans for the day after Christmas.

"Of course I don't mind if you take her, Paul! But don't you think she, or you, might have asked if I had plans? It is Christmas, Paul!"

"Lia, why do you get so damned upset over trifling things?"

"It's not trifling to me! I am not some roach on the floor. I am your wife!"

I wanted so much for Paul to see how this was affecting me, for him to stand with me, support me, and get this ugliness out of our lives. In the end I knew it had all been useless.

It seems miraculous to me today that I was capable, during this period, of even getting a meal on the table. Yet I ran my

The Healing of Lia

house, cooked, cleaned, and functioned when necessary as Paul's support at business dinners when the wives were "inspected" by the top brass of his company. In truth, these dour functions were the only social events or outlets Paul and I ever attended. By now, other than an anniversary night out or a movie once or twice a year, I never was taken anywhere at all.

Paul is very much a homebody who hates going out. To get out meant meeting his resistance and apathy, which usually turned into a full-fledged screaming match that exhausted both of us. As ill as I was becoming, and as fearful of meeting people as I was, I would find myself, on the days Paul had free, standing like a child, sounding him out.

"Paul, it's a lovely day. Could we maybe take a drive . . . or if I fix a picnic, maybe we could go out somewhere?"

I could feel his no before it was ever voiced.

"Lia, you know the fence needs mending. And my spark plugs are due for a change. Maybe next week. Some other time."

But next week never seemed to come, or when it did I might be ill, and it would be too late for me. And it began to seem to me that I had but one enemy, and his name was Paul.

"Goddamn you! I don't need to go next week! I need to get out now!"

And one time, when I asked if we might go out somewhere nice, so that I could wear a long dress, and was told that we would go out "nice" to the office party (one month away), I hurled myself at him in a rage that would be difficult to tell of on paper.

Dimly, some inner voice told me that no matter what I did, it would do no good. Paul was immovable. Paul was strong. Paul was unhurtable. And so it seemed. So instead of smashing Paul, I smashed myself until the awful need to live dimmed and finally went out completely. I found that when your body is battered and bruised, and your head pounded until thinking is impossible, it somehow doesn't matter quite as much whether anyone loves you or not.

It was now my firm belief that Paul not only did not love me, but that he deliberately did things to hurt me. Destroy me is perhaps a better word. That is a word I found in a journal note; I felt that I was being "destroyed."

Often, for no discernible reason, I began to have strange and violent spells of anger. Afterward, Paul would hold me close and try to comfort me. He also told me he could always tell before "it" happened by looking at my eyes.

"They change, Lia. They are not your eyes any longer. The skin around your eyes looks frozen and tightly stretched. It is like looking into the eyes of a complete stranger, some other woman."

What he didn't know was that I, too, could feel it begin to happen, but didn't know what "it" was, and I didn't know how to stop it. After it began . . . I no longer wanted to stop it.

These physical feelings became more evident and more severe, and the violence I tried to hold back began to seep out in awful ways. Fear drove me inward and I began to leave the house less and less. The only people I would see were those I had to see: people at the grocery market, Aunt Nettie, Paul's family, the fuel man, and Harry, who came by to service the antiquated furnace.

I would remain quiet and docile for long whiles, spending all my time cooking and baking treats to "make up" for the other times. The thing was that I was having trouble even remembering the other times.

I think the violence began the day the family began to ask me about lunch before I had swallowed my last sip of morning coffee. I went slightly mad, standing at the kitchen sink with all the debris of breakfast spread about: toast crumbs, sticky jam pots, egg hardening on the plates. All of a sudden the appliances looked menacing, and the kitchen itself, a cell . . . and my family, the jailors.

All these years I had been a docile servant of them all. I had asked for little for myself. But somehow, this particular morning was different. And, yes, they responded by looking at me as if I had truly gone mad or insane.

The terrible Christmas that I "spoke up" was also the last time I visited with my own relatives. These visits to my family were, for me, like entering an unmarked danger zone. I have, in the years since, tried to discern just what sort of pleasure these people derived from our visits; I know I derived none at all.

The Healing of Lia

This particular season Collin and Joy had toured Europe and it proved to be an especially rich resource of goods.

"Lia! Have you seen Joy's Waterford crystal from Dublin?" voiced Aunt Addie before I had been relieved of my coat. Adding her barbed pièce de résistance, "You *do* know what Waterford *is*, don't you?" (Yes, Aunt Addie, but people who live in dark, deep holes have little need of such.)

It was rather like sitting in an arena, letting carrion birds pick and tear small pieces from my being, not large enough pieces to kill, just causing a slow agony of seeing my children's eyes linger on the incredibly beautiful Aubusson carpets, Boulle cabinets, silver appointments softly reflecting hidden lights, and Cousin Joy vaporously drifting about with trays of pâté as Collin poured his liquors and wines which often cost as much as my weekly grocery allowance. It was cruel and it was unnecessary.

If I had not been ill and had been able to shed a little levity on events, perhaps they would not have affected me so deeply. At this point I seemed to have lost any ability to defend myself from others.

This day I sat for the better part of a three-hour visit until Collin got around to describing a magnificent piece of art in Rome. When he said he didn't know whose work it was, I gained a perverse pleasure in interjecting bluntly, "Bernini. I believe you are refering to Bernini, Collin. He is widely known in the art world," and leaving them all peering at my backside, I went into the bathroom where I sat, sick, shaking in an angry resolve never to let my family humiliate me again.

On the trip homeward each of us sat quietly dulled with diminution, and I told Paul that I would never go again.

I, Lia, had disappeared into an unknown latitude, away from family, friends, neighbors. Away from the world of myself. The zephyrous young girl who once shook hands with a governor and had hopes of being Somebody became a bestial, slavering creature—exactly as predicted. I lived wrapped in darkness as voices screamed within. Wrapped in the black shroud of ignorance with no one to open me to the light of Truth. Drugged, battered by my own hand, silenced by fear. Living in death, but not quite. This Lia had still, within herself, some anchor of hope. Nobody knew this, not even I.

The contradictions came because a part of me allowed me to get up, tend my duties (my home was clean, my meals well prepared), and sit in my eyrie watching the play below.

Home. Home became a trap, a prison, and all within it my enemies. I was now unable to see any of what Paul did for me, only what he denied me. The more angry I grew with Paul, the more I smashed at myself. Like a tentacled leviathan, the disease crept in and crowded out reason.

"Lia, why on earth are you pulling the linens out of the closet at three in the afternoon?"

"Why not at three in the afternoon? Damn it, Paul, I feel like cleaning the closets!"

One day as we were having a pleasant visit with his sister Lois, while I fixed tea and cinnamon toast, Paul stood in the kitchen directing:

"That's enough butter, Lia. Not too much cinnamon, no more," until I felt my neck tighten with unreleased anger. *Rules, rules, rules! Directions. Directions. Directions!*

Later, Lois laughingly asked, "How do you stand it, Lia? Doesn't it make you mad?" It did, but not in the way she meant. Mad has other meanings, too.

Whenever I exploded, Paul was shocked because of his efforts to help.

"Lia, all I was doing was helping, making suggestions!" But to me they were not suggestions, they were orders.

The days Paul worked away from home, I relaxed more, functioned better. But I felt great guilt because I knew I should want him home with me. Guilt. Anger. Each played against the other until I heard myself screaming at Paul, whom I love so dearly, "Leave me alone! Let me breathe! Let me discover myself, *my own way!*"

"Okay! I'll leave you alone! I won't ever tell you another thing!"

There was no way to stop it, no way of reaching each other. Words became weapons and we used them against each other.

I never knew that I could have done as I liked and just ignored Paul. But this is easier said than done.

Paul had certain things he wanted our home to be. Rather a perfectionist, he wanted a clean home but made this difficult (I

The Healing of Lia

felt impossible) by objecting to any noise. He would wander about idly during a work break, asking questions.

"Lia, why run the dishwasher *now*? Why not wait until tonight?"

"Because dirty dishes are not a set thing, Paul! If I don't run them now, I'll have an overload tonight!"

Suggestions? Questions? I didn't know anymore. I felt as if some sort of bomb were about to go off in my mind. In my mind Paul grew from a pedant into a martinet and any remark that he might make was interpreted as intended to destroy me. He was in a terrible position: he had a sick wife, but every piece of advice he gave was thrown back in his face angrily!

Economy demanded that our home be a tightly run ship. Used to making do, doing without, conserving anything usable, I enjoyed being creative on my budget but felt that Paul had become a fanatic about our lifestyle.

"Lia, why don't you save that?"

"Because I don't know what to do with two spoonfuls of cauliflower!"

"What happened to the rest of the gravy from the roast?"

"Dammit, Paul! The dog has to eat, too!"

"Did we eat *all* those chops last Wednesday?"

"Oh, hell no, Paul! I sell food on the side for spending money!"

Paul had good intentions, but his constant, hovering questions, and my accountability to these questions, were to me like being caught in some awful web that drew tighter and tighter as I fought it.

Waste was simply not tolerated, restrictions were drawn, and in our home there was a rule fitting every action.

When the children were younger, Paul would get them to run mirthfully and turn off lights, shut open doors, and practice economy by enforcing the law of the Great Huckleberry. It was against the law of the Huckleberry to waste anything. They cheerfully obeyed and it seemed a sensible psychology when carried on within reason. Carried to an extreme it chafed deeply.

Most of it I didn't mind, not even sorting the garbage: one dish for the soup pot, one for the garden compost, one for the dog. If I mistakenly put something in the wrong dish, I found myself in the humiliating position of knowing I was too incompetent to even properly sort garbage.

"Lia, not bones in the compost! It will draw every dog in the neighborhood!" And, of course, he was right.

My next-door neighbor Merri remarked one day as she sat watching me, "Mercy, Lia! I feel my time is more valuable than to do things like that!" As time went on, I felt that not only my time, but I myself, was not of any value, so why not sort garbage?

The rules of home were inflexible. No issue ever of great importance, yet no issue small enough to be overlooked. When my infractions were brought to my attention, even kindly, I began to hide and sneak rather than experience humiliation.

In fairness to Paul, he never denied me anything I needed, but when sometimes I asked for a small item, I felt great resentment to have to explain my need.

"Do you have to get the bras this week, Lia?"

"Well, I'm hanging lopsided if that answers your question!"

Why are you so *angry?* I just asked a simple question!"

"That's the whole point! That's my whole life, answering questions!"

What I wanted to scream was that he should have *known* I never asked unless I had a need. I began to feel like a horse with a barbed bit in his mouth—and the rider was reining in hard.

It never stopped. Each week we vowed to "begin over again" and each week we grew exhausted from the endless tension. The more tense Paul became, the more rigid he was. Now, well into the troublesome years when our girls were reaching maturity, we were one snarling, unhappy family with me feeling compressed, squeezed by agonies over simple restrictions that we must follow.

Like some fire in a profane temple, fed by the tinder of daily events, my anger grew. I totally lost my sense of humor or ability to take a joke with myself as the butt of that joke and felt brutalized by the man I worshipped.

I seemed to know that when I was "out" the miasma lifted, and I began to drive out and around, often "awakening" to find myself in a place I did not remember going to.

On one of these days, as I wandered about a shopping center, I heard my name called and looked up to see Meg, my cousin.

The Healing of Lia

She invited me to lunch and instead of running, as I normally would have, I accepted. This luncheon brought about so many changes in my life that if given full account, it would be a story in itself. These changes brought me closer to the top of the ladder of trauma than ever before, and as quickly cut all my remaining supports from under me; they brought joy and agony, peace and confusion. And at the end, brought about the greatest bodily harm a woman can sustain and still live. With this came my final break with reality.

A pleasant luncheon of crêpes and coffee ended some time later on a floor in an unknown place, with a cruel, oily hand smothering my screams and the rapine destruction of the small balance that survived in my mind.

"Lia! You wouldn't believe the changes the prayer meetings have made in our life! I never felt such joy! We go each Wednesday evening, and we all sit in a circle praying for the Holy Spirit to come upon us—and, oh, Lia! He does! A miracle! Out of nowhere He comes, and we begin to witness and speak in strange tongues! It *is* a miracle, Lia! Won't you come with us . . . share with us. . . . Say you will try!"

Draining my coffee dregs, I fumbled for my purse, thanked Meg for the luncheon, and left.

I went home in a strange mood, feeling a strange calm. I was not lost, not frightened, and I had actually enjoyed the meeting with Meg. Her words kept hitting the sides of my head: charismatic . . . miracle . . . healings. Healings!

After dinner I ventured to ask Paul if he had ever heard of the charismatic movement.

". . . yes, Lia, but I honestly don't think it is for us."

Later in bed I took the gift Meg had given me and began to flip through the pages. A small paperback Bible entitled *Good News for Modern Man*. Although it was a new book, it fell open to a page and my eyes found a sentence: *"You did not choose me: I chose you."*

I looked across to Paul, sleeping so far away in his own bed with his back turned to me, and realized that I didn't feel alone. Putting the book under my pillow, I turned off my lamp and when I next knew anything, it was light. It was the first night of peace I had had since . . . I could not remember.

The next day I found the courage to ask Paul if he would take me to the Wednesday meeting.

"Please, Paul. Just to see—"

"Lia, those meetings don't have the bishop's approval yet."

"Bishop's approval! Paul, what difference does that make?"

"A big difference. Wait a while. Wait for a month or so, then we'll see."

"A month! I can't wait a month! I've got to go . . . now . . . Paul!"

In tears, I explained to Meg, Paul's refusal.

"Let it rest, Lia. Don't insist. Just pray." And Meg gave me a certain passage to read when I hung up the phone.

Bible thumbing had always been foreign to me, so I had a difficult time even locating the passage. When I did, I began to get an eerie feeling that this book contained messages just for me:

> If the world hates you, you must remember that it has hated me first. . . . I chose you from this world, you did not belong to it: this is why the world hates you. . . .

From the moment of this reading I *knew, believed,* that if I could get to the meetings I would be healed. Healed! I made myself a promise: somehow I would get Paul to take me. Somehow.

My somehows ran the gamut of asking, begging, pleading (at one point I knelt at his feet like an animal), but it took a terrible and damaging episode to convince him of my need.

The last time Paul refused me, I tore into him like a berserk beast and I believe that it was only his superior strength that kept me from smashing him. Instead, I smashed myself. The following week he did drive me, and thereafter I knew that I could find my peace here with these people. After this I did what I never thought I could, I drove out into the night alone because Paul would no longer take me. An edge of hate grew and hardened because I saw Paul as denying me help in my attempt to live again as a normal being and find my way back to God. For twenty years I had gone with him to worship in a way I could not accept; now he would not go my way at all. My confusion said: is *this* the world that hates you? Isn't Paul a part of that world?

The Healing of Lia

Each Wednesday night we sat, a grouping of lost souls numbering about twenty, black and white, rich and poor, sinners and saints. In a circle, hands joined, praying and chanting in tongues that God alone understood.

The first evening Paul had taken me, we were met at the door by a smallish young priest in sandals and another member of the group, a physician of some prominence in our community. We were both embraced and given the traditional charismatic greeting, "Peace, I love you!"

Paul was more than a little put off at being hugged and kissed by strangers, and men strangers, at that! I admit that for all my need for physical affection, it rather took my breath away, too.

The group sat in a small room in a circle of chairs set so close that our knees touched our neighbor's. At first, some merely read Bible passages and witnessed how faith had helped them in the week gone by. Then a subtle change took place and one by one they closed their eyes, lifted their hands in a gesture of supplication, and from their mouths issued what I can only describe as an eerie, unworldly melodic chanting. As I listened (I sat by the sandaled priest), I tried to intellectualize that he was chanting in Latin and that I sorely needed to bone up on my basic translations. As the chanting increased in timbre and fervor, the very walls of the room seemed to hum and quiver with the poignant cacophonous cadences. Almost as if they had a will of their own, my arms lifted, palms upturned to receive the Spirit, and I was swaddled in feelings I could not begin to describe; more nonphysical than physical, as if another sensory passageway into my being had opened, I found exactly what I had been seeking for a lifetime: peace. Peace and God.

My mentor for the seminar was the physician, Dr. Bryan. A gaunt, middle-aged man whose eyes reflected tiredness, he took me under his wing and began to initiate me into the life of the charismatic. I found that Dr. Bryan had given up a lucrative private practice to work in this way to help the lost, give succor to "hopeless" alcoholics (he gave each of his patients a routine prescription: the address of the prayer meetings and the time he expected them to come each week for "treatment"), and find his own place in God's plan. These choices had cost him his marriage, his family, and in the end his practice. Rather than being broken by all this, he seemed to burn as a man on fire from within.

Exactly four weeks after my learning seminar began, I was baptized in the name of the Holy Spirit by Dr. Bryan, and as the group encircled me, chanting, laying their hands upon my head, praying me into the community, it was affirmed that from that moment my healing was begun. As I drove home through the empty streets of unfamiliar neighborhoods, heading my car over the cloverleaf onto the interstate, I remembered vivid holographic words written across my brain: *Lia is healed! Praise God! Healed!*

At midnight when I finally settled in my bed after reading my daily Bible passages, I awoke with Paul pulling at my arm, shaking me.

"Lia! For heaven's sake, what is the matter?"

"Matter? What do you mean? Nothing is the matter, Paul."

"Well you've been sitting bolt upright for ten minutes jabbering words that I can't understand! For heaven's sake, if those meetings upset you like this . . ."

"Paul, I'm fine. Really. Just go back to sleep. I was probably dreaming."

But I was not dreaming and I knew it. The following week when I told Dr. Bryan about the incident, he embraced me happily and said, "Lia, it's the sign we have been praying for! Don't you see? Your conscious mind is so troubled it had not been able to let you receive the gift of tongues . . . but while you slept, your subconscious mind reached over into God's world and you spoke with the tongues of angels! Lia, God is in you! Now and always!"

And I believed him with all my heart. I believed them all.

I went weekly to the prayer meetings and prayed that none of my friends had noticed any changes in me. Gradually I began to feel a sense of aloneness even with them and a gap of difference between my friends and me grew. If I felt the earth slipping and knew I was in danger of falling into the chasm, I held on with a death grip. I witnessed, confessed my weaknesses, begged acceptance, and tried to file away my rough edges to fit into their mold.

The Healing of Lia

One evening as my seminar group sat drinking coffee and discussing everyday things, including books we were reading, I laughingly iterated my library list for that week: a book on Etruscan art, an Agatha Christie, and a look into the religions of the East. A tenuous silence fell and my words seemed to lie exposed and somehow obscene while everyone sat and looked into his coffee cup. Finally Dr. Bryan spoke in his soft way.

"Lia, we are not judging you, dear, but we have found it more enlightening to read only works of inspired reading, material concerning the religious way of life."

Not judging? Then why didn't they *look* at me? Why did I *feel* judged? Inspired reading only? What of the beauty of metered verse? Of art, history, adventure? Wasn't God in all these things? Everywhere? As I looked around the group, they had suddenly changed: they were no longer with me, they were against me.

As Meg and I drove home later, her face alight with fervor, she chatted on in an attempt to explain what she thought I had misunderstood.

"Lia, I don't miss any of the rest of it. My shelves are bursting with books! Bible stories, stories of nuns, priests, saints! And I get such comfort from reading them!"

"But don't you want to learn *more*, Meg? To know more this week than you did last week? How can you bear to limit your reading?"

"Lia! You're missing the whole point! We cut ourselves away from anything that might be a danger to us, just as contemplatives do, sort of a safe seclusion from the sins of the world."

Neither Meg nor any of them had any idea of what reading and learning meant to me. Nor of the years I had spent relearning *how* to read, regaining my comprehension of the written word. Each precious printed word, each grain of learning I absorbed, meant an infusion of life after the emptiness following the shock treatments.

Glancing sideways at Meg's earnest face, shadowed now by what she mistook as her failure to reach me, I felt tears of humiliation, and something else, anger. Welling within me was the ubiquitous feeling that again I was being rejected as not-quite-good-enough by persons operating cruelly in the name of Christianity. Telling me to be "in the world, but not of it"! How? After fighting so hard to be allowed entry into this world, how was I now expected to reject it as evil?

Tears spilling, I ground the gears and spoke to Meg.

"Want to hear something funny? My book list for the past two weeks included books on Gypsy folklore and witchcraft . . . and *The Godfather!* Talk about your 'inspired' books! Meg, face it, my interests run in strange directions for someone imbued with the Holy Spirit!" And vividly in my mind was a dinner-table tableau of two weeks past with Paul telling me, "No, I'm not interested in reading or watching anything about the Mafia, Lia. I have better things to do and better things to fill my mind"—the clear implication being that while he was keeping his mind undefiled, I was not.

The person who on the next Wednesday drove my car out of the yard, onto the interstate, and walked into the prayer meeting was someone they would not soon forget. Not often does one attend a prayer meeting in a see-through blouse and slit skirt. The only remembrance I have of this night was revealed through brief journal notes that had lain hidden, until it was too late to mend the damage. This night was the end of it, a final humiliation, and a final break with any attempt to relate to people or to God.

One short week later, according to my own notes, my body, which for forty years had been morally unblemished, lay brutalized in a pool of human corruption, somewhere on some lost street in some lost place, while the world played its games, watched its television, and ate its lunches. Raped. As God was the only witness to this, other than one, it must have been He who took me, guided me home. Perhaps seeing one of His children hurt, who had been a living monstrance, a repository for the body and blood of Christ, brought forth an act of mercy and help. I have no way of knowing this or of little else. But the circle I drew around myself now was no longer an attempt to draw others within, but rather to wall them off from me. Even God. Perhaps most of all God, and even today I can't explain why.

There is no doubt that when God designed the human mind, he installed a built-in safety device. Exactly when it is triggered is certainly different in each of us. Mine went quietly into operation at this point. Why it waited so long and allowed me to endure so much is a moot point, except perhaps to students of psychology. The empty shell, the rind of me, lay bruised, silent, voided of any evidence of life for many days. Except to breathe and evacuate, I might have been dead. As if some inner pressure exerted an effortless depression of the carotid arteries, I slipped away to where I had always known I belonged; counterpoised, moribund, the bed becoming my bier, I let Lia go peacefully away. And like a fragile waxen taper I watched as she melted to extinguishment in a warm pool of self.

What residue of flesh and bone that survived got out of the bed sometime later to face what lay outside the door to the bedroom. The only perceptible emotions that functioned in this automaton were fear, despair, and guilt; the only intellectual knowledge was that of being condemned for reasons I could not comprehend, of being unloved because of being unlovable, of being alone because of being an alien in a world of normal people.

Like a creature who tunneled in dark places living in shadows, at times I caught glimmers of light. Half blind from the darkness I tried to reach this light. I had lain abed for over a week before I rose to bathe and tend my body. I stood under the stream of scalding water, soaping myself over and over, still feeling filthy. It was the first I had ventured out of the safety of my room since I fled to Dr. Russell's office days before.

"Lia, my dear! You must ignore what happened! You have been raped, but it's over. Consider it just a social incident in your life that should be forgotten!"

Dr. Russell had sat on the table after examining me and ordering large injections of penicillin to be shot into my backside.

"No need to take chances, Lia, but don't worry, you're all right."

All right? I wasn't, but nobody seemed to sense that. I had gone home and lain with my buttocks blackened from the injections, my arms with clear, distinct finger marks up and down them. Blue, red, purple. The house carried on without me. Paul was silent, confused, and hurt. I tried to tell him what had happened, or rather, by now, what I thought had happened, for it seemed not to have happened at all. At least, not to me.

I found no possible way to explain, because my mind pivoted between points of rationality and blank unawareness. As if my body was attending life without the mind attached. Some inchoate holocaust whipped my brain cells first in belief, then in disbelief. When Paul shouted at me, as well he should, to tell him *why*, tell him *where*, I sat like a mumbling fool not knowing the answers.

"That oily sonofabitch! Harry! Why on earth would you have gone, Lia?"

"I didn't, Paul. I wouldn't—"

"What in hell do you mean by that?"

"I don't know . . ."

"Well, did it happen . . . or didn't it happen?"

"It did. At least, I think—I don't know anymore, Paul."

And Paul told me he could not talk with me and wanted only to be quiet and think. Somehow, the world stopped then for both of us. He didn't understand; how could anyone expect him to? Nor did I understand. Only God understood and He was silent.

Finally, my body mending, I got up and began to live again. I knew Paul was having thoughts about leaving me or sending me away, and each day I arose to face the fear: would this be the day? I spent hours trying to remember the past months and I could remember nothing. But something led me to know that *out there* was a world of sunlight, music, wonders, mountains, fields, salty oceans. Life. Life that I would never know if I didn't leave the tunnel to experience it. So I tried, I truly tried.

After a time which was unmarked by clock or calendar, Paul took me out to a park one day, and as we sat on the soft grassy lawn he bound up his hurt and pride and gave me his forgiveness. If he never did another kind act in his lifetime, Paul had done what few men would do, for in his mind he felt he was forgiving an erring, unfaithful wife. I preferred him to think this rather than what I believed to be the truth. I firmly believed myself possessed by an entity of evil. I believed myself cursed, lost, damned. There were good reasons for this belief and one made its emergence during this day of reprieve.

While we sat in the sunlight speaking of our future together, a grisly metamorphosis occurred. I suddenly felt a welling of

The Healing of Lia

uncontrollable anger, and heard very distinctly in my mind words that I *knew* had not been spoken:

"He's actually forgiving *you!*"

As if wired to some remote-control machine, my body and mind seemed not to obey my will. The body was shaking with uncontrolled mirth! I felt my face twisting into a grimace which I hid by spinning around until my back was to Paul. To stifle the sounds I feared might come out, I put my fist to my mouth in terror. I realized that while my body might be my own, my voice and tongue were not. It is only by the grace of God that the words running in my brain did not escape my mouth. This spiritual incubus romped through my brain, making a mockery of me, and Paul sat, still holding my hand, unaware of what was happening.

Why, God? Why me? And because His voice was silent and the future so bleak, my thought was that I must destroy myself. Such a lovely thought, that of entering the peace and quiet of death I had longed for since my time began. At home, hanging over my bed, was a small wooden plaque on which was lettered:

> Death is not extinguishing the light
> It is merely putting out the lamp,
> because the dawn has come. . . .
> —*Tagore*

This became the only thing in my life that comforted me.

Still I hung on and lived.

I was home now. At least, physically. Exactly where I really was is still in question. Judging from the journal notes and my own spotty memories, I was trying very hard to "cure" myself and succeeding only in momumental failures. Paul and I continued having terrible fights, physical fights. He had no comprehension of what was wrong with me. Never the same two days in a row, anything at all might trigger an episode. After these times I had no memory of what had happened. I knew he blamed me for "things," but I had done nothing, nothing at all. Often I would awaken with bruises, painfully throbbing puffs of flesh on my body, and the house would be empty, Paul gone, the girls gone. Lying there, trying to remember, the answer would be there, standing clearly like a dead birch, silver against the blackness of the night, shafts of knowing.

But memory, or what we refer to as memory, was no longer within reach. Wreathed in confusion, hearing directives voiced by a manic muezzin . . . calling . . . shrieking from high balconies only I could envision, I would lie listening, listening, listening.

Sometimes the drugs quieted the voices, dulling them until my arms and legs felt leaden, until food or sleep or love or living no longer mattered. Only the quiet. Please, God, only let the quiet come into my mind. This was my prayer, my only prayer. Pleasegodpleasegodpleasegod—until the drugs wore off and the voices began again louder than ever. It was no good to fight, I knew this. I always lost and when I did, they were so angry with me that the damage had to be dealt more severely because I had not obeyed.

Perhaps the largest clue to the illness at this time was what hung in my closet. My everyday uniform had long been dark slacks and tops. My dressy clothes were black with high necklines, schoolmarm clothes.

Strangely, even in my teen years I had a sort of favorite uniform costume: a severely cut black dress worn unrelieved except for a demure cameo pinned to a velvet ribbon about my neck, and my long hair pulled back in a tight bun. I remember feeling very safe when dressed in this manner, and I noticed that if anyone did ask me out, he was interested in *me*, not in the way I looked. This was very important to me; I felt more "me" at these times than any other.

Except when I wore the flaming red velvet cut down to the bottom of my ribcage. Except when I wore the outlandish gold lamé, or the hobble-tight skirt with the brilliant pink see-through blouse, or the clinging white sheath with yards of rhinestones wound about my neck. . . .

Sequined, bespangled, bejeweled. I wasn't taken for a schoolmarm at these times. But I wasn't safe, either.

"Where do you teach, Mrs. Farrelli?"

This odd question came from a young associate of Paul's at a dinner dance. It seemed to be a question I had answered all my life. Even in high school one of my nicknames had been

The Healing of Lia

"Teach." Everyone laughed about it who knew me. Lia may have looked like a teacher with her thinness, horn-rimmed glasses, braces, and severe hairdo, but anyone knowing me would certainly laugh at such a name!

"I don't teach anywhere! I'm not a teacher at all!"

The young man seemed very embarrassed. Later, when I entered the ladies room to fix my makeup and caught sight of the woman in the glass, it made me catch my breath.

The woman in the mirror wore all black: long skirt, black top. True, the top had tiny sparkles of silver threads running through it, but the impression was one of conservatism, modesty, inhibition. Little makeup, wire-rimmed granny glasses, tiny unobtrusive earrings—the schoolmarm was squarely facing me.

I remember feeling slightly ill when I returned to our table. For the rest of the evening I sat and regaled everyone with caustic, risqué remarks and double entendres of an obvious vein. The men began to laugh with heartiness and Paul took me out on the dance floor and asked if I felt all right. I did not feel all right. I felt dizzy, ill, and frightened. I heard myself saying things I would never say, making remarks that were crude, vulgar, embarrassing, even to me. And yet, there seemed to be no way to stop. It was as if I were on a runaway train and it was moving too fast to jump off.

I could feel the winds of things happening, cruel winds that whipped my face, taking away my breath. But I couldn't get the train to stop and I knew if I jumped it would be the end of something—the end of me. I was riding the train hard in those months that are lost to me. And apparently was riding in terror.

Perhaps it was because the part of me that carried on through this period was a clever, energetic, and apparently able part. This speaks loudly in the fact that follows: after years of terror and sickness I took on a part-time job as a secretary in a doctor's office! The Lia who had spent half a lifetime cringing over her inabilities to make decisions, drive cars, and be a wife and mother just marched out and obtained a job that entailed public contact, quite a lot of responsibility, and a very small salary. None of which seemed to matter. The job was a symbol, a signpost that I still had some value in the world.

I was fighting not only the illness but pain. Terrible pain. It was almost impossible for me to do my essential work at home and totally impossible to do well in my job. I went to Dr. Ling, begged pain pills, tranquilizers, antidepressants, sleeping pills, anything at all to stay on my feet. I saw Dr. Russell and after telling him of pain that ripped from my vagina backward into the rectum he sent me to surgical consultants who wrote complexly worded letters that said: "This woman is imagining the whole condition." As he pitied me and was my friend, he gave me bottles of tiny barbiturate pills to calm me and help quell this "imagined" pain.

Over a period of a few months I saw two more physicians, one an expensive internist who, after giving me a pelvic and rectal examination, said he found everything in a normal condition but wondered why my cervix had been left intact.

"But it was removed! I'm sure it was removed."

"Apparently not, young woman. It's there, that's for certain."

I left his office vaguely disquieted, still feeling the dull throbbing from the sensitive area he had palpated. Out on the street I faced the fact that the markers on the road were signaling one thing: each of the doctors felt (and stated frankly) that all my problems were in my head. Perhaps many of them were, but *one* was not and it would be a full year before the mistake was discovered. One more year of agonizing, debilitating, unnecessary pain.

During this year Paul and I made desperate efforts to find a "solution" to our problems. He agreed to see a marriage counselor and psychologist with me, even though the added expense was a hardship. Each week we left this man's office fifty dollars poorer and devoid of any hopes at all for a future. The only thing we might have gained from this doctor was a vastly increased vocabulary of words we could never use in public.

"You have *both* made a success of fucking up your lives! You particularly, Lia! When are you going to realize that there is no frigging payoff to pain or illness or depression?"

Not having the least idea of what he meant, I sat muttering things that made no sense whatever. As far as I could ascertain he recommended freedom of *self* and living in a sort of unaccountable way which included not accounting to each other, to anyone (including God), for anything.

"How many drugs are you on, Lia? How many a day?"

"Two—two drugs. I take them every three hours."

"At night, too?"

"Yes. Day and night. Why?"

"Did it ever occur to you that you are addicted? That you couldn't stop these drugs if you wanted?"

"Addicted! Certainly not! Dr. Ling assured me they were nonaddictive!" I was appalled and angry at this man for suggesting such a thing.

"Well, don't believe it. Test yourself. Stop them now." Deriding me, he sat rocking in his chair.

"Do you know how ridiculous you are, Lia? You say you have left the church in one breath, but in reality you possess one of the most rigid, self-destructive Catholic consciences I have ever seen! You are more tied to obedience to the church than most practicing Catholics!"

Finally, shuddering under his verbal barrage of *shits, hells,* and some epithets I had to ask Paul the meaning of later, we left, paid our fifty dollars, and never went back.

Our next choice seemed a better one. It may not have solved our problems or given us an answer as such, but the weekend we spent at a Christian Marriage Encounter was one that made a profound change in both of us.

The weekend had not been a planned thing. We were both exhausted emotionally and physically and were financially unable to bear more expense. The decision to go was made after a night of despair.

I don't know why I ran out that night. I cannot remember the reason that sent me out into the dark empty city streets after midnight. Miles from home, so far from home! As I ran, the headlights of a car beamed down on me. The car stopped and a door was thrown open. A voice shouted in anger.

"Get in this car, Lia! Stop this! Get in the car!"

Paul's voice. Paul, with so much anger in his voice.

"Goddamn it, Lia! I've got to work tomorrow! Get in the damn car!"

On and on I ran. Running from Paul, from hurt, from the pain, until my lungs would pump no more air, until I stood rigid, sweating, against a filthy brick wall and let him take the case from my fist and lead me into the car.

Whatever happened to send me out into the black streets in a section of town noted for muggings, robbery, stabbings, and drug pushers is gone from my mind forever. I know only that this was the night Paul told me it might be better if I went away for a while. I didn't know how far "away" he meant, nor where "away" was. But I did know if I allowed myself to be put back in the hospital with the shock treatments and drugs, I would never return as the *I* that was Lia. They would take my mind from me this time and it would be for forever.

The next day I called Dorrie, my sister, and that afternoon I flew to her home. I carried with me only one small bag and my Bible, the gift from Meg. Why I carried it I don't know, but I remember feeling that it was quite, quite necessary that I carry it.

Dorrie opened her home to me with generous words.

"Stay as long as you'd like, Lia. Just rest and enjoy yourself, use the pool and the sundeck. . . . We'll talk when you feel like it."

Talk? How do you tell your baby sister you are losing your mind? And your marriage? How could she understand?

I did rest. Each day I got up to total quiet (no demands, no phones, no pressures, no hurts), had breakfast, and went up onto the deck where I sat, my body turning a healthy brown, holding the book on my lap. For many days I sat, as if having gone past the point of rigor mortis, I now became limp, numb . . . unfeeling, unknowing, nonexistent. If there was an epicenter to me, then it would have taken a miracle to have reached it.

After a week or so Dorrie planned an outing of sorts to help me. She and her fiancé took me on a boating holiday. They took along delicious foods, plenty of fine wines, and accoutrements of the good life. They also took along a surprise "friend" for me.

There was no problem in knowing what to do with the foods and wines; there was most definitely a problem in knowing what to do with the friend. On the boat, cabin space was at a minimum and as Dorrie and her fiancé were examples of modern,

The Healing of Lia

liberated living, there came the night when the problem presented itself: I had no place to sleep—at least, not if I wanted to sleep alone.

We were all sitting, listening to taped music and drinking a fine Reisling when it dawned on me that Dorrie did not intend to share bunk space with me that night. Frantically I signaled her that I wanted to speak in private. Behind the curtained partition I asked in a lowered voice, "Dorrie, what do you expect me to do? I'm not a complete prude, but I don't do these things!" Suddenly out of patience she hissed, "For heaven sakes, Lia! There are other people in this world besides yourself! You're a big girl! Take care of your own decisions!"

When we came back into the open cabin, the two men sat, seemingly unperturbed by what they must have heard or suspected. I sat across the table from Dorrie, my face splotched with anger that she had put me in such a position. I had no idea of what the "friend" felt about me or of what he had been told of my presence. Whatever he may have expected, I never learned, because shortly after, Dorrie and her fiancé had a tiff (probably owing to the situation) and she and I retired with a silence between us that ended the trip. The next day we were back at her home and I realized I had absolutely no right to cause a problem in the lives of others because I had problems of my own. I called Paul, who came to take me home with not a word of complaint or a mention of the reason for my leaving. A week later he agreed that a Marriage Encounter in a cloistered atmosphere away from the children might be one answer. It was. For that weekend we "encountered" each other in a spiritual and emotional way that gave us insight into the fact that we each still had a deep love for the other. Except for the illness, we might have carried this feeling of peace and happiness home and nurtured it always. Except for the illness. But neither of us knew it *was* an illness. We knew only that whatever it was, was ugly, despicable, damning to our marriage. Not knowing what to hate, often we hated the wrong thing. More often than not we hated each other.

Paul believed that prayer would put an end to it and he prayed so hard it hurt to watch. I no longer carried such a belief. Only in the most terrible moments would my strength give way and cause me to sink to my knees behind closed doors, praying,

"God! God! You have eyes to see, ears to hear, how can You let us hurt so?"

Again I ran to Dr. Ling, this time because the precious bottles of pills were empty. I began to take double and triple doses just to numb myself, to keep the horror away. It never did for long. For a while, perhaps, but not for long.

"I am sorry to see you feeling so bad, Mrs. Farrelli." (I was never *Lia* to Dr. Ling, not even after almost twelve years of weekly visits.) "My job is, of course, not to solve personal problems but to keep my patients functioning and on their feet."

When I had broached the subject that I was having sexual difficulties and experiencing terrible anger whenever Paul approached me, he expressed concern and suggested, "Perhaps you might see a family counselor?"

As usual I left his office with less hope than I had when I entered, but richer because of the papers for drugs he gave me to keep me "functioning."

At home I barely was functioning. Feeling guilt at not being a good wife and mother, I tried to be a super wife-mother when I was able to function at all. I vacillated between being an invalid and doing jobs that were beyond the strength of a normal woman. I seemed to pride myself in doing everything the hard way. On days that I worked, I still tried to have freshly baked hot breads and homemade cakes for dinner when I was tired beyond telling. The Christmas of this year I made twelve cakes and hundreds of varied treats and complex dishes. (In April we were still eating Christmas cakes from the freezer.) I felt a constant and immediate pressure from my house duties. Whatever plans I had for a day, my family always had needs that seemed to overide mine in importance.

"Lia, must you do that *today?* These papers really should be taken to the bank."

"Sorry to bother you, Mom, but could you pick me up at three? I have a class tonight and need to get to the library."

Rush! Hurry! Run, run, run! This became the rhythm of my life. Dinner was always a hectic affair with the bolting of my carefully prepared dishes and a dashing off to classes, cram sessions, client interviews. They were always ready for dessert while I still had a plate half full of uneaten food. I would jump up to pour Paul's coffee and whisk my remains into the dog's dish so no comment would be made about my growing thinness, while the girls argued about "whose turn" it was. The table was cleared often with my not knowing exactly what I had eaten. To still the pains in my stomach, I turned to my small bottle of Butisol. Lovely green nectar to quiet the pains.

There seemed to be no break in our lives at this point. Neither Paul nor I took a day for solitude or pleasure. I was well into my forties and had the belief that if I took an hour to sit with a cup of coffee and a book, I was guilty of some bad act. Work was a narcotic for both of us. When you work hard enough you can't think. Right then we couldn't afford to think.

Keeping my job was of supreme importance to me, but was becoming nearly impossible. I spent more time in the bathroom doubled and bent than I did at my desk. Patients began to complain about a machine answering the doctor's phone, because each time I left the office I put the phone on the automatic recorder.

Each day as I headed homeward I promised myself that it would be different. This day I would control my anxieties, my temper, my fears. This day I would begin to feel less pain and would get better. At home they had no idea of what I was fighting. They were active, healthy, and accustomed to my being the housekeeper, cook, chauffeur, augur of the future, answering service, seamstress. Their needs and demands on my strength overpowered what little I had left. They did not realize it, not any of the children or Paul, but my physical strength was simply running out. Each day the pain drained a little more of me, and one day as I looked in the mirror at the vacuous visage, I saw Nobody. Nobody. And that day my prayer was to ask, "Lord, can it be over now? Can I let go? Lord, can I end it all now?"

I seemed to know when I was "myself" that everyone except me was in control of my life. To counter this I tried to withdraw from everyone. I practiced not caring what the girls were doing, feeling they had shut me out long ago. In the past when I made attempts to reach out to them, I often received cold, half-hearted, often rude answers. Perhaps they were in a normal phase of rebellion, or perhaps they were just sick to death of my illness. Whatever the cause, their attitudes were more than I could bear at the time. I stopped the family breakfasts and ate alone, and spent hours sitting, weeping in my bubble of drugged spacelessness. Without knowing it, I was on the point of launching the bark of my life into new waters.

Like a stream, it began as a small trickle. Later it grew into an uncontrolled river, rushing over the rocks of confusion and boulders of pain, pulling me into whirlpools of searching, questioning, discovery.

On a stormy weekend I saw a small notice in our paper:

USE AUTOHYPNOSIS TO CHANGE YOUR LIFE!
IMPROVE YOUR HEALTH! ALTER YOUR PERSONALITY!
IF *YOU* WANT TO CHANGE, CALL THIS NUMBER TODAY!

Such an anticlimax began my introduction to hypnosis.

The next evening Paul and I were sitting in a large, comfortable room with about twenty people, listening to a placid, soft-spoken, elderly man describing the phenomenon called hypnosis. I signed up for the eight-week course in autohypnosis and Dr. Ricker discovered to his delight that I seemed to go deeply, swiftly, into a trance state, often having some difficulty in "returning" to my normal state. He encouraged me to use this ability to my advantage.

"Hypnosis is only a very deep and relaxed state, Mrs. Farrelli." A very *normal* state! There can be no possible harm in using it to the fullest degree of your ability."

Nor could there be any possible harm in using it to block my pain, or in using it to remove negative thoughts and replace them with healthy, positive thoughts. So I was taught and so I believed.

I could barely wait to begin my program of self-improvement! Each morning, noon, and evening I sat quietly in my room with the door locked and put myself into an altered state. I used routine exercises, mentally instructing myself that the past *was* past and would be forgotten, that I would concentrate only on a happy future. Good thoughts, wonderfully positive thoughts. But instead of getting better I began to be severely agitated after each session. Agitated, angry, and more destructive to my body each passing day. I began to react violently to any upsetting situation in the house. The degree of the problem was something

The Healing of Lia

I could not weigh. Often it took only a word or a critical look to trigger an episode that would end in violence against myself. I began to look like a battered person, which, in effect, I was. Terrified, I upped my drug intake and began to take double and triple doses of the pills prescribed by Dr. Ling, in the hope of calming my "nerves." Dreams tore my sleep at night, voices tore my days.

Then came a day of sunshine, release. I awoke to feel my body relaxed, my head clear. After my coffee I put the dog out, watered my plants, and set out for the forty-minute drive to the office. Stopping at an intersection to await my turn to hook around the plaza, I noticed the vehicle in front of me driving erratically. Fast. Slow. Brake lights winking rhythmically. With growing impatience, I kept a safe distance when, suddenly, a monstrous hatchet cleaved my brain and I knew who the red truck belonged to and who was driving it! For an instant a keening sound went through my head, the multiplied, magnified scream of every woman who has been torn and damaged by a man. The infusion of terror was accompanied by the sure knowledge that for me at that moment there was no escape. The lanes moved forward at the green signal, and caught in a moving line of cars, I maneuvered around the plaza with its open cobbled spaces a concentric circle of planned beauty.

Harry did not follow the roadway around the plaza as I did; he cut the red truck diagonally across the cobbles and as I reached the open highway, he cut in front of me, edging my car closer and closer to the ditch. As most of the traffic headed in the direction of the business area and I was headed in the opposite direction, I was virtually alone on the roadway. Not quite alone. The red truck moved inches from my window, close enough for me to catch the smell of oily rags.

The red truck clung side by side with my car as I drove in blind terror. The horn honked and from the corner of my eye I thought I saw his arm motioning in some strange way. One mile, two miles—and then I remembered—the school! If I could make it to St. Dismas's, there would be a traffic officer stationed with his patrol car! All I had to do was make it less than one more mile! Passing the village intersection, I slowed not at all, hoping that my speed through the zone would call attention to my car.

It didn't. The siren I prayed to hear was nowhere about that morning. The school! Aloud I chanted, "God, God, let the officer be there."

But he wasn't. Nobody was. The road was empty save for two vehicles: a red truck and an ancient Volvo driven by a madwoman. Then, from a hidden lane, came an old man driving a tractor and I slowed to allow him access. He pulled out and, swinging widely, caused the red truck to veer into the left lane. Taking advantage, I put my foot down to the floor, ran the red lights blinking at the railroad crossing, and didn't look back until I had pulled into the parking area at the office. The road was empty. Completely empty.

Not waiting for the elevator, I ran the two flights up to my office, put the key in, and opened the door. Shutting it behind me, I sat with the blinds still closed, like a blind cretin, not moving, hardly breathing. The phone rang and I let the machine answer it. Beth, from the office across the hall, knocked on the door to join me as usual in our morning cuppa. Knock, knock.

"Lia? You in there, honey?"

One hour. Two hours. Patients came, the mailman came, but the door stayed locked and the blinds shut against the light. My boss would not be in until late afternoon, so the office was empty except for me. I was alone and I knew it was not safe to open that door to *anyone*. I also knew other things, that Harry would find the place where I worked, that I'd never be safe there again. Exactly how long I sat in that frozen condition I don't know. I do know that I drove myself home and later lay in bed too ill to move. Not being able to talk about it with Paul was the worst of it, but something told me not to reopen the old wound. The subject of Harry was closed in Paul's mind. He went about life as if Harry had never entered it. Wanting to spare me, his silence closed the door on ever bringing the subject out into the light, and even now in my terror I would not tell Paul what was the matter with me. "Grow up! Deal with it!" I told myself. But I couldn't, and I knew I couldn't.

That night Paul reached out for me and held me, sensing perhaps that I was slipping again. Some hours after we had made love, I awoke needing to void. I tried to move my legs and get up, but they felt as if they were attached to some devilish pain

The Healing of Lia

machine. When I finally did get out of bed and to the bathroom, I found I could not stand again to get from the commode. Perspiration formed on my face and I slipped off onto the green carpet, breathing in short gasps. I tried to crawl back to bed, but from my waist down nothing moved except the waves of pain. Thinking I was screaming, I began calling to Paul and Lori, who later awoke, and hearing strange raspy grunting sounds, found me. I could feel the hands lifting me, helping me. After swallowing a liberal dose of Butisol, I lay awake saying over and over, "It's all in your mind, all in your mind," until I drifted off in a haze of drugged comfort.

Waking was like rising to the surface of a murky, dark pool. Cold, with my damp gown clinging to me, I slipped from the room and down the stairs before I pulled my robe about me. Opening the back door, I stepped out on the flagstone patio and sat in a wet deck chair watching the transparent little earthworms that come onto the stones each morning and that often stay too long and drown. I sat and watched, knowing that later as the sun came and the day began, I would have to sweep the little dried worm bodies away. I sat there alone until the softness of the new day came and I felt the pain slip back to being bearable. I dressed and drove myself to work, determined to deal with the pain as I dealt with the fear, silently and alone.

At midmorning I said the first honest words I had used for months: "I can't make it any longer."

10

As I suppose with everyone, there comes a point when one cannot go on, and yet from some deep reservoir comes a last ounce of energy. From somewhere that came for me and I alone made the decision to call Dr. Ward's office. Now the day was here. This was "tomorrow," the day Paul had told the girls I was to see the new doctor. Again alone, I sat listening to all the voices telling me what to do and what not to do.

"Away," one voice said. "You already know what it's like to be away! Don't go! Just call and cancel the appointment."

And my pragmatic self replied, "But there's nothing wrong with me! Maybe only a chemical deficiency, or some gland out of whack."

Fear. Nothing to fear?

It's very dark under the eaves where I lie listening as sounds begin to diminish, fade, blend into the stillness. And again the steady drumming of the dog's tail against the washing machine. . . .

I look up, hoping to find the shaft of light that will show me my way out. I know that my safe place is guarded by only the one small entry door, but I can't seem to find it. I begin to move forward, crawling like some night-blind arachnid, slowly, very slowly, because my knees are skinned from the roughness of the boards. Past the tennis racquets which Lori keeps here, past Kara's old easels, Katie's ice skates, and boxes marked Monopoly, Parcheesi, Candy land. Past my box of doll furniture which no one is allowed to touch or play with because Papa gave it to me and it's all I have left of him. I lick away the tears and rub my hand across my eyes to shut out the light which is so bright that it blinds me. Crawl, crawl, just a little bit more. . . .

I come out through the little access door only when I feel it is safe. Thrown across the chair in the bedroom are my new slacks, with a neat, clean gash across the rear. On my left buttock is a matching inch-long cut, now bruised, encrusted with dried blood, and throbbing painfully. The gold hoop in my left earlobe hangs lopsided, the ear lobe torn. Blood has dried around it in a brownish blob.

As I walk barefoot through the upper hall I can feel under my feet the scattering of chips and slivers of broken glass that are still embedded in the carpet. Towering over the carpet and the slivers of glass is our old Adams secretary which hides its secrets from me in the bottom drawer. I go into the bathroom through the door that has one panel splintered, the paint chipped away, where something has smashed it again, again, again. And the pounding lumps on my head bring waves of nausea and then violent vomiting.

Standing under the warm shower was more to comfort the purplish green bruises that covered my upper body than for any desire to get clean. I had not been clean nor had I felt clean for over a year. Not since the day I lost myself—and found myself somewhere I did not remember going.

Mechanically I bathed my body, carefully avoiding the cut on my buttock and all the other places that hurt. First one washcloth. Then another. And another. It was very important that certain parts of my body must not be touched by a cloth that had bathed other parts. And that my hands never touch my body at all. I *knew* what wickedness was and I didn't want it in my life. Just to be clean. And good.

Carefully I chose what to wear for my appointment. Dark, conservative, and mature clothes. "Well" clothes. Anything except the gaudy, bright things that I never wore at all, but that hung in the closet. . . .

I sat before the mirror, taking time to use enough makeup to hide the scars on my cheeks as I gathered courage for the long drive to Richmond and to the man who might help me find the answer to my illness. I needed this courage badly because it was daylight and I had to leave the house and might be seen. There was always the possibility that I might be caught, detained, questioned. . . .

I had shut my door to the world for good. The telephone might ring, letters might come, neighbors stood hanging their laundry and chatting, planning coffees. And I would run into the shuttered bedroom to hide.

Most of all I knew I must avoid all the loving, well-meaning people with whom I had shared so much at the charismatic prayer meetings. Each morning as I sat choking on my eggs and toast and tears, I knew the persistent ringing of the phone meant one of them was concerned about me and that if I answered that person would try to guide me again in a direction I could no longer take. I had taken it once, believing that I was healed, cured.

The day I realized that the miracle had not happened at all was the day I began to hate even them. They, who of all the world had opened their hearts and arms to me and accepted me as I was. They would have accepted me if I had walked into the prayer group and announced, "I am a murderer," or a thief, drunkard, or pervert. I knew this.

I didn't walk into the prayer group as a murderer, or a thief, drunkard, or pervert. I walked into the meeting one evening as something far worse, as someone they did not know or recognize —and they loved and forgave me. But I did not. And when in bits and pieces the knowledge came to me, I shut myself away from everyone while words echoed in hollow places and settled to confuse my thoughts.

"Your healing must have agreed with you, Lia! You seem different somehow. Really beautiful!" said my friends.

Different? Beautiful? Or perhaps cheap? Tawdry?

I might have shut the door to people, to family, to hurt, and reality, at least that is what I tried to do, but instead of escaping I only took them in with me and sat while they banged away at the door of my brain.

Ring! Ring!

Growling, Sarg would bark and look up at me to ask, "Don't you hear that? Someone is at the door!"

The Healing of Lia

Letters were dropped in the box. Neighbors called out, "Lia! Are you in there, Lia?"

Inside my head I screamed back, "Go away! Don't hurt me anymore!" And other voices said, "Run! Hide! Close the shutters!" And when I had done this, I knew that for a time I was all right. Safe, alone, all right.

During that last long year I burned all the letters from my family and if any calls came, I begged Paul or the girls to take them. After a while all of my enemies left me in peace. But it was not peace, it was a tortured loneliness that I chose rather than face the agonies of listening to differing, confusing, and often badly advised remarks.

"What you *really* need is this," they would say. "What you *should* do is that." Get a job! Get a hobby! Get out more! Smile!

All those years I listened to them. My family, his family. And somehow I lost myself, if there ever was a real *me* at all. I thought if I did it all, everything they all told me, the family, the church, the whole damned world, that they would love me. But they didn't. I gave up self, the part of me that could have been so fine and good, to be what they wanted. They had killed me and I let them. And I didn't know why.

What I needed was not a job, a hobby, or any such thing. What I needed was a doctor who would look at me, listen to me, and not shuttle me out of his office in twenty minutes because my "time" was up. I had a job, the biggest job I could handle: living until I found that person.

Hobby? Mine was challenging. I spent hours each day searching in corners and dark places trying to find the twenty-two caliber revolver that Paul had hidden since wrestling it from my hand not long before. I had first pointed it at my body and then at my head before I realized there was something one must do other than just pull the trigger. When Paul found me clawing at the vile metal thing, he tore it from my hand and later hid it. I thought that there was no place in our house where it could remain unfound and, with that hope, I searched a room each day. I wandered idly opening drawers, lifting socks and shirts, feeling behind cushions. Even if I never needed it again, it, like the bottles and pills, represented a security to know that I *did* have a choice. God knows, I had little choice in other facets of my life.

Knowing that I could wait no longer if I was to take the long drive to Richmond and be on time to see Dr. Ward, I left the safe darkness of the house, got into my car, and began the drive that was to be an ending and a beginning for me. From that day onward I would learn the full implication of words such as pain, acceptance, trust. And later what it meant to have hope, help, and a future. But more than any of this I was setting out accompanied by this new doctor to find out who I was, where I was, and why I was. It was not to be a journey with mutual trust or even of willingness on my part. I had learned the bitter price of trusting the wrong person and would not soon make that mistake again.

In a way we began this journey together with Dr. Ward shackled hand and foot and with me lame and limping. We stumbled, and often I slipped and fell. But we made it, make no mistake about that!

The drive into the city went quickly and I shortly found the building where Dr. Ward had his offices. Parking in front of the brown brick complex, I sat looking at the area in front of the building. There was a small park, complete with a duck pond and shade trees. The day, typical of early summer in Richmond, was scorching. Before I got out of the car I did as I had been doing for over a year; I looked to the left and right, behind me and before me. There was no red truck in sight. Safe.

Getting out, I locked the car, went into the building, and headed for the elevators, taking one more quick look behind me to make sure that I *was* safe, that there *was* no red truck driving through the area. The guard asked me if I needed help and I said no, that I was fine. I got into the elevator and pushed the button that read "4."

Getting off was not as easy as getting on had been. There was the hallway to check—both ends—and only after doing this did I open the door to Dr. Ward's office.

I spoke briefly with a pretty receptionist, took my seat, and picked up a magazine to hold. Not to read, to hold, while I watched the door and the other patients. Were they all as afraid

The Healing of Lia

as I, I wondered? Did they have to hide from something as I did from the red truck?

Even in the cooled office I was too warm. Warmer than the others because of the clothes I had to wear as my cover. I wondered if any of the others had bruises to hide, too. I sat thinking how nice it would be if I didn't have to be there at all, and then I heard the soft, quiet voice in my head say, "Just tell the receptionist that you are going to the powder room. You could get out and into the elevator and back to the car without being caught."

"And punished?"

"Stupid!" my voice said to me. "Who is going to punish you for not going to a doctor? Nobody forced you to come here!"

"Then why am I here? Why can't I just go home and be happy like other people?"

. . . Oh, God, did I say that out loud, I wondered. Were the other patients looking at me? I heard my name spoken and looked up to see the receptionist standing in the doorway to the inner offices. She was asking me to follow her.

My voices directed, "Walk casually. Smile. Do just what is natural and everything will be over in half an hour and you can go home and never come here again." I followed down the hallway, saying to my voice, "How nice! You know, I really am feeling much better. I probably don't need any doctor at all."

After asking me to please have a seat, the young woman filled out a long form while I answered all the usual queries about full name, address, place of employment. Then she left me alone with my thoughts and my voices, one of which said, "Just don't cry. Whatever you do, don't cry!" When I looked away from the window-wall, Dr. Ward came in, took his place behind the desk, and asked me in a very relaxed way what my problem was.

PART TWO

11

As I entered the consultation room, I was immediately awed by the woman before me. Lia Farrelli sat, her hands clasped in her lap, her legs tight together. She was entirely in black, and she appeared to be frightened—a look about her of the caged animal that may well strike. What I was about to hear was the story of an unusual illness, unusual to me even as an analyst; unusual in its severity and duration. How Lia had kept her thread of sanity under the circumstances of the story I began to learn that day is difficult for me to understand even now. Looking back, I understand the dynamics of how and why it developed, but her self-destruction was so strong that I am amazed she didn't succeed in suicide at some point. I only thank God that she didn't.

As I have gotten to know Lia, I realize I was given entrée into a life in a far deeper way than usual. Utilizing hypnoanalysis, I was able to examine her emotions to such an extent that maintaining an objective, clinical attitude was often difficult. It was a phantasmagoria of life laid before my eyes.

I found myself caught up in the intensely emotional and touching story of a woman who had survived a lifetime of mental illness and twelve years of constant, and unsuccessful, psychiatric care. She had had various labels and diagnoses heaped upon her, none of which had been correct, as I was soon to discover.

The decision to begin the book was made one day after Lia and I had had a short visit during which we decided to leave the subject open for both of us to sleep on and ponder awhile longer. As Lia gathered her papers and gloves, she placed on my desk a small newspaper clipping dated the day before. After she left I sat wondering what decision I should make. I picked up the clipping and began to read. It was short, and concerned views of a prominent psychiatrist discussing various methods of therapy for treating the mentally and emotionally ill. Marked in red, Lia had circled one sentence. In answer to a query from the newsman about how electroconvulsive (shock) therapy "feels" to the patient the doctor had replied, "Well, that really is a moot point. They are insane, you know." I crumpled the clipping into a little ball and that night at dinner I asked my wife and daughters how they'd feel if I became an author.

I had many concerns about collaborating with Lia on this book. I knew it would mean months (eventually these months grew into four years) of work in addition to my practice. Mainly, however, my concern was for her welfare. Did she, so soon after her therapy and recent surgery, have the strength to carry it through? I had a good idea of the pain she would experience while the writing was taking place, but I do not believe she did at the time. She seemed determined, however, that the book should be written so that others who might be approaching hopelessness in their lives might find some tangible reassurance.

Getting to know Lia has proven to be a unique experience in my life. I have seen a human being so weak and full of rage and anger, so afraid of life itself—convinced that she was meant to be self-destructive and emotionally ill for the rest of her life— become a vibrant, strong, attractive woman, a remarkable woman, full of desire to live life to the fullest and to use an intelligence so great that at times I find it frightening.

Lia was what is commonly termed a multiple personality. The incorrect diagnosis of hysterical depression had been applied to her in the past. Though she was a hysteric when she would have an emotional division or splitting, she had managed to hide the disassociative component for years and also hid it from me for the first few weeks of therapy. In fact, there was no time that a "new" personality appeared for Lia's appointment. It was all more subtle.

Subjected to traumatic experiences in her life, living in a family that was void of anything but self-serving feelings, a marriage wherein love was like the beautiful crystals of a phenocryst embedded in porphyritic rock, her mind had chosen a means of escape. Somehow Lia had to have a means of dealing with the

The Healing of Lia

emotional and physical traumas that came from her mother, her husband, her priests, and, lastly, but certainly not to any lesser degree, her physicians. So her mind resorted to the development of other personalities to handle certain phases of her environment.

After our first meeting I came away with the feeling that she didn't trust me, and it was not long before I knew why. Exposed to those twelve long years of psychotherapy, all the time becoming progressively worse, why *should* she trust another physician? Or another therapist? More to the point, why trust another man? It had been the men in her life who had, to a great measure, served to put her where she was that day. The old childhood rhyme that ends, ". . . doctor, lawyer, Indian chief," in her case could have been changed to, ". . . doctor, husband, Catholic priest."

On a conscious level, Lia was screaming for me to help her ("You are my last hope"), but subconsciously there were so many conflicts working at one time that I knew I faced difficulties when I accepted her for therapy. Even assuming she *could* be helped with hypnoanalytical procedures, I wondered if I could manage to break through her wall of distrust.

Most assuredly she had no specific reason to trust me. I was only another in her long line of physicians. Physicians who, the facts were to reveal, were not attuned to this woman's problem. It's always easy to judge in hindsight, but from the beginning it was apparent that the last thing Lia needed was to swallow another pill or to undergo further electroconvulsive therapy, although she seemed an ideal candidate for this "miracle of modern science."

She had twice received electroconvulsive therapy with no evidence of long-term benefit either time, and her positive response was as filled with holes as was the torn tissue in her lap, and the torn tissue of her memory.

". . . and you are my last hope. . . ."

These words have been said to me frequently, but never with more emotion than I heard on this day. Before me sat this thin (almost emaciated), terrified woman in funereal black, who was about to give to me a history of far-reaching ramifications. She had been under the care of a psychiatrist for over ten years. She had reached the point where she was frequently confused and was unable to account for increasing periods of time in her life. Days would go by and she would have no recall of what had transpired during these times. Now we know that her altered personalities were in control on some of these occasions. Medications had become her friend to enable her to survive, but they were actually destroying her body. Her marriage seemed a twenty-year disaster, having Catholicism as its main focus. In this marriage there had been few happy times with her husband, who seemed to have little or no understanding of his "strange wife."

After our initial greeting, which was polite enough on her part (it was even accompanied by a slight smile, the last I was to see for several weeks), I asked her the all-important question: "What's the problem, Lia?"

Addressing the window (she looked everywhere during the consultation, except at me), she replied in short, broken, and often unfinished sentences.

"I've been in the care of a psychiatrist, Dr. Ling, for over ten years . . . it's getting worse, not better. I have fits of rage. It keeps happening. I try to hold it in but it hurts me all over I . . . just can't get up and do it."

At which point I noticed that she looked toward the ceiling and made a steeple with her hands folded under her chin. "Yes, go on," I told her.

"I feel confused . . . take so much medicine. . . ."

I was to find that drugs played a large part in her problems. The personification of the legal "walking drugstore," she could not recall just when or why she had been given some drugs. One significant thing to me as a physician was the combination of certain drugs and the dangerous amounts prescribed and available to her. One particular drug had been given in such strengths and for such a duration that it had actually caused a paralysis of the large intestine.

"How long have you felt you had a problem?" I asked next.

"All my life . . . always. . . ."

At this point she said that she had been able to hold everything together and under control until the birth of her third child, which, she related, was "difficult . . . for me."

The Healing of Lia

"Difficult in what way? What made it harder for you, Lia?"

Again she looked toward the window and said in almost a whisper, "I went berserk . . . right on the table in the delivery room . . . they told me I did. . . ."

At this point she broke into tears. I reached over, handed her another tissue, and resumed my questions. "Tell me about your marriage and your family life, Lia. Just begin anywhere."

Responding, she described to me her marriage of twenty-two years to a very rigid (here she corrected herself and said "devout") Catholic, her three children, each born within a year of the other (". . . before I was ready. My first baby was only twelve weeks old when I got pregnant again"). Her animosity was turned inward and she began "hurting." Two subsequent miscarriages caused feelings that she could no longer bear up, and as she related that after seeking solace from her parish priest she had been told how "evil" it (and she) was for not welcoming all her children, she began weeping again.

"But your marriage itself. Is it a happy one?"

"I do have a happy marriage . . . Paul is so forgiving . . . he's my number one forgiver! He's done so much . . . I owe him so much. . . ."

Forgiver? What is she seeking forgiveness for? Why does she feel indebted to the point of "owing" her husband something? Trying to fit these questions in with my standard ones, my shorthand flew over the chart. I asked, "Do you and Paul agree on most things? Any problem areas? Arguments?"

"Agree? We don't agree on anything! But that doesn't mean we don't love each other! We're just different sorts of people!"

I sensed a feeling of anger almost to the point of aggression that I had even dared to question such a point!

"How 'different,' Lia?" I asked. And as she began to tell me how different, I had a sense of wonderment that the marriage had endured two months, much less twenty years!

As I listened to this woman, what I was hearing might, at first, have been construed as the common complaints of a typical housebound wife who is suffering from "jailhouse blues." Many normal, well-adjusted women suffer in this way, an army of women who have moved from the protective/restrictive environment of their parents' home into an even more protective/restric-

131

tive environment of marriage. As these restrictions are dispensed with such "love" and are imposed by the person the woman most desires to please, often extremes of guilt are felt. After all, when a woman is lucky enough to have such a caring person looking after her every need, she must be a very ungrateful person to resent him! Not only ungrateful, but just plain bad—at least in her own eyes.

As Lia unfolded the beginnings of her illness and life story to me, I had many thoughts and questions concerning her extremes of emotions. Was she really as ill as she and her physicians felt, or was she merely a very likely candidate joining the lines of pill-addicted or alcoholic wives ensconced in comfortable, well-equipped homes who suddenly find that they never really learned to be *people?* We often read of wives (most frequently of notable or public figures) whose feelings seemed to parallel what I was hearing now. Perhaps one of the most common, and most painful situations, is when a sensitive, creative woman marries into a structured family and finds her sensitivities and need for beauty—music, poetry, or whatever—buried under a rigid structure that stifles creativity.

Later, as I began to know my patient better and found that she was, indeed, a person desperately in need of beauty in her life, I knew many of my original feelings were correct. No one is going to survive well in a home situation that is repressive, oppressive, and finally depressive. That much is certain for the healthiest of women. But Lia Farrelli was *not* the healthiest of women—far from it. My question was how much of her illness *was* illness? And how much was simply the pain of being told by the world that she, as Everywoman, was free to live a happy, fulfilling life? She knew she was repressed physically, emotionally, and financially, and was outraged when told otherwise. My job was to sort through the maze and find the answers to this and more. This job was inhibited in part by the fact that I saw only one side of a two-sided picture, and that was Lia. The other side was her husband, Paul. I was to find, before this ended, that I often wished that rather than having Lia in the therapy room I might have had Paul Farrelli.

For now, however, I sat as Lia began telling me of her happy marriage and of her husband, the "forgiver."

The Healing of Lia

"Paul had a good home even though there was no father in it. He . . . left. At least that's what I was told, but that's a story in itself. Paul was fairly smothered with love from his mother and sisters: he lived in a sort of cocoon of love, which I suppose I envy him. He went to parochial schools and was thoroughly weaned on religion. He had everything except . . ."

"Except what, Lia?"

"I don't know how to say it! He thinks I'm a snob—his whole family does! I guess the word I mean is culture. We just don't share the same meaning of the word! Not only that, but . . . I've always felt that he never even *tried* to understand my needs, not even from the beginning. We always seemed to end by doing things his way, the things he enjoyed, his friends, his choice of this or that, while—it wasn't even a matter of fifty-fifty! He was miserable when he was dragged—and that's what I felt I was doing—to things that I loved! I enjoyed beer at his Knights of Columbus Club, too. I liked his friends. But sometimes . . . I'd get so bored! In our whole marriage he has taken me to only one or two operas, and I just stopped asking. I never begged or insisted and . . . we never do anything at all now. Maybe a movie or two a year. Nothing more. . . ."

"And how do you feel about this?" I asked her.

"Cheated! Angry and cheated! God knows I have sat and listened to more Tex Beneke with him than he ever listened to Paganini with me! Just like church . . . I went his way—*everybody's way*—but mine, for years and when I asked him to go . . . to share—oh, shit! I don't want to talk about it."

"Well let's talk about it anyway. What about church?"

"I left it. I had to. I'd go each week and get . . . sick. I'd have to come out and . . . vomit. . . ."

My shorthand notations were reading, "Can't stomach it. What? Environment? Herself? Why guilt?" And again I noticed that strange gesture, the steeple under her chin with folded hands.

"Okay. You left the church. What was the turning point for that?" Lia then began to tell me, with more distress than her former anger, that this point happened when she found she needed major surgery some years back. The surgery involved and necessitated sterilization. She tried in desperation to get the sanction of the church before the surgery. Not only would the church not sanction the surgery, but the priest laid down obstacles to the point of giving her verbal suggestions that later were to prove almost fatal. She was told after the sterilization surgery she would be living in mortal sin and would have to do penance the rest of her life. As Lia said this she slammed her forehead with the heel of her right hand. It impressed me enough to make a notation on her chart to this effect. Little did I realize then the full impact of that statement.

"How did this affect you and Paul? Did it cause arguments?"

"Not really arguments directly. Paul doesn't argue . . . he's very much a pacifist. He hates what he calls my 'deep discussions.' He just turns away and this is harder than if he shuts me out. He seems to get angry over all the wrong things and to just accept things he should get angry about!"

"In what way, Lia? What are some of the things he 'should' have been angry about?"

"His family! Paul has a fine mind and should have gone on to college. Even without his father . . . there were others . . . aunts, uncles who might have encouraged and helped him! They're sickening to see! They're so damned great on hugging and slobbering over Paul, saying what a 'smart boy' he is . . . but not one of them dug down to help their brother's child!"

By now Lia was fairly choking on anger. Pressing on the issue, I asked, "This would have made you feel better—if Paul felt anger toward these relatives?" She thought a moment before replying.

"No. I just feel Paul shuts his eyes when he should *see* things. Especially things in his own family. But the money part is painful. Money is not important . . . unless you don't have it. Most of Paul's earnings have been diverted into the pockets of my doctors. There's nothing left for pleasure . . . or some necessities. He does without many things. I turn his shirt collars to hide the worn places . . . we do argue over money . . . we fight over his tithing to the church when I'm short on grocery money or having trouble meeting bills. I resent his giving after . . . my . . . trouble. I would rather . . ."

"Rather what, Lia?"

"Burn it. I would rather burn the money after they . . ."

The Healing of Lia

As each facet was revealed, I realized that for every one thing I was being told there were one hundred I must find out about. Veering off, I approached another topic.

"Is your sexual life satisfactory? What percentage of the time do you experience orgasm?"

"No trouble at all. We have always had a very good physical relationship. Tremendously great. Only our mental communion is not . . . so great."

Well that takes care of that, I felt. Or does it? "Lia," I asked, "if you could eliminate any aspect of your life this moment, what would it be?"

"Paul's family. I fear them . . . whispering, manipulating . . ."

Here she broke down again before I could make much sense out of her story. Between choking sobs I caught the words— Greg . . . telephone . . . sneaking—until finally I firmly told her to just close her eyes, relax, and begin at the beginning. She sat quietly and then spoke.

"Paul's brother called last evening . . . I was preparing dinner . . . I answered but he was barely civil . . . just asked for Paul. I put the phone down and called Paul, who took it on the extension upstairs. I completely forgot that I hadn't hung up the phone in the dining room. Then I heard noises . . . I went to replace the phone and I heard Greg saying, 'But don't tell Lia!' I don't know why, but I felt sick . . . and afraid . . . after all the other things that had happened.

"I began to sweat . . . but I put the phone to my ear and listened as Greg asked Paul to meet him today . . . up behind the service station where they could talk . . . and to sign a personal note for almost one thousand dollars! And not to tell *me* he was doing it! I felt so ill . . . sick . . . my head pounded. I knew I was in terrible danger. . . ."

As Lia related this story I wondered many things: What "other things" had happened that caused her so much fear? What sort of paradoxical family situation did she really live in? Why did she react with such intense fear? I asked quietly, "What did you do? What happened as a result of this situation, Lia?"

"Last night in our room I kept waiting for Paul to mention something. He didn't, and so, humiliated that I had eavesdropped, I admitted to hearing part of his conversation. I asked Paul if he planned to meet Greg. He said, 'Yes, but I'm not going to give him the money.' Then—then I asked why he had not just *told* Greg that and . . . Paul grew very angry and told me to mind my own business. I think I just lost myself then. Just went crazy. I began screaming at him.

"Your business? My God! I have done without all these years, too! Behind a service station! Out in the street like a couple of criminals! Sneaking! How crass can your family be? Whispering . . . hiding things. . . ."

By now Lia was in such a state that she was practically sliding out of the chair. I had a fairly good idea of the picture but not of what came next. After a moment she calmed down and finished the story.

"Later, I don't know exactly how much later, Paul closed the windows as he often did before a confrontation and angrily told me he would not stand for any more of my 'crap.' I believe it was then that I picked up a five-pound lead weight from his barbells and began to smash at myself. Not at him, although this is what I had wanted, but at my own head and body. He grabbed me, with the strength that only a man has, and flung me bodily across the room onto his bed. I was screaming words of hurt, anger, hatred, when he took his pillow, put it over my face, and pressed down to shut off what he couldn't bear to hear. How long it lasted I don't know, but when I could no longer reach for air, the burning went out of my brain and the will to live went out of my body. I believe that I blamed him more for releasing me and letting me breathe again than I did for his way of quieting me. . . ."

So Lia's "happy" marriage had other elements to it. I sensed many things here: that every element she mentioned was merely the tip of an iceberg; that each of her fears seemed to intertwine with others until the end result was a tangled skein that threatened to choke her. Moving on, I looked at a sheet of paper on which was a typed list of her surgical procedures. Ordinarily I do not allow "prepared statements," as I want to hear everything from the patient at the moment, to observe his emotions and whatever linkages he makes in his history. I did glance at the paper, however, and could hardly believe my eyes. There were twenty-one entries for a period of twenty-three years! More surgical insults of all descriptions than would normally occur outside of a war zone! One entry would perhaps have been overlooked except that Lia had attempted to strike through the typed line: listed among the "surgical" procedures as entry number two was "marriage."

At this point Lia began speaking reflectively, as though she had told me nothing. Obviously her subconscious wanted to make sure I had understood certain things.

". . . Twelve years . . . it's getting worse and worse . . . the rages. Can't seem to hold it in. . . ."

I was puzzled about one thing in particular. Even after I had read over the sheet with lengthy details of her surgical history, she continually made references to an "it" that was making her hurt. What "it" did she mean? "Lia, have you ever attempted suicide?" I asked.

"Yes."

There was a brief pause before she added, "Not really, I . . ." and with that unfinished sentence (most of her sentences were unfinished, I had noticed), she just sort of stared into space.

"Have you ever seriously thought about it?"

"Yes! Last . . . year . . . with a butcher knife. . . ."

My chart entry here was: she wants to lay it open, get rid of "it." That she had formulated a means of self-destruction, physically and mentally, was clear. My notes were running off the edges of the chart. The puzzling correlation between her references to "it" and her action of making the steeple with her hands pointed to a problem concerning her religious attitudes. One must be set on, almost programmed on, a goal of self-punishment that incapacitates him. And guilt and religion crept into many of her replies.

Continuing, I asked if she considered her childhood to have been happy or unhappy. Her reply exploded, "No! She hated me! My mother never loved me—No!" Our communication almost ended right there as I realized that I had touched something that was so painful she could not discuss it.

"How about deaths, Lia? Deaths that have touched you in a particular way?" I could sense a tensing against this question as she withdrew her attention from the bookcase and turned her eyes toward me. As she answered I almost wished that she were again looking at the books. "She laughs and laughs . . . in my dreams. I try to kill her . . . make her stay dead . . . stop hurting me . . ."

Now weeping, Lia sat as I watched her. Had there never been kindness, love in this woman's life? I asked, "And your father? What of him?"

For one short moment as her face softened, I knew what Lia should have looked like. Without the lines of hurt and hate and sickness on it. With the scars of a lifetime wiped away, she looked childlike and very pretty for a moment as she said, "My Daddy was so very loving . . . but he died. He was only fifty when his ulcers perforated. I was just seventeen. . . ."

So there had been devotion, but sadly for Lia it had been cut short. Months later, when I had access to Lia's journal, I found entries which verified some of my feelings that spoken or unspoken, Lia received suggestions at a very early age that she was unloved. Worse, she developed the idea that, perhaps, there was something wrong with her or her body. She felt untouchable.

During my search for avenues to probe, Lia evinced an almost tangible flowing of emotion, shifting from agitation to fear, to anger, and back to fear. The transfer was so rapid, so volatile that I found myself wondering if I wasn't imagining it. I decided to ease up a bit and asked, "Can you tell me how you feel? Not just physically, but every way. How would you describe yourself? How do you think of yourself . . . of *Lia?*"

"As . . . fearful. I feel lost. Literally lost. Without . . . direction . . . identity. I don't know who Lia really is. Don't laugh, please don't laugh. . . ."

After assuring her that I would not think of laughing, she seemed to relax, and seeking out her friend the bookcase, she spoke in a kind of reverie—very softly, almost poetically. It rather raised gooseflesh on my arms because I knew that what I was hearing had an odd—no, an eerie—sound to it.

"Sometimes I'm invisible . . . other people don't see me, not really. That makes me a phantom . . . a stranger. Sometimes I find characteristics . . . which must mean I have a character. Prudish . . . but another part is like a . . . daredevil. Gentle . . . violent . . . hater! I'm literate. I know I'm knowledgeable, but sometimes . . . with people I'm . . . stupid. I believe things that . . . I don't know any halfways . . . I love deeply and hate just as deeply. I fear God but don't trust even Him! . . . I am very obedient . . . I always obey . . . and sometimes it hurts and hurts . . ."

Here she gave me a small smile and said, "Conundrum! That's me. A conundrum!"

I had to agree. It is exactly what all my notes added up to.

Clocks have a way of chiming at exactly the wrong moments, as mine did now. I pushed my buzzer and in the quietest tone manageable asked my secretary to juggle my next appointments to allow me more time with this patient. This was my initiation into a new phase of scheduling: whenever Lia was due for an appointment, we all knew we had a choice of clearing the office of other patients, working on our lunch time, or running into a very sticky situation!

During the remaining time of this consultation I felt I would try, perhaps, to get a better, broader picture of some of the problems of this new patient. Casually I asked, "Is there anything else you want to tell me at this time?" Seeking the comfort of the bookcase again, she answered.

"Yes. Last year I was . . . hurt. By a man who . . . he was someone I trusted . . . I am so afraid . . . now. I hide from the red truck all the time. . . ."

"Hurt? How hurt?"

With this beginning I took the first steps in a very personal journey. Almost as if she had taken me by the hand, Lia led me into her world, a world of unending fear, of the inhumanity of people, one to the other; into a lifetime of unspeakable pain which I wished could not possibly be true. Lia had been raped by a man to whom we have given the pseudonym, Oilcan Harry, by nature of his occupation. The few brief bits of information that Lia gave me that day were appalling enough, but later in her therapy, as more facts were revealed, I found these not only to be true but also in some instances to be far worse than I had imagined.

The journey I began that day was one that many times I have wearily wished could have been averted. Viewing mental suffering and illness from behind the therapist's desk is one thing, feeling the pain of it is another. I find it a bit harder to laugh at "crazy" jokes, watch movies about "sickies," and generally join in the public attitude of "We all know it exists—we just don't want to see it."

Lia's account of her experiences in mental wards may be one of the strongest indictments against current methods written in this decade. Her experience with drugs—drugs that were literally pushed into her, addictions she fought alone because her doctors felt it unimportant that a mental patient had become addicted —was horrifying to hear. When asked about her first breakdown, she said at the end of the accounting, "For months and months I had been going to church each day during the quiet hours of the morning. I would sit for long whiles and talk to God, begging to be made whole again. Never for the physical pain to be removed, only the mental. 'Please make me well,' I used to ask. 'Please, God. . . .'

"Then . . . they took me . . . and I walked down the long hall to the door and turned the handle. Locked. It was, of course, locked. I remember standing for a long while there with my hand on the knob . . . and putting my cheek against the cold metal door."

Lia's memories are something every doctor should read if he is to understand the difference between treating patients and treating humans. The experience to me is rather like one might feel after reading about a trip to the moon and then suddenly finding oneself on the ship, en route. It was jolting. During this first meeting I didn't realize the extent of Lia's pain or of her self-punishment—that she was literally a mass of bruises from self-torture.

When ending my initial consultation, I always request that the patient tell me in his own way just what it is he wants me to help him do. Lia's entreaty was, "Make it go away, all this hate and anger. . . ." She was a very angry woman. She had expressed this anger when talking about her husband and her mother. Though she realized she was angry and even filled with rage, she had not been able to focus the anger even on a conscious level. As a result, she had directed the anger in toward herself. Her means of expressing this was through self-inflicted physical trauma. She had told of hitting herself with the weights

The Healing of Lia

in her first visit, but I did not realize it had been an ongoing event during the past several months.

Another thing that Lia did not realize was that her hate and anger were only symptoms of deeper emotional conflicts. She must first sort out her underlying feelings before it would be possible to make anything "go away."

How long it takes for a person to reach the point of self-destruction is a moot issue. Five years of pain, or perhaps fifteen minutes of pain? Ten years of mental torment, or just one, enormous, blinding shock? Each individual has a threshold for pain and suffering, each different; some unbelievably long in endurance, some unbelievably short. A tiny inconvenience to one person may be all it takes to break another. It takes wisdom, cunning, interest, to look for this in others. And sometimes it takes even more; it takes a tool, a weapon, a probe to strip away the fears, defenses, and layers of conscious clutter that mask and disguise illnesses and cause them to appear as what they are not. Quite often physicians are handed a wealth of red-light indications by a patient and if they are lacking in receptivity they miss them all. Lia's did for most of her lifetime. The common viewpoint that the "person who talks suicide seldom does it" is very far from the truth. They may not succeed the first time but each try becomes more nearly successful until the day the job is finished. Each time, a scream for help becomes more feeble, less hopeful, and the screamer comes to believe that no one cares—for it would be unconscionable that they *do care*, and yet do not help in some way. There is an entry from the journal that I feel fits here particularly well. Even in her illness, certain things were crystal clear to Lia:

One might say that each of us contains a complex "fail-safe" mechanism, and compared to the one that operates the atomic bomb protective system, ours is far more intricate and sensitive.

Our first fail-safe warnings may (or may not) be physical; mine were, for a certainty. The cause-and-effect theory was never more obvious, but as humans are wont to do, they all looked in every direction for the cause, except in the mind. That was unthinkable . . . that a child may be destroying herself willfully, out of misery and hurt.

When a small child, one who has not yet reached the age where introspection is possible (indeed, many adults never reach this point), begins a pattern of illnesses, none of which are physically attributable, these are the fail-safe warnings operating on a physical wavelength. As I *was* a child when the illness began to manifest itself, my body was desperately giving a nonverbal message to my parents and the doctors who treated me. *Why did none of them pick up the message?* I was a thin, anemic child, skeletal in appearance, who found relief only in expelling whatever life-prolonging nourishment I was given. A child's way of rejecting life, a slow but determined suicide.

Killing the body is not an easy thing. Through my life, at different stages, I have found this true, over and over. When the subconscious mind realizes this fact, there are seasons and times of revitalization of the "self"; the body tries to repair itself and go on with the business of life. These times are the ones I refer to as my "well" times. My fail-safe mechanism had done its job successfully.

When, however, a human being (whether it be a small child or an adult) is subjected to one shock after another, his life becomes one perpetual readjustment. Sooner or later a wearing down begins, and like a continuously run motor, changed intermittently and with random speeds, high/low, up/down, and after trying to adjust itself . . . finally it simply quits. All the world understands the malfunctioning machine; not so with the human machine.

Lia's story is the story of a damaged child who grew into an even more damaged woman. To her the realities of her life were insurmountable and so, in order to survive, a system had to be designed, a backup fail-safe that would enable her to handle the overload to her emotional system. The transformations into another state—into other personalities—were her only means of survival. And the fact that she not only did survive but survived with an extraordinary will and burning intelligence is a miracle.

The Healing of Lia

12

Lia returned one week after her initial visit. I realized that the information I had gleaned the previous week gave me only a cursory understanding of her life with Paul Farrelli or, in fact, of her life in general. It was apparent though, even at that early point, that Lia's relationship with Paul was a fantastic turning point in her life. A turning point, yes, but even more it was like the never-ending thread of a gigantic screw that, as it continued to be turned, turned, turned, caused Lia to become wound tighter and tighter within herself and within her life.

Though Lia felt that all she needed in life was the love of this one man, it did not take long for reality to unfold to her: she found she had married not only Paul, but the Farrelli family. In ordinary circumstances this may seem the ideal—in Lia's case it was tragic.

Although I had gone through an extensive interview with Lia during our last session, there were still areas of her history that I had to uncover before beginning therapy. We had only touched on the subject of her sexuality and I needed more specific information. The fact that she had experienced the trauma of rape was a cause of great concern to me, as I realized I must tailor my approach and timing in order to encourage her full trust and confidence in me which, as I said, she felt little of at this time.

It was apparent that there was no conscious history of sexual experiences during her childhood. She did recognize that she had certain feelings, but she had quickly learned to suppress these just as she had learned to suppress so much in her life. Her first sexual act of a conscious overt nature occurred on her wedding night. I have often felt that as Lia and Paul's physical union

143

was one of the better points of their marriage, it's sad their conversational intercourse could not have been as good.

Lia was open and frank concerning their present sex life. Although she showed a normal shyness in answering such direct questions, she was soon relaxed and giving information to me freely: intercourse, twice weekly; climax almost one hundred percent. As I noted her answers I found this all startling, at least until she added her next bit of information.

"I don't really have any problem that way at all except when I have the bad times with pain . . . sometimes I swell so badly that he . . . can't . . . you know, penetrate. . . ."

She smiled at me faintly and looked down in her lap. And my notes read: the subconscious is still king!

Since Lia and I have had some of our best horn-locking sessions over this point, it is of particular interest to me. For some months before she came to me Lia had been having severe pain in her abdominal area, during which times there would be an exacerbation of the symptoms she described and an associated swelling within the abdomen. This pressure was such that it would occlude the vagina. Yes, we were later to discover that there was indeed a physical problem, a large mass growing, but what she was reluctant to see was that it all worked as a *subconscious* means of rejecting her husband "in the bad times." The mass was found to be a large ovarian cyst which obviously fluctuated in size. I felt that her subconscious could control the swelling of that cyst.

Easing my way into the subject, I asked her to tell me more of the rape. As expected, when I posed the question her fear became much more pronounced. Before she replied, she did an odd thing that continued the entire time we were on the subject: as if she sensed some danger, she looked around the room and then over her shoulder at the door. Again and again, almost furtively, she looked at that door, but it seemed no reassurance to her. Hands and body trembling, she replied, "I have times when I can't remember things . . . and one time . . . this man . . . but it was as if I really wasn't there! . . . just like it was in the room when Lori was born! I was standing across the room . . . watching . . . watching . . ."

"You were standing across the room watching what?"

The Healing of Lia

"Watching it happen . . . to . . . someone else."

"Both times you remember standing across the room and watching it happen to someone else. Do you know who that person was, Lia?" I had to ask because I wanted to see her reaction and I had to know. She looked at me, faintly puzzled.

"Who? No, just someone . . . someone I don't know. But I was there! I saw it all. . . ."

"Did you feel any danger to yourself? Any fear for yourself?" I asked.

"No! Not for myself. I knew I was protected . . . I had the protection of the Holy Spirit! I had nothing to fear!"

I don't know if I sighed then or not, but I probably did. Here we were back again at religion. Marriage/religion; rape/religion. It was like sitting on a burr while someone sat on your lap. So many avenues, so many doors. Which one should I open first?

"Let's begin with the Holy Spirit, Lia. Tell me all about you and the Holy Spirit that protected you."

"Well, it's really so wonderful if you truly believe! And I do . . . I mean, I did then. You see. . . ."

Whereupon Lia embarked upon a most horrifying, discomforting tale of her year-long devotional attendance to what she termed a charismatic life with a group of persons who proselytized her. Clearly, at that point Lia was too ill and confused to have known what she believed, but as she related the story of her "baptism" and subsequent miraculous "healing" (which she also believed), I found not only my horror but also my anger mounting.

She was very willing to talk of the charismatic life, but it was next to impossible to get any further information concerning the rape at that time. Lia's mind had done a beautiful job of suppression. Or was it really suppression? In the realistic sense it was. However, if the rape had occurred as she had said, then she may well not have been able to recall what had transpired in the altered state of consciousness. In this dissociated state another of Lia's personalities was "in charge." This was to be one of those segments that had to be brought back to a conscious level by the use of hypnotic age regression. The rape had taken place and was, perhaps, one of the vilest experiences any woman has had to endure.

Lia came home from the market one day and had been having profuse abdominal pain, for which there seemed to be no relief. When she had entered the house and had placed her bags on the washing machine, she spotted the bronze sundial. It was beautiful and just the type she had always wanted, made of antiqued bronze with Roman numerals. Paul knew that Lia had wanted the antique which had an inscription bordering the circumference: "Count Only the Sunny Hours." Harry, their furnace repair man, had shown Paul and Lia the dial several weeks before, and there was some discussion of their making the purchase. When she first spotted the dial with its beautiful patina, she was thrilled. Was it possible that Paul had bought this as a surprise for her? The joy gave way to concern that only intensified the abdominal spasms. After spotting the sundial on the drier, Lia was unable to recall further what had happened that day, but knew that somehow Harry and his sundial related to her physical and emotional trauma.

At this time Lia was aware that her rapist was still out there and she was constantly watching for him. Thus, as we talked, she persistently looked over her shoulder. My big questions were, *why* was he still out there? Why wasn't he behind bars?

"Lia," I asked, "what did Paul do when you told him of this experience?"

"Do?"

For a moment she looked at me strangely as if offended that I had asked such a thing.

"There was nothing that he *could* do. You see, he told me that to pursue it would implicate the children and legally would mean going 'public' with it. So he could do nothing."

That left me sitting in shocked disbelief. Nothing could be done about a rape and a rapist walking the streets because of the embarrassment of going *public!* Had this all just been discussed in a very calm, rational manner and then put aside? How in hell can one just set aside the fact that one's wife has been raped in order not to let the general populace know? Just to avoid the feeling of public shame?

Or had it been put aside? There were two avenues of possibility here: first that Paul Farrelli did not *believe* that his wife had been the victim of rape and that instead he believed her unfaith-

The Healing of Lia

ful, and secondly (and I hoped I was correct here), that he had acted in what he felt was her best interest.

So, after allowing myself my moment of "shocked disbelief," I realized that considering the deeply complex nature of Lia's home situation, perhaps Paul felt he had acted wisely and for her good. I pondered momentarily the current attitudes about rape, the courtroom traumas endured by the victims, the simple fact that often the victim suffers more condemnation in the press than the rapist. This may account for any man's reluctance to report such an assault on his wife. And there were children to consider. Having daughters of my own, I tried putting myself in Paul Farrelli's place. Given the same set of circumstances, what would I have done? Many normal, well women have stated that seeking "justice" became more of an ordeal than the actual rape, and Lia was most certainly *not* a normal, well woman, not as she sat in my office this day. For the moment I swallowed my anger and tried to understand Paul's state of mind and his reasons for his actions and reactions.

Still, the other possibility would not let itself be dismissed so casually: the possibility that Paul Farrelli did not *believe* this incident to have been a rape, that not understanding her illness or the fact that the rape occurred in a state of mental blackout, he had adjudged Lia an adulterous wife. I later discovered that Lia herself had only a hazy understanding of what had happened to her, and *she* considered herself as adulterous rather than victimized. How exactly did her husband see all this? I phrased my questions in this vein very carefully and was stunned by the acceptance in Lia's manner.

"Lia, what exactly does Paul feel about this incident? Do the two of you ever try to talk it out? How does he react?"

"Paul won't talk about it at all. When it first happened I wasn't even sure it *had* happened. I couldn't remember, not really . . . only just a flicker, then nothing. You know, like an old movie, with the pictures flickering and then disappearing. He thinks, he believes that I was unfaithful, he doesn't let me talk about it. He's just not the same anymore. He shuts me out."

Well, that told me what I had hoped would not be the case. I don't know which caused me more anger, that Paul chose to brand his wife and, as a tribunal of one, condemn her without discussion, or that Lia sat in such accepting fealty to his judgment!

I later discovered that Paul had indeed "shut out" all chances of discussion with his wife—and anyone else. Lia had begged him to talk with someone, if not to her then to me, or his pastor, to anyone. And he steadfastly refused. Lia had apparently been told by Paul that he had "forgiven" her, and that ended it in his eyes (and this I questioned). But it did not end it for Lia. She knew, by means that any woman could tell, that she was far from "forgiven" and that her chances of being vindicated in Paul's eyes were slim. What sort of barrier did this man have that he refused to even seek out the answers for himself? Why, after over twenty years of her total fidelity, was he willing to judge her in this way? What rendered him incapable of understanding or of digging to find the facts along with her? Why wasn't he with her now? I had no answers to these questions but I did have an answer to something else: I began to see the torment Lia must live in each day in her own home. The damage she suffered at the hands of Oilcan Harry would fade and heal in time; the thousand pains she suffered at home daily, knowing Paul's judgment of her, would never heal until he reached a final understanding of her illness.

Lia seemed to know (without realizing it), that there was an answer to her illness and that once she found it she would be all right. What Paul Farrelli needed to understand was that Lia's damage had occurred when she was in a state of unawareness, just as if she had been a five-year-old child in total innocence of any provocation. She was a victim and nothing else. I did not myself know *all* the facts, but I did know this much: Lia Farrelli was again in the position of being "forgiven" for a sin she did not commit and was being subjected to a "penance" that went on daily. My job now was to find out finally what had happened and why.

A pleasant luncheon of coffee and crêpes with Meg was the beginning of my odyssey into the charismatic life. During the next weeks I lived apart from reality and spent hours in prayer to the Holy Spirit. I truly lost all my fears and felt safe in His protection. This ended sometime later, my body lying brutalized in a pool of human corruption.

The Healing of Lia

Somewhere on some lost street in some lost place. While the world played its games, watched its television, and ate its lunches. The empty shell, the rind of me, lay bruised, silent, void of any evidence of life for many days after . . . and I slipped away to where I had always known I belonged; counterposed, moribund, the bed became my bier and I let "Lia" go peacefully away. . . .

Lia had, by this time in her second visit, gone through an extensive interview, and she had completed the psychological tests. These tests reinforced some of my initial feelings and impressions: she is afraid of emotional involvement, distrustful of people in general; there is a likelihood of some form of psychological deficit, such as an inability to concentrate and periods of confusion; anxiety, tension, and depression are prominent; suicidal preoccupation is likely; patients with these patterns are frequently described as schizophrenic.

Now all I had to do was to get her to recognize *what* had happened in her life that had produced her present condition, not only what had happened but the sequence of events and how each had affected her. That sounds simple enough! I felt I had the diagnosis though I did not realize the multiplicity (there is a therapist's Freudian slip!) of her diagnosis.

Now it was time to introduce Lia into hypnosis for the first time in my office. She came to me with an abundance of knowledge about hypnosis, having been trained in the use of self- or autohypnosis by a layman. And she was extremely suggestible. These were positive points for therapy. On the other end of the scale, she had been misdirected in the use of her self-hypnosis. Her instructions had been to attempt to utilize her autohypnosis for self-analysis, which I am convinced is impossible; one cannot be analytical or objective about oneself. During her periods of hypnosis she had actually created more confusion, anxiety, and a deeper suppression of subconscious material, material that was vital for the alleviation of her symptoms. Using this inadequate knowledge and her profound suggestibility, a two-edged blade developed: she slipped into very deep hypnotic states so quickly and easily that even in her self-hypnosis she often frightened herself. Discovering she had this ability, to hypnotize herself and not having the proper training to handle it, she often used it as an escape route from reality. Lia was like a child with a loaded gun—and she was pointing it at herself. On one occasion she recorded in her journal the effects of a morning "relaxation" session:

I knew I was drifting too deeply when I was only five minutes into my morning "relaxation" session using self-hypnosis . . . but even though one part of me warned *stop*, another stronger part was pulling me toward the soft, shadowy places where I can wander freely, painlessly, where no one and nothing can reach or hurt me. This time, however, was different; somehow the unexpected happened and I lost track of my *self* lying on my bed in my safe room, and I "awoke" to find myself sitting in a nest of pine needles in the rough log lean-to in which I played as a child.

I sit Buddha-fashion, very much alone as is my habit to do, and I cannot feel any physical sensation in any part of my body. "I am wood," I think with my child's mind, and make no effort to move because I know that I cannot. I don't know how long I have sat here in this odd position, paralyzed, immobile, but I know the date and I know that I am twelve years old, and that Gina, my sister, has just been given a beautiful new bicycle and I have been given nothing. Nothing at all.

Today I think it very strange that even though I am over forty years of age, with an adult's accumulation of knowledge, that I am sitting here only twelve years old, . . . sitting on pine needles, turned to wood. All at the same time, the adult, the child.

Sitting alone.

. . . it is bright red with black trim and chrome handlebars. The word "Streamline" is stenciled on it, and it has lights, a horn, and a luggage carrier. It is the loveliest bicycle I have ever seen and they gave it to Gina.

I don't remember walking the path to the lean-to, I am just here, and I don't cry because I am made of wood and wood does not hurt, does not cry.

On the way back to my own bed in my own safe room, I can remember many times being the wooden child sitting alone in the woods. I don't know how I ever forgot her. But I don't think I shall want to relax this way anymore . . . not for a long while.

Patients vary in their ability to attain a hypnotic state. Lia took to hypnosis like the proverbial duck to water. She was found to be a fantastic subject and easily attained a somnambulistic state in a very short time. Her ability to get into hypnosis so easily may partly be responsible for her illness. The easier it is for one to get into hypnosis, the more suggestible one is. It follows that one is then more prone to have harmful suggestions seat themselves in the subconscious mind.

What is hypnosis? What is it not? How does it work? There are no simple answers to these questions. I wish I could say there were! Hypnosis has been around at least as long as recorded history; hypnoanalysis is not quite so old. History has recorded for us very clearly the presence of "sleep temples" which the ancients used. Tribal chants, voodoo trances, firewalkers, and some of the Eastern religions all use forms of the hypnotic phenomenon. One does not have to be in a state that could be described as a *trance* (a word I dislike because I feel it conjures up visions of witch doctors and zombies) to be in hypnosis. I dislike the theatrical Mandrake concept often connected with hypnosis, as it is inaccurate and misleading.

Waking hypnosis has occurred in all of us throughout our lives. We have been susceptible to suggestion from many sources —teachers, parents, religious leaders. Frequently we move from the state of waking hypnosis into a deep hypnotic state without ever being aware of it. This brings us to the fact that there does not have to be a "formal" induction into hypnosis. It can easily be brought about by conditions such as intense fright or fear.

Fear brings about a concentration of the mind, and when this occurs people may receive and accept harmful or negative suggestions. The person is not aware of what is taking place in his mind, or, if he is momentarily aware, he will immediately suppress the material and "forget" it. But not quite. Only consciously is it forgotten. In the subconscious the memory lingers intact. We will see as we go through Lia's history that this is what occurred in her life. Owing to a bizarre family history, she was a terrified young woman who had been bombarded with negative suggestions.

Because it has been used for so long, it would seem that we would have gained a much better scientific understanding of hypnosis. Sadly this is not the case. Some of our hypotheses are based on other hypotheses that are over a hundred years old.

Some of our newer awareness has actually been brought about by investigators who were trying to prove that there is really no such thing as "hypnosis"! Perhaps hypnosis as defined by Milton Erickson, one of the foremost hypnotherapists in the world, really tells the story: ". . . a state of intensified attention and receptiveness, and an increased responsiveness to an idea or set of ideas." Clearly, then, intense concentration is a prime factor and, as a therapist, I tell my new patients that hypnosis is akin to the presleep state with this exception: the wandering of the mind is controlled by the therapist so that the mind is directed along a single path, rather like the daydream state wherein all external stimuli are excluded in order to focus on one subject. Anyone who has sat through two green lights while horns were honked and fists were shaken will know the feeling! Suddenly you are back again, aware, but *back* from where?

There are two basic schools of thought concerning hypnosis and its effects on us both physiologically and psychologically. We are aware now that the theory of Mesmer, who felt there was some form of animal magnetism within his body that could be transferred to the patient, is not valid. But there well may be physiological changes that do take place within the brain during the altered state.

Hypnosis is not a panacea and has itself cured no one. If a therapist has in his armamentarium *only* his ability to hypnotize, he should not be practicing either psychotherapy or hypnosis. Any person who enters into psychotherapy with a therapist who guarantees results should head for the nearest exit.

Only if the therapist has a profound belief in what he is doing and in his ability to do it, should he attempt to give therapy. At *no time* is a patient more aware of intonation, projection, and the very confidence of the therapist, than when the phenomenon of hypnosis is present. Just as a nursing child is able to sense the anxieties and tensions of the mother by a radiation of feeling, the therapist with any neurotic problems will be unable to separate these from the therapy, thus creating a situation of "counter-transference." In such a case he would be reckless indeed to even attempt therapy on anyone. Only when the therapist is able to manifest his ability to search, diagnose, and

The Healing of Lia

analyze the patient's problem, and then utilize his ability to formulate positive suggestions, will he be able to make successful use of hypnosis in his practice.

The problem is not that it is difficult to hypnotize someone. Quite the opposite—it is, in fact, too easy! The sad reality is that many people are so *easily* hypnotized that undetected damage to their psyche has occurred throughout their lives. Again the problem is not *how* to hypnotize someone but what to do with him once he is *in* the state.

During the hypnotic process, two basic changes can be observed. One, the most apparent, is that of increased and profound relaxation in the body. The other less outwardly apparent change is an increase in concentration which brings about marked suggestibility. This open, suggestible attitude enables the therapist to work toward a change in mental attitudes or behavior. There have been in our recent history great political figures who used increased suggestibility in what has been descriptively called *mass hypnosis*. The adjective *great* as I use it here blankets greatness both for the good of our world, or for its destruction. Churchill had exceptional ability to utilize phraseology and intonation in such a way as to rally his people in their time of need. Counterposed in his uses of words and rhetoric to stir the masses (and probably one of the best practicing hypnotists of the century) was Adolf Hitler. Both of these men influenced masses (who were unaware that they were being influenced), one using his influence for great good and the other to foment a hysteric mobilization to carry out his mad wishes.

At any seminar where hypnosis is the basic subject, one question invariably arises and after being heatedly discussed is tabled without any firm conclusion being drawn. The question is this: are there certain persons (labeled questionably as prepsychotics) who should never be exposed to hypnosis? My use of the word *questionably* is deliberate, because whenever the label of prepsychotic is applied the next question to follow will be, Just what *does* constitute a prepsychotic? In the liberal sense, anyone who is *not* psychotic might be prepsychotic!

But where did this place Lia? Since I personally believe each individual must be evaluated *as* an individual, and I knew that some of the finest therapists in the world utilize hypnosis with schizophrenics with good results, I felt I must do whatever I could to help her.

Deciding against using only the application of direct suggestion (wherein the therapist works with habit breaking or behavior modification by using positive suggestions), I elected to use hypnosis with analysis for Lia. I knew full well that in her distraught, disturbed condition it would have been fruitless to suggest to her subconscious that she would "relax and have a feeling of well-being." Her subconscious mind (and most likely also her conscious) would have only laughed. Also, this method had been attempted by her lay hypnotist with, I felt, the results only contributing to the exacerbation of her symptoms. With hypnoanalysis (which may vary in its meaning from total personality analysis to analysis of a specific problem), it was possible for me to deal more directly with the problem at hand.

Before we began her analysis, I discussed with Lia the various ramifications of importance to her concerning hypnosis. She did not need to have explained to her one thing that patients often wonder about, "Suppose I don't awaken?" Since the patient wills or allows himself into the hypnotic state, it follows that he has only to will himself to awaken again. An extremely resistant or fearful person will simply not allow himself to go into hypnosis in the first place, so this fear is only one of many centered about myths and fallacious old wives' tales. It is virtually impossible to render impotent all of these myths, and it is the therapist's job to educate his patients in order to dispel any reserves of fear they may have.

Another myth that patients often bring into therapy is that they might "wipe-out" during the sessions and be unable to remember what transpired. The fear of hypnotic amnesia is quite common and is usually an adjunct of the Mandrake concept of stage hypnosis. Amnesia can only occur during very deep stages of hypnosis, and in the deepest or somnambulistic stage there may be spaces or areas that may not be complete in recall. It is possible—and in Lia's case it was expedient at certain points—to instill amnesia if the therapist decides that it is to the *patient's advantage* and that the material would be better forgotten. Such definitive decisions are all a part of the therapist's job. Only recently, as we discussed certain of her more painful sessions in order to correlate our notes, Lia grew upset that she couldn't remember a session of some import, while she had vivid recall of things that had happened long before. "I can't believe *that* was what I said, "she insisted, and asked, "For heavens sake, why can't I remember it—it's horrible!"

It was horrible. That is precisely why on the day in question, while Lia was still in a deep hypnotic state, I suggested to her that, "Upon awakening you will feel safe and comfortable and have recall for only those events that have been pleasant or helpful to you."

Lia has discovered that as time passes some of what she remembers as her "pain" of therapy begins to subtly diminish. This is not to imply that it will disappear magically. It will not. But as we have worked on some of the more traumatic subject matter and at times have had to bring back to her conscious mind painful areas of her life, this is being used by Lia as a way of cleansing her mind of certain things. A painful catharsis, to be sure, but for her very beneficial. It is helping her develop a powerful reserve of inner strength that is heartening to see. Used properly by an experienced therapist, hypnotic amnesia, rather than being looked upon by patients as something to fear, should be welcomed, much like anesthesia is welcomed in surgery; it is one more way to remove pain.

Lia could attain a trance level in which she had total disassociation of her body from her neck down. By this I mean that when she is in the hypnotic state, it is as though nothing of her exists from her head down. At times she related that she felt she was nothing but a concentrated area of thought, existing all unto itself, and functioning as an entity.

Thanks be for all little favors! Lia had gone through her first session of hypnosis in my office without any problems. In a patient so highly charged emotionally, I feared she might have a flooding of material for which she was not prepared. I wanted to do nothing that would cause her to flee into her mind, but more importantly, to do nothing that would cause her more emotional harm.

Lia's third visit. This was the week we began the word-association testing, the word *testing* being perhaps a misnomer as this is not a pass-or-fail type of testing.

13

I looked forward to this visit, knowing that these tests can be richly productive, because in the hypnotic state the responses of the patient may be quite different from those that are given in the waking state. Often following such a session, the patient will say, "I don't know why I should have said that! It doesn't even make sense!" And perhaps to the conscious mind the answers do not "make sense," but to the subconscious—that's another matter completely. And these answers are the ones I am seeking.

The word-association testing was extremely difficult for Lia. Her emotions were quite high during the testing and she had several abreactions during the testing periods. Abreactions occur when the patient suddenly goes into a very emotional state that may be accompanied by a spontaneous age regression or a violent purging of suppressed material. As the unexpected must always be expected in hypnotherapy, the therapist must assimilate this material on a here-and-now basis.

Age regressions do not always occur during abreactions but interestingly, they may be induced by the therapist during the sessions when he deems it expedient to do so. Many psychotherapists feel that regression to past episodes in a patient's life is unnecessary, and frequently patients are reluctant to go into their past, feeling that they only need to handle the problem with present-day investigation. It has been verified in my personal experience and practice, however, that when the predisposing factors have been brought from the subconscious (where they may have been suppressed for years), the patient feels an almost immediate response in his general well-being.

The Healing of Lia

The subject of hypnotic age regression is probably one of the most fascinating for the general public. I have had laymen and professionals in the field alike ask if I have ever regressed a person to a previous lifetime. My answer is, "No, I have never done so." There are, I am aware, some very reputable physicians in the country who feel they have accomplished this, and I cannot give a definitive explanation as to what may have occurred with these patients. In some cases I feel that it may have been what I would term a cerebral short-circuiting such as may occur when, after extensive and exhaustive researching into past periods of time, a person develops a firm belief that he actually lived a life in another time, another place. In Lia's instance it was necessary to regress her to her birth experience, but having obtained the information I sought, there was no need to press further.

Age regressions may be of two types. The most frequent type occurs when the patient is regressed to a certain age and time and will begin to speak in the past tense, as in a deep memory recall. The second type, a true revivification, occurs with the patient actually *reliving* the scene, speaking with the voice, mannerisms, facial expressions of, say, a three-year-old. The former type may occur in relatively light states of hypnosis and be very beneficial; the latter type occurs in a deep hypnotic state and, associated with extreme emotional release, is perhaps more expedient, causing as it does a greater purging of material quickly. While the person is in the regressed state we "insert" suggestions utilizing conscious materials. As an example, suppose a patient received, at a very early age, negative suggestions that he was a "bad child" for having done a certain thing and, because the suggestion was accompanied by fear, absorbed this suggestion into his subconscious mind on such a highly charged level that it is totally accepted. In his mind he *is* that bad person from that point on. Once having accepted such an idea, he may have then proceeded to act out "bad" behavior. In treating such a case using therapeutic age regression, I point out to the patient that now, using his adult mind, he may accept the idea that he is a good person and relinquish the negative suggestion. I then proceed to plant positive suggestions to be integrated into his subconscious. He can then safely discard the damaging idea and live his life accordingly.

Lia was deeply in hypnosis when we began her testing and I was to find that, rather than her answers just not "making sense," it was in my view akin to being ringmaster at a three-ring circus.

The weeks of the association tests were terrible. All those awful words! I don't know why I couldn't have retorted with some zippy little words and answers, but somehow my mind just wouldn't respond. I must seem such a prude to Dr. Ward. Or just plain stupid.

When I found this journal entry much later, it exemplified how differently the patient and the therapist interpret results. Lia bemoaned her lack of "zippy" phrases, while I rejoiced that she responded explosively, like a well-oiled furnace without a thermostat! As her entire word listing was well over 150 words, I include here only those that merited the most valuable responses. I will not attempt to give complete verbatim answers, as often the patient tends to ramble, dissemble, and have long silent pauses. When necessary I shall relate the total verbal exchanges.

FARRELLI: Terrible.
LIA: Sick . . . has to be . . .
FATHER: Lonely . . .
MOTHER: No! No! . . . awful . . .

Here, there are two responses of particular note: the first, "sick," followed by a sigh and "has to be," serves notice that Lia's subconscious had accepted the fact that she had *no choice* other than to be just that. This "sick" implication was to a child as destructive as is the syphilitic spirochete that invades a human at an early age only to destroy him twenty years later. The second notable response was that to the word "mother"; Lia began to reply in an almost hysterical manner. Her respiration became rapid, almost a choking sort of breathing, and when asked what was the matter she cried, "Hates me, hates me, hates . . . I try so hard . . . she diminishes me!" Whereupon I noted she was responding in the present tense, even though her mother had died many years before.

Continuing with the testing, and because of certain ponderable statements Lia had made in reference to her sister, I inserted this phrase:

The Healing of Lia

[Sister's name] ALWAYS: . . . was the queen.

I thought at the time it was an interesting answer, but it became even more meaningful later. The Latin word for queen is *Regina,* and it was the pseudonym Lia chose to be used in this book when referring to her sister.

"How was she the queen, Lia? In what way?" and I waited as the answer came slowly and disjointedly as is common in hypnosis.

". . . don't know. Gina was the only loved child . . . she looked like Mama. She had everything . . . even the nose. I looked like Aunt Addie . . . my nose, too . . . and this made Mama mad. . . ."

Here I admit to being fairly well lost! So far I knew that family noses came into all this and for some reason Lia's mother wasn't too pleased with Lia's nose. As it seemed a rather acceptable nose to me, I knew this would be one of those things to get into later. We did, and I am glad we did. During a less formal office visit one day, Lia and I sat chatting about her family, and the full story she told me concerning this segment of her life, of her mother's terrible envy of her own sister, Addie, and of the venting of this emotion on Lia, was astonishing to me. I found myself getting more and more hooked on learning about this family. It was becoming something of a horror story with the main victim sitting totally unaware, telling me about it.

Not long after this conversation I saw some snapshots and portraits of the family—both sides—and of Lia's siblings. They were exactly as Lia had described them. If I had seen them anywhere I believe I should have known immediately who was whom! The biggest shock, though, came as I looked at a portrait of Lia as a baby of about nine months. Without doubt it was a picture of the saddest, most dejected child I had ever seen. The other children all appeared with big smiles and "cute" professional poses; Lia had apparently just been plopped down on a covered piano bench, and the most painful thing for me to see was that her wispy baby hair had not even been brushed for the photograph. She did indeed look like an unloved, unwanted baby.

It is my firm belief that impressions are formed by children as young as this, and even younger. Lia simply was not able to comprehend such treatment as she was getting. Not on a conscious level. On a subconscious level she was comprehending one hell of a lot! Her interpretation was, "I'm different. I don't belong to this family. I am only a visitor," but she knew even this couldn't be so, because visitors are treated nicely. The upshot was that she didn't know what or who she was.

The word association continued.

FEAR:	Terrible . . .
MY RAGE IS:	Bad . . . me too . . .
PAUL ALWAYS:	Hurts me . . . Stop! Stop!

Her first spontaneous abreaction occurred at the word "Paul." Lia was building a crescendo of screams, moaning, crying, "He's hurting me . . . hurting . . ."

"What is it? What is happening, Lia?" I asked her.

"He's hurting *me!* I haven't . . . healed . . . hurting . . . please don't! Can't tell him . . . can't tell . . ."

"What can't you tell him?" But I thought I already knew the answer to this. By now she was thrashing about in the chair in definite pain, as revealed by the expression on her face. Perspiration broke out on her forehead and around her neck. It seemed to intensify minute by minute.

"Oh! . . . it is only going to . . . pregnant again . . . don't! . . . please understand! No! No!"

Obviously, intercourse was taking place during this regression, and she was experiencing not only marked physical pain but emotional pain. The expression, "haven't healed," referred to her episiotomy from the birth of her baby. She was emotionally anguished by the fear of another pregnancy, which was actually what did happen to her. Here, she was experiencing a crossover of remembrance: her conscious realizing that the pregnancy *did* occur, her subconscious warning her that it *might.* Her reference to "Can't tell him" told me that she lived in fear that to refuse meant he might reject her and withdraw his love, and so although intercourse at this time might have been agonizing, she needed that love badly enough to endure pain. Having never felt really loved, anything to her was worth the price she paid, even agony.

Lia took many steps into the depths of suppression. It is easier to suppress, to suffer even physical pain, than to cope with rejection. One cannot surmise what might have been Paul's thoughts and reactions if Lia had told him what she was feeling. In Lia's narrative she gives a vivid description of the early years and of the religious aspect that entered to damage and virtually destroy the happiness with which this young couple began life together. However, at this time in her therapy I was unaware of all of her story. One thing was certain, that Lia considered painful love better than no love. What she had not bargained for was the price she was to pay when the suppressed anger and pain surfaced in the future. The part of her personality that had the ability—the need—to strike out would surface. Within a few weeks I was to find out about just one such episode, recorded here in the journal.

Paul stood looking from behind the half-open door. A strange thing passed over his face and he laughed—at me—at the creature I had become. "You're a crazy woman!" he said as I knelt crouching, clutching at the bent remains of the shattered lamp, broken glass underneath my feet. A creature, not a person; lips apart, saliva collecting at the edges of my mouth, breathing air that burned my lungs. And I smashed again and again at that door and the wall with the brass lamp frame. Plaster crumbled, paint chipped, and I didn't care.

Paul grabbed me with one arm and with the other hit me a blow with his open hand. The heel of his hand caught me on the temple. Stunned, I fell backward into the pool of broken glass. His finger caught in my earring, tearing my lobe, and the blood ran down my neck. Lying there with a jag of glass cutting my buttock, stunned, bleeding, barely human, I knew that there was only one way out. I had to die.

Lia's protective personality would indeed use any means, even self-destruction, if it felt threatened. Frighteningly, the very act that should have been the most healing for Lia, the act of love, was becoming the trigger mechanism for the release of this personality. But why? Was Lia's fear of sex a cohesive point? It seemed to weave its way in and out of this whole terrible story like warp and woof. There were still in this woman facets that only time and she would be able to reveal.

We were now into the fourth week of therapy and I felt we had had a good week of work
last time. Today I had hopes of being able to
conclude the word-association testing, but as Lia's emotions
were so highly pitched, I gave her extra time, making quite sure
that she was in a very deep state of hypnosis before I continued
the testing. Once again we began.

SEX:	Lovely.
MY PAIN:	Terrible.
BEING BORN:	I'm all . . . dead.

When I first saw Lia, one of the questions that I asked her
was what she considered the worst thing that had ever happened
to her in her life. She had replied, "Being born." This was my
reason for having inserted this particular phrase in the test. Her
response did not coincide with what I had preconceived it to be.
I simply did not understand "I'm all dead." It really haunted me.

DOCTOR:	Don't like them.
GOD:	Hurts me!
WHEN KARA WAS BORN:	Was so sick . . . I wasn't ready . . . I wasn't ready for another baby . . . what did he care?
HOSTILITY:	Mine.
BEING MARRIED TO A CATHOLIC:	Oh God! It's awful!
HAVING THE STERILIZATION:	I had to! It was necessary but they told me . . .

The Healing of Lia

Here there was no further response, but from her history I knew it related to the priests and what she had been told about mortal sin.

MOTHER ALWAYS: WHEN IN THE DELIVERY ROOM WITH THE THIRD BABY:	Left me out. I went crazy . . . they kept making me have . . . that baby . . .

Without prompting, Lia suddenly regressed to the delivery room where again she was giving birth to her third child. Her screams pierced the walls of every room in my suite of offices.

"No! No! You can't make me do this againnn . . . I won't . . . won't!"

More screams. At times her screams were intermingled with words I could not readily understand or capture in my abbreviated notes. Then suddenly there was silence. Observing Lia, she seemed frozen, still. And in a strangely quiet voice she began in calm, measured words to describe, exactly as one might describe a scenario, what she "saw" happening to the "woman across the room."

". . . Dr Obgee looks very perplexed . . . she seems a madwoman," Lia said faintly. She described the "woman" as cursing at the doctors and nurses, and noted in an objective manner that "she" seemed in agony, sweating, contorted. She said that "the woman" obviously was enraged. After a few moments there was no sound at all from Lia. She was motionless in the chair.

When I attempted to intervene to glean more information, her guard went up. The self-preservation defenses raised their shields and she began, in answer to my questions, to rationalize about what had just happened. I was impressed mainly by the fact that she did not remember a good measure of what I had just heard. I could push no further. The patient had served warning to me that her subconscious had released all that it felt safe to release at this point.

What was I just witness to? I was at that minute glad my associate was not in the office. Within myself I was not willing to deal with what had just happened, so I surely wasn't ready to discuss it with someone else. Was this a dual personality I had just interviewed? It is not that the subject is verboten, but I had been caught off guard and preferred to have more data to support my feelings. Patients will often describe events that take place in hypnosis as if they were an observer to the action, just as so frequently occurs in dreaming. This was how I explained the episode to myself that day.

I began again to speak, directing Lia to breathe deeply and to go into a more deeply relaxed state. During the fifteen minutes of self-sorting, as I catalogued my thoughts, she had dropped back to a deep, deep level and, I felt, was prepared to resume the session.

MEN ARE TO ME:	Only hurt . . . and more hurt.
RELIGION TO ME:	A trap!
IF I EVER LET GO:	I would hit him in the head!
SUBMIT:	Always, to him.
VIRGIN:	I still am . . .

Well! It was just that kind of day! Here was my patient, a woman who had experienced five pregnancies, had three grown children—and she is still a virgin! So at first I had my smile for the day. But only at first. Again I had the distinct feeling that I was missing something. What? Why such a denial? Only to deny her own sexuality, or perhaps her marriage to Paul Farrelli? I didn't think so. I did not realize then that Lia's response, "I still am," was so absolutely logical and appropriate. But not for Lia as I knew her then.

PUNISHMENT:	Church.
I REALLY DESIRE:	To die . . .
WHEN MOTHER DIED:	I was so happy.
DIVORCE:	Unthinkable.
IN THE HOLE:	That's where he always wants to be . . .
TO FEEL CLEAN:	I never feel clean! . . . I wash and wash . . . and I can't get his filth off me . . . [*screaming*]

There went my plans for a calm, peaceful hour. Lia had told me of the rape, but now her real fear was breaking through her controlled facade. The abreaction occurred as suddenly as had the one before—to be honest, before I was prepared for another emotional trip. Within a matter of seconds Lia was experiencing the rape by Harry.

"Can't get away . . . from the filth . . . all over me! . . . there! . . . there! . . . I never feel clean! . . . I wash and wash and I can't get that man's filth off of me! . . ."

"Who's filth, Lia? Who's filth can't you get off?" And she screamed her replies to me.

"His! His!"

"What is it? What is happening to you, Lia?"

"I can *never* get it off. I rub and rub . . . but it won't come off! . . . That man's filth all over me! I'll have it with me always . . . I know it! . . ."

Intervening, I said, "Okay, Lia. Right now your mind is beginning to drift. It is taking you back. You are going back, getting younger, going back and back in time. And on the count of 'three' you are going to be right there, right there as you go into that time with Harry. One. Two. Three."

There was a short pause and then Lia spoke saying, "No—he's our friend! He has always been a friend. This is not right! He would never hurt me . . . he has always been our friend . . . no! no! . . . please don't . . . please, please . . . no! Not right . . . no! no!"

"Come on, Lia! Tell me what is happening!"

"Oh, my God! No! No!"

Her screams were becoming louder and she began to breathe in short panting breaths. "Now," I asked, "what is he doing to you now?"

"He is sitting on my chest! His weight . . . crushing me . . . the smell is so horrible . . . oily . . filthy . . ."

"Let it all out, Lia. Let it go! What is happening?"

". . . *Crushing me!* He's killing me! . . . saying I can . . . take it in this end or . . . in the other end . . . either one that I want . . . it is . . . so horrible! *Horrible!* . . . no! No! Why am I here? . . . where is here? He says . . . that nobody will believe me! Nobody will believe me . . ."

Every phrase and word that came was studded with anguish, fear, crying. Then there was a momentary silence. Lia lay motionlessly in the chair. There was no movement whatever and she seemed to sink to an even deeper hypnotic level than before. When she again spoke, it was with an air of detachment or separateness.

". . . raining, raining so hard. And I am all dead. All dead. Now I know how it feels and it is awful . . . it smells ugly . . . like dirty oil . . . it even tastes like oil . . ."

"Lia, what tastes like oil?" I pushed, only to find that momentarily I was being shut out. Lia was lost in her regression and continued to breathe with short, struggling pants.

"It hurts to breathe, so . . . I just stop trying to . . . there is some enormous weight . . . on my chest! . . . on my body . . . crushing me! Don't open my eyes! As long as they are closed I'm safe! Safe in darkness . . ."

"Are you in darkness, Lia? Where are you in the darkness?" I asked, hoping she would again open her communication with me. I waited.

"I'm in church . . . alone with God! I look forward to my special days, my days alone in the church with God! I'm here and I'm safe. My special day . . . my place . . . my pew. My own God!"

Something warned me to remain quiet and not intervene at this point. We were headed somewhere, and I wasn't too sure where. Then she began to cry again and her words ran together in a jumble.

". . . he's saying . . . his voice saying strange things! . . . hissing sounds . . . his teeth are clenched . . . words make no sense! A choice. This end or the other! Woman, you smell so goooood! . . . no noise. Keep your mouth shut! *Nobody will believe you!* . . . my mouth is not there anymore . . . something terrible pressing my . . . breath out. Pressing my lips against my teeth . . . and it hurts. It hurts all over . . . don't have any arms, any hands . . . all gone. I lost them somewhere under me . . . I know they're under my body . . . twisted in back . . . but they're not arms . . . they're just two more pains. Inside my body something . . . is hurting me . . . pushing my life right out of my body! . . . there is nobody to help me . . . I called them . . . all. Gently, now . . . very gently, out . . . safe . . . dead."

The Healing of Lia

In this pause I felt she would permit me to enter. "Lia, is it all over? Now what?"

"Yes. It's all over. I'm dead. I'm dead . . ."

"Did he kill you, Lia?"

"I wish . . . I wish he had . . . I died, I died . . ."

"Her voice was very weak and without any hope in its quality.

"How, Lia? How did you die?"

". . . so dark . . . I don't need lights! I carry a special light of my own within myself. I can kneel here, close to the tabernacle where the Host lives, and tell Him how it is to be lost . . . and I am lost, God. I don't know who I am anymore . . . sometimes I don't know where I am, or why . . ."

At this time I believe the thing that caused me the most horror was to realize that this woman, another Lia who was speaking now, must have been taken from this atmosphere—in this frame of mind—and by some hideously destructive design led into another more brutal reality. Though I believe she would have had to be in some altered frame of mind to allow this with Harry. During the next two hours I sat as Lia relived physically and mentally all that had occurred that day. I watched and listened, intervening when necessary, as she excruciated, and knew that it must be done if I was to discover what I needed to help her.

". . . there is nobody to help me. I called them all! Paul! Mama! Papa! Godgodgod! . . . I don't want to be here and . . . there isn't any way out! . . ."

And here there was a pause. Her voice resumed in a flicker, but it was not the same voice. Coolly, placidly, she said:

". . . there is. Let go. Just let yourself go down the corridors in your mind. Gently, very gently. Out. Out. Safe . . . dead . . ."

Dead! The word Lia had reiterated over and over and over. Although she was not dead physically, on a subconscious level the acceptance of death was complete and the culminating event was now revealed. Lia had, I realized from the beginning, excessively strong subconscious feelings of death. There were other events in her life that had primed her mind into the acceptance of this suggestion and that had, in many ways, placed her in the chair today. Shown clearly in her journal are such instances:

This cannot be a real dream because there are so many people here! I am very small, just a child, and it's summer . . . stifling hot here in church. All the people are crowded into the pews and I can't see and I can't breathe! I am so hungry because of the long fast before Communion . . . not even a drop of water may be taken. The candles are hot . . . and smoking; the incense is so thick and all the voices are droning . . . I feel so ill. I want to vomit, but they will be angry if I do. Then I feel very funny . . . and a lovely darkness comes . . . and I don't feel anything anymore. I know someone is lifting me in his arms, so gently, and when I look I see it is Mr. Blakely, and I let the darkness come again. It's so nice, so lovely to be dead and not feel so ill.

Mr. Blakely, I later learned, was a local funeral director who was a member of Lia's parish church. What could be more perfect symbolism than for a child to find herself in the arms of one who cares for the dead? To her, death was a means of escape from that which was intolerable to her on this occasion, and also on the following one (from her journal):

I am seventeen and I can hear Mama talking and saying, "I don't know how I ever had a child like her!" and I know she means me. But I just go on playing the piano, and the music sounds very heavy and sad, like the funeral march I had to learn for my last session. I go upstairs to the bathroom and drink the whole bottle of medicine marked *poison*, but it only makes me sick and I throw up. But I feel so much better because I know that Lia is dead anyway. She must be dead . . . only my body still keeps on going and I can't figure out how to stop it. Then I know. It must be done when you are a baby.

Again the use of the mechanism of death to avoid the pain of a situation that is intolerable. Even the playing of the "heavy" music, reminiscent of a funeral march, shows how suggestible Lia has been. And though she had heard on many occasions the "rejection" from her Mama, this time, no longer able to live with it, she attempted suicide. Even that was a failure, so she simply accepted an emotional death. Having once said that being born was the worst thing that had ever happened to her, in this excerpt from her journal she has said clearly that she recognized it had to be done "when you are a baby," like a litter of kittens that

The Healing of Lia

are unwanted—to the bag, to the river—death being the only answer.

Lia's very strong religious education in the Catholic church had indeed embedded itself well. When the "adultery" (the rape) had occurred, she again had a moral death. This, coupled with the "mortal sin" of her sterilization, left her no choice but to accept moral death.

There was still one very important factor that I felt had to be pointed out and examined. The rape obviously had not taken place in her home. Where had it happened? And why had she allowed herself to be somewhere with this man? I hit home with one further question.

"Why did you go, Lia?"

Immediately Lia's voice seemed to change and she spoke with a very offended, defensive air and flatly stated, "I *didn't!* I wouldn't have done that, I wouldn't have! I could trust him. He was my friend! He has always been our friend!"

Her denial was more than just one of indignation. It was a declarative statement spoken by one who truly believed what she said.

I now gave Lia suggestions to relax and to clear her mind completely. Further emphasis was made to her that even though she had felt that she was morally dead, she could live again, that she was to breathe in the good breath of life, to feel her blood coursing through her arteries, and to even feel that close associate of hers, pain. This may seem like a negative suggestion, but as soon as she stated she felt pain in her abdomen, I then gave her the suggestion that it would disappear, which it promptly did. By this means I was able to show her that *she* controlled her body and therefore could make it live a full and beautiful life.

A long and exhausting session was drawing to a close. It was time to prepare for her next visit. She was given the suggestion that she would have a dream; it would awaken her in the middle of the night and she would write it down and bring it with her when she came to my office the next time. The dream would contain very useful information about her problem. Again she was reassured as to her well-being, and was awakened.

This was not the time for a triumphant cry, but that is exactly what I wanted to give! As I was moving from one room to another in my office, I spotted Lia being escorted to her treatment room by one of my assistants. She was like a breath of spring walking down the hall toward me. The reason? Today Lia was no longer dressed in black: the shroud of death was gone! I did not need to ask if she had had a dream as I had given her the suggestion to do on her last visit. I could see that she *had* responded to the suggestion, and the very visible fact that today she was attired in a soft yellow dress told me that she had integrated the work concerning her feelings of subconscious "death." I felt a great sense of exaltation within myself because Lia was making such progress. If we could keep things going now, we would have a good end result.

The dream that Lia had handed to my assistant was written very legibly and on one side of the paper, as had been directed. As I read through it, I realized that here was a deviation from the usual, in that portions of the dream were factual and portions were symbolic. Only she could tell me which were which, but I could recognize certain statements that fit into her history.

Lia was escorted into her treatment room, correctly positioned, and made comfortable. I placed her dream paper before me with her chart, and brought about hypnosis by progressive relaxation. It is somewhat slower than some other methods, but I wanted nothing to jolt her emotions. I felt we were going to be dealing with material that might contain some of the origins of her problems. The dream as presented by Lia was as follows:

The Healing of Lia

It is 2:30 A.M. and the dream was this: I am all alone in the dark bus and I have my baby in the mason jar where Paul put it, in my lap. Every time the bus hits a bump I can feel the blood bubble out of me and I'm afraid someone will know that my baby is dead and my husband wouldn't take me for help because he was too busy. He got so angry when I began, and he just pulled it out, put it in the jar, and went back to building the closet. The bus ride seemed forever and I notice I'm not alone now. Mother is up front, looking at me with the look that says, "I'm right again!" She and Paul always seem to be right. Then he is there too—God! he really came to help! —but then he says, "Get up! I'll tell you when you've had enough rest!" But I'm so weak I can't get up and I know if I don't do as he says he won't love me. His mother is now on the bus—where did she come from? She sits chanting on her rosary beads: "My Paul! My Paul! My Paul!" and I break out in a terrible cold sweat. I want to scream, "But I have our baby—right here!" but I can't seem to make any sound. Then all the prayer group is surrounding me, smothering me. Dr. Bryan lays his hands on my head, begins to speak in tongues, and tells me I am not living in the spirit because I am so angry, so full of hate. And then the jar cracked and that shriveled dead thing begins to grow, and Father Jon, who married us, pats my head and says, "See, Lia, it's all not real anymore!" And I scream at him, "You mother-fucking old bastard! You said each time was like a sacrament, something holy! And it's *not* loving and beautiful at all!"

Then I'm not on the bus at all. I'm locked up with Aunt Ava in Lofton State Hospital and Mama is on the other side of the window —it has bars—laughing and saying, "See! I'm right! You ended up right where you *belong*! In the crazy house! I told you so!"

And then suddenly I am back on the bus (I have ridden the accursed thing since it happened) and I awaken.

I read the dream back to Lia, asking her to visualize it again in her mind as I read. At this point I reminded her that dreams were very symbolic but now, on a subconscious level, she could understand these symbols. She immediately screamed back to me that it was *not* symbolism at all but was exactly the truth as it had transpired. I could recognize that this was not exactly as it had happened, but I could not be sure exactly what was what at this time.

"What do you mean, Lia? It is exactly how what happened?"

"I'm in bed, having a miscarriage. I call for Paul and he is so upset with me that he just pulls it from me and flushes it down the toilet. Then he goes back to work on that closet."

For a moment I was confused. "Flushes it down the toilet" did not agree with Lia's dream material of the fetus being placed in a mason jar. I knew from her history that Lia had two miscarriages, which in her hypnotic state had been combined into one during this dream interpretation. Her first miscarriage had been flushed down the toilet; the second had indeed been put into a mason jar for her to carry alone on a nightmarish bus ride while her husband had been working on a closet. It is not unusual for a patient to combine facts of two similar events when in the state of hypnosis, and in this particular situation it really made no difference.

"All right, you have passed the fetus and Paul has flushed it down the toilet. Now what?" I asked, continuing. She had begun to sob and there was both fear and anger in her voice. The correct ingredients were all there; she was feeling neglected and threatened.

"I'm still bleeding . . . bleeding . . . it seems to be so much! I'm feeling weaker and weaker . . . why won't he *help* me? I call to him . . . ask him to take me to Dr. Obgee . . . and he says he is . . . too busy and for me to get my friend Maggie to help." (By now she is crying profusely.) "My friend takes me to Dr. Obgee's office but she can't wait . . . she has to leave me. Afterward . . . I'm ashamed . . . and I don't tell Dr. Obgee that Paul didn't bring me . . . that I'm alone. I take the bus back home and . . . the trip is so long . . . I can feel the blood bubbling between my legs. I have a diaper stuffed in my underpants . . . but I can still feel the blood bubbling . . . down . . . horrible! Each time the bus bounces more blood comes . . . how can I stand to *lose* so much? Why doesn't it *stop*? I don't want to go home! I don't want to! I'll . . . just go back into that same place where nobody wants me . . . just go back and get . . . pregnant again. . . ."

"Lia, right now you see yourself caught in a dilemma. You see no way out for yourself, but you are going to be fine. You are doing just fine. Now let's get back to the dream. If you will look toward the front of the bus, you can see your mother standing there."

Without any questions being asked, Lia begins.

"She has that same look on her face again, that look! That look that is so hard to describe. But a feeling that I am . . . that I am. . ."

With soft-spoken urging, I broke in, "Yes, Lia, go on."

She knows that she is right! She and Paul . . . they are *always* right! Everybody is right! . . . but me. He's very angry . . . I'm causing him so much trouble! And . . . I can't let him feel angry . . . I don't dare! He's the *only* one who ever *loved* me . . . if . . . if I don't do just as he says . . . he will stop loving me and . . . I'll be totally . . . alone. . . ."

"Lia, there is someone else on the bus, and according to the dream, it is your mother-in-law. She is saying her rosary and repeating, 'My Paul, my Paul, my Paul.' What does that mean to you?"

"Yes, she is always doing that! She is trying to take him away from me so that I will be totally alone!"

It was very clear that Lia felt little or no security in her life. And that her fears of being left "totally alone" were becoming unbearable.

Going on with the dream interpretation, I said, "Lia, the next segment of your dream is where you are with Dr. Bryan. He is laying his hands on your head and he is speaking in tongues and he tells you that you are not living in the spirit. For whom is Dr. Bryan a symbol, Lia?"

"He's the church group . . . I . . ."

"No, Lia, I want to know who he *symbolically* represents in your life. I realize that he was with the church group when you were with the charismatic movement, but I believe he stands for something *more* than that in your life."

"He's . . . all of them . . . all of them with the church! All of them who condemn me! He says that I'm so full of anger and hate . . . and I am . . . . I am full of anger! Very, very angry! So *angry!* Ha, ha, ha!"

Here, as Lia spoke, she broke into a strange intonation and her sobbing evolved in a transposition from sorrow to a shrill, almost threatening quality. A strident harsh laugh ensued momentarily and just as suddenly stopped. She said harshly, "I *will* show them! . . ." and when I questioned her further her voice switched back to its normal, softer tone.

I did not feel at this time that I had enough background information to pursue this line of thought. Also, I had not gotten a voluntary response which might have helped me identify just what this new voice might mean. Again I drew her back to the facts of the dream.

"Lia, in your dream the jar cracks and the shriveled, dead thing begins to grow. What is this 'thing' symbolic of, Lia? What does it mean to you?" When she replied, it was with a very weak voice, similar to the voice of a child.

". . . that is the baby . . . the baby who was unwanted . . . and it begins to grow. It begins to grow into full size . . . it is not wanted and it begins to grow. . . ."

"And what meaning does that carry for you, Lia?" I asked her.

". . . it means . . . all the unwanted babies . . . all the babies. Even if they're not wanted they grow . . . up. And that was . . . me . . . me. . . ."

"All right, Lia. They all grow up. Now, in your dream there is another religious person. There is Father Jon. What meaning does Father Jon have for you?"

"For me? He is the one who started me in . . . all this! By telling me that each time was like a sacrament! Something holy! But when it's like this, it's not! It's *not* holy. *It's not!* It's nothing but . . . pain . . . and hurt . . . and hate! It can't *be* holy! Oh, my dear God . . . it can't be holy, not when it's like this! My God would not hurt me!"

"It is all right now, Lia. I want you to know that you are *safe* and I am going to protect you in every way. You must trust me to take care of you at this time. You are going to go back now in time . . . back in time. . . ."

An age-regressing technique was done now to take Lia back to a very important event in her life, a time that her own mind would choose.

"You are going back, to be at a time in your life when you were made to feel very guilty. Or to a time when you did something for which you felt guilty. The most important time in your life—when you were made to feel *very, very guilty.*"

After an interval I asked, "Lia, what's happening to you right now?"

"I'm in church . . . talking with the priest . . . telling him about all the . . . the pain and bleeding . . . that I need to have surgery . . . and the doctors won't do it . . . not unless they can tie my . . . tubes at the same time. But . . . ."

"Yes, Lia, you are telling the priest. But what is happening now?"

He doesn't seem to be hearing me! I tell him over and over . . . all the troubles I have been having . . . but he just sits there . . . asking me if I have prayed! Oh, God! How I have prayed! . . . doesn't he have any sense at all! You stupid bastard! I'm dying! Can't you see that? No! Of course you can't . . . You can't see your fucking nose in front of your own face! . . . ."

Choking on angry sobs, Lia was experiencing anger in a very extreme way. With very little prodding from me she continued.

"How in the name of heaven can I expect you to understand? But you're a priest! . . . you are supposed to be able to understand people . . . and problems . . . even women's problems. Paul is no better . . . he won't help me! . . . won't give me advice . . . won't even discuss it . . . why can't anybody hear me, help me? Why can't God hear me? . . . ."

Here I asked, "Lia, what is happening now? Tell me."

"The priest is telling me . . . telling me . . . " (Lia is by now crying almost hysterically) that if I have the operation . . . the sterilization . . . that I will be living in mortal sin and . . . and . . . ."

"Yes, and what?"

"And I have *been doing penance* . . . ever since then! Every day I do penance! Every day of my life!"

Lia was no longer in the age regression. She had left it of her own will and I did not feel at that moment that it was important for her to continue in that phase. I had the significant information I needed at the time.

I asked, "How have you been carrying out that penance, Lia?"

"All the torture I have endured . . . all the . . . ."

"All the *guilt*, Lia! How have you atoned *for all the guilt?*"

"Yes! All the guilt! . . . so much to bear! I have punished myself . . . for years and years . . . and I've let others punish me! Even Paul said . . ."

"Yes, Lia, even Paul said what?"

"That it was my guilt! That it was the price all women pay for their sin . . . of tempting Adam in the garden! That's why we all hurt . . . even the church says it's so! . . . our guilt! . . . and I've paid and paid . . . I've ridden that bus in hell ever since. . . ."

"That's right, Lia. You have ridden that bus in hell for so very long. But how have you been punishing yourself?"

"Bruises . . . the sores . . . pains . . . everyone who looks can see what a horrible person I am! They can just look at me and see . . . they will know just how bad I am. . . ."

From the journal:

The terrible picture in my mind was one that we all had to draw on the blackboard when we were in the fourth grade. Sister had described how our little souls had been born with a blemish, a tiny spot on them, and all in the class had been told to draw their "souls" on the board. I drew mine in a sort of womb shape and put the little spot (original sin) right in the middle. Then Sister explained that our baptism had cleansed this spot (we were allowed to erase it) and that henceforth, using our free will, it was quite up to us to keep this little spotless soul free from sin. We all promised that we would try very hard. Then we were told to picture a soul with several venial sins, which we depicted by placing several small dots about on this poor soul on the blackboard (one lie, two angers, one disobedience, were inflicted on mine) . . . and finally the pièce de résistance . . . one mortal sin. We were all directed to take the chalk and completely darken the soul. Cover it right out to the edges with this terrible sin. And the only way to erase this one (by now we were all in terror) was to recognize it, hate it, confess it, and do penance for it. And if one dared to receive Communion while in this state . . . it compounded the offense, and you were worse off than before. (And just how one got worse off than total damnation I never knew.)

I am sure that by recess all my little classmates had forgotten the exercise on the board and gone about their play. But I did not. And to this day I have a terrible picture of this evil, darkened soul I carry within me because I seem to always be questioning those in authority over my

The Healing of Lia

spiritual life. I remember much about religion during this early part of my training. Either, for some reason I took it much too seriously (Paul, my family, my classmates, and friends all had the same training, and none of them lived in terror as I did and still do), or I was not able to cope with the fact that I was unable to live a stain-free, sin-free existence and consequently lived in fear of the judgment of a God who did not seep into my child's consciousness as a very kindly, loving, understanding God. I was taught to fear God, and I was obedient in this directive, as I was in most others. I did. And I do, still.

Today I spoke to Father in confession, once again trying to make someone understand that I did not do this thing by choice, but in pain. But it was all not a bit of use. When I left the confessional, I left to carry the heaviest burden of my life, and I do not know if I can suffer it anymore. He gave me a penance that I must do for the rest of my life, to beg for forgiveness. It isn't a long penance, or a very hard one . . . but, oh, God! . . . it is such an unjust one!

So now I knew one part of the puzzle. One answer to one of my questions. I knew why, or at least part of the why, of Lia's self-punishment. Lia was one more victim who, like many before her, had been taught the negative "fear God" philosophy by experts, who apparently failed to recognize the counterweight directive: "God is love." I made a decision, albeit a quick one, as to how I would handle the immediate situation. I was not at all sure at the moment that it was the correct tack to take, but since religion had played such a predominant role in the creation of her problems, I decided I would use it in the solution of her problems. If, I felt, it could be used to her detriment, I now figured that I would finally put it to work for her benefit. For this woman, I felt it would work—that is precisely why I chose to emphasize it so strongly. Religion was now going to be used to give her love rather than fear.

"Lia, you do believe in God. You know that and I know that. Even though it has been hard for you to believe in the past few years, you still do believe in a loving God. But you have allowed religion to put you where you are at this moment. Now, I want you to accept the *other* side of religion, the side in which we know that God is a forgiving God and, even if you *had* committed a crime against Him, He tells you that He will forgive! I want you to put it back into His hands. Let Him forgive you! If there ever was a sin—and it is difficult for me to conceive there ever was—can you do that, Lia? Give up this eternal hell? Return to a happy life and recognize that you were condemned *by a mere man!* Think of that, Lia! A mortal man, just as you and I! You *can* do it! I know you can, Lia! Starting today you will know that you are worthy and were created in God's own image. In His eyes you *are* beautiful and you have a *right* to live free of torment. I want you to *accept* these suggestions now into your mind, your body, and your spirit.

"Relax, now, again remembering that you are a worthy person who must answer only to yourself and to God, who loves you very much."

I continued for some time with relaxation suggestions coupled with suggestions to create a feeling of peace, self-forgiveness, and reliance on her ability to create her own future. I realized that the material I had gathered from this dream was just a bare scratching of the topsoil, but it was an indication of how terrified she was. It was a small step, but an important one, into her life, her home, and later into her childhood, into the world of a terrified child, of adult injustice and facts that caused me to wonder how, with no positive counterweights, Lia had survived. For now, however, Lia was given the suggestion to have another dream, and following more comforting and relaxing words from me, this session was terminated.

16

I had told Lia that I wanted to see Paul. Right now I needed all the help I could get, not because the therapy was failing but because Lia's home situation seemed to thwart and impede her progress. Often, in my experience, the families of patients (and the mates in particular,) feel threatened when they witness the progress of the person they have come to accept as "sick," and subconsciously set about to undermine this progress. I had the distinct feeling this might be true in Lia's case.

Paul Farrelli came to my office the day before Lia's next appointment. He was a very pleasant, soft-spoken, neatly dressed man. My first impression was that he was uneasy and would have preferred to have been anywhere except in my office. As we talked he volunteered little information in response to my questions, answering in short, polite phrases. Slightly puzzled, I realized he was not to any degree discussing either the severity of Lia's illness or the illness itself, as he was bound to have experienced it. He handed me a sheet of paper, saying only that it was Lia's latest dream. I took a moment to glance at it and—there it was! Exactly what I had been looking for! The second personality had left cold, hard, written proof on the paper.

I glanced at Paul, surprised at how still and quietly he sat there. He must have seen it too, read it too! Incredulously I watched for some reaction, feeling that any husband concerned for his wife's welfare and paying the costs for her therapy would have demanded to know, "What the hell's going on here? What does that paper mean?" But in this man there seemed to be a complete absence of what I would term just plain old normal curiosity. I'm not sure what, if anything, I said to Paul Farrelli about the paper, but remember just sliding it into Lia's chart and out of sight.

I was even more amazed when, after having given me the paper, he relaxed and began talking as to an old, comfortable acquaintance, as if he had completed his duty. Intrigued, and in order to see where the conversation would lead, I let him take the ball, and we sat for the better part of an hour chatting about everyday things. I did feel that perhaps he, too, needed some soothing encouragement, as he had been dealing with a very sick wife for many years. But silently I questioned exactly what had been the method of his "dealing." I noticed if I tried to lead the conversation back onto the subject of Lia he sidestepped and dodged like a professional boxer.

Paul Farrelli was, as Lia had described, a very handsome man. I couldn't help but wonder, having seen Lia only as she looked today—ill, scarred, terrified, dressed in funereal black— how she might have looked when he first met and loved her enough to marry her. I wondered, as children often wonder when they see the very ill or elderly, what she was like when she was twenty and she could still smile, dance, and play? Paul was dressed in very presentable clothes; he was tanned, slim, and fit looking. He was, in fact, the picture of the secure, satisfied businessman. The contrast with his wife, as I had seen her, was staggering, and it gave me cause for reflection on some of the statements Lia had made. I began to wonder about some rather elementary things.

First, he *must* have known that Lia had told me of the incident with Oilcan Harry, and that I could see for myself at least some of the bruises on her. Yet he made no mention whatever of either of these things which, in normal circumstances, one might expect a husband to at least say, "You know, my wife was rather badly hurt last year," or "My wife sometimes damages her body." Anything! He might have said anything at all, but for some reason he chose to say nothing. My expression "in normal circumstances" perhaps explains this anomaly; the circumstances here were far from "normal." Lia and her illness were most assuredly not normal, but neither was the situation with her husband in my office this day.

The second thing I wondered about was, how in the name of

common sense, would a husband refuse his wife's plea to relocate their home, when to stay meant that she must endure living less than two miles away from the person who had assaulted her in such a manner? Lia's actual terror, as evidenced in my office, was increased each time she had to drive to the market, to the shopping areas, or to the center of her town, because each time she went she had to drive by the business place of Oilcan Harry. Paul must have been aware of this. I myself recently had occasion to visit the town in which Lia lives, and while taking some papers to her home I realized, as I drove by the home and office of Oilcan Harry, that an angry shudder shook me. I knew that Paul's business firm had numerous branch locations to which he might have requested transfers. I knew that Lia had repeatedly asked him to do this, not merely since the "incident," but as far back as the beginning of their marriage. She had told me, "I have begged Paul to leave this place, to go away," and apparently Paul had always given Lia the same answer, and this was that one did not "run away" from one's problems. Lia seemed to feel that Paul's refusals had nothing to do with her "running away," but rather were saying something quite different. The message Lia was receiving was: "Home and family is what matters, and you *will* stay even if it kills you." She saw herself trapped by destructive elements, even her geographical environment, and saw Paul's refusals as his method of punishment. Lia later compared living where she did to forcing a survivor of Buchenwald to live in a nice housing development just down the road from where the internment camp had been. It was torment, and the absolute absurdity was becoming a wedge of anger she wanted to direct at Paul. Instead, she directed it elsewhere.

But for now, sitting, chatting with Paul Farrelli, I waited for him to make an inroad into the subject concerning Lia's illness. I waited in vain and so, when the time came for him to take his leave, I tried to give him some encouragement, telling him that I felt better days were in store for both Lia and him. After he left I sat for a time contemplating Lia's description of her home life and the type of person she had described her husband as being. All things considered, why was I bewildered by what had just occurred in my own office? But, dammit, I asked myself, *how* could a man of apparent intelligence just close his eyes to all this? Or had he? Even if he was sick to the teeth of his wife's illness, how could he ignore the paper he had handed to me? Was he, as Lia had told me, a man compelled to deny whatever was unpleasant or might not fit the contours of his ideas of the logical scheme of life? Was what I had witnessed an attitude of disinterest, or had this all become an impossible reality for him to face?

Then it hit me as only an "it" can—I was angry as hellfire! Didn't this man realize his dilemma? My dilemma? My job was not to pander to his inability to face his realities. This was not Paul Farrelli's therapy, it was his wife's, and my job was to help get his wife back on the road to sanity. To do this I needed his cooperation if not his help. And then it dawned on me that I was angry all right, but not so much at Paul Farrelli as with myself. I had, godammit, let him waltz away from me without learning one thing from him. *How*, in blue blazes? I'd had him right there in front of me! And I'd let the interview get away from me!

Perhaps some of my anger was caused by the embarrassing fact that after handing out some pretty lofty advice to Lia about controlling her own life and what she might do to alter Paul's behavior, I had blown the whole thing myself. Well . . .

There it was. I sat staring at the paper, attentive not only to what I was reading but to *how* it was written. The dream Lia had written was in two totally different handwritings. In the upper portion the dream had been a voice (mine) directing her to finally tell the truth to me.

> I am in the therapy room deep in hypnosis. I feel none of my extremities, they are gone, completely gone. And out of the darkness came his voice telling me that I must now tell the whole truth —about the other.

Okay, that much was fine. It was written in delicately feminine script. It would have all been fine had it not been for the words that slashed across the bottom of the page, the pen pressed so forcefully that the paper puckered:

> *If she tells you one word I swear I will kill her, doctor.*

The truth. I had an idea that the secondary personality had surfaced for one reason, and that was because in Lia's dream she

The Healing of Lia

had *assented* to the voice (mine) saying, "I want so very badly to tell . . ." Clearly this other entity was becoming a danger to Lia. I had a part of the story now, but only a part. I needed times, places, episodes, reactions—all the things Paul Farrelli might have given me and didn't.

The answers all existed, but they were in a place I knew nothing of. They were hidden in the journal in the desk, hidden from Lia and me. And the ones that weren't there were locked inside Lia's head. The journal pages were a headway leap into exactly what her feelings were and why:

I am vaguely aware of a beginning, a subtle sort of rebirth within myself. Dr. Ward has thrust brutally, necessarily, before me that I must accept things as they are.

I admit to my deepest self that while loving Paul, more than that, *worshipping* him, that I have hated him for what his beliefs have done to my life. He did all that he did without having the slightest knowledge of the damage . . . I have to believe this, or I could not bear my own life.

My spirit was damaged, deformed, when I married Paul. But not beyond healing! Had he been other than he was (a Catholic), he might have seen things in another light.

I believe with every fiber of my intelligence that *every human condition is created in the mind.* All the pain, the violent vomiting, the tumors, were but a manifestation of my anger, my hatred, and were a way of shutting him, and everything, out of my life, my body. Hatred of an institution that warped Paul's mind, blinded him into unthinking submission, that caused the loss of my physical health, mental stability, and marital happiness. Rules instituted by celibate men—never by God, Himself! Never, never would a loving father inflict such anguish on his children.

Saved. I have been saved for some reason. I do not believe the Creator would grant a gift of intellect, sensitivity, and creativity, only to snuff it out with mental illness.

I am allowed to drift, however, into the untold, unspeakable horror of illness . . . and then be pulled back again. It is very necessary that I record this journey back and forth as not many tread the path both ways. A journal. A journal that looks inward, probing into the nature of a spirit that burns in a torment beyond understanding.

The dream came as Dr. Ward said it would. I was in the therapy room, deep in hypnosis. I felt none of my extremities . . . they were just gone . . . completely gone . . . and out of the darkness came his voice telling me that I must now tell him the whole truth. God! I awoke, and Paul was sitting on my bed . . . comforting me . . . and I felt so released! I knew for a certainty that I must do as the dream directed, tell *the whole truth!* About the other . . . please let him make it easy for me . . . the humiliation, the burden, is so terrible. I hurt so badly . . . my chest bones are beginning to show . . . I can't eat. Please *let Dr. Ward listen* . . . and help. Thursday, so far away. A lifetime.

Next day's entry:

I must tear up the paper on which I wrote my dream. No one must ever see the terrible writing at the bottom of the sheet . . . plainly the words are there, but when were they written? By my hand? *No! Not my hand!* . . . I am so tired of the fight. Fight her, deny her existence . . . and she will keep surfacing and eventually destroy my marriage and my life!

I have begun to swallow the barbiturates I have left—just a few pills left now. This is a defeat for me, to go back to the drugs.

How can I tell Dr. Ward? Who would believe me?

So one part of Lia had known of the danger in the dream paper—but which part? Lia herself didn't know. Later I was to find in the journal a note Lia had written after her last visit and before I saw Paul.

Yesterday I saw Dr. Ward. It is getting harder and harder to hide the truth and yet I cannot seem, even under hypnosis, to tell him of the other entity within myself. He wants to speak with Paul next week and will do so before my next visit. If Paul had more understanding, he might help me—save me—but I have begun to lose hope, any hope at all. I know well enough this other being, this other woman, will not reveal herself, or let me do so, because by doing so she destroys herself —and by now I realize that it is I she plans to destroy, not herself. Only during the rages does she come out fully, lurking deeply at other times, just surfacing enough to drive me deeper into torment. My mind is a boiling, seething, ebullient mass of torment. Oh, God! How I want to go to sleep and just sleep on forever. The thought of a dark veil of peace slipping its cover of comfort over my mind—sleep, peace, and at the

end a quiet merciful death. But how? How is one sure? How many pills
are enough? How deeply does one cut? I am not so stupid as to want to
turn myself into a vegetable because of an overdose that didn't quite
work. Wired to monitors and tubes for months or years to grieve my
children and embarrass them. One must be practical. I want my children to remember me not as a madwoman, but with some remnant of
dignity and love.

I longed for release from the drugs! How I thought my mind,
stunned so long, would begin to whirl into a myriad of lovely thoughts!
And all I did was release *the other*, the thing I have dreaded since she
came from nowhere in the delivery room at Lori's birth. I can still chill
at the memory of the screams—laughing, terrorizing even Dr. Obgee
who had to leave the room and search out Paul. But he never told him.
I cannot imagine why. He let me go mad on the table, and perhaps he
might have spared me all the pain that followed, because I, in my
humiliation, could never speak of it to anyone. What would I say—
"There is, within me, another woman, whom I fight to keep deeply
hidden, but who is stronger than I." Black, evil, like a malignancy, one
who lives only to destroy. And it is I she is bent on destroying.

I wish I might pray. Might believe and feel comfort from a loving
God. But I am steeped in hatred. In evil. Dr. Ward says it is a sin against
God to hurt myself as I do, but I cannot tell him that it is she who does
this, not I—never I. Who is she? Where is she now? Why does she come
out for no reason at all? I cannot bear to be host to such an entity. If
she is Lia, then surely Lia must die.

I'm glad this material was not available to me at this point in
her therapy. With the implication of self-destruction, I may well
have pushed intervention harder. Doing so at that point may
have led to suppression of the altered personality once more.
The basic journal was not discovered until Lia had been in therapy about two months. And then she kept parts of it from me.
Later she would find even other entries hidden about her home.
Obviously a subconscious battle was ensuing, a battle that was
resulting in the physical and emotional destruction of this tor-
mented woman.

From the different handwriting on the note I could begin to
see Lia was striving to reveal that there was some form of alteration existing in her personality, an alteration that she had written

wanted to harm her and ultimately destroy her. Over the years Lia had developed tremendous anger, hatred, and rage, and she needed a mechanism to handle all of it. She long ago learned that she did not have the authority to express rage, and to do so would only verify that she was a "crazy woman."

As in the delivery room, Lia was able to detach herself and stand across the room and observe the actions of the "she." "She" was able to strike out, to rage, to confuse, to laugh inappropriately, and cause utter chaos. Lia had to shrink in the corner watching this horrible transformation, denying that she could ever be a part of that thing across the room.

What sort of *non entity* was at work here? Obviously it was a personality that was capable of great rage. When "she" appeared in the delivery room, there was rage and abuse to the nurses and doctors. Why to them? Surely Lia could see that these people were there to help her, to provide her with relief from pain, to help her with the birth of her third baby.

As I sat in the dark of my office that morning before my appointments, it all just continued to roll over and over in my mind. Why? Why?

She had said that she had had repeated pregnancies and that she was not ready for them to come with such speed and with such regularity. Were nurses and doctors "helping" her? No! They were *forcing her*. Forcing her to have another baby that she did not want, that she was making a last ditch effort to prevent. It was a losing battle again. Lia could not handle the thought of what was happening, and the idea of having another child at home was too much for her. So "she" came to strike out for Lia as a means of protection. But with all this great deduction, I was left with the *who* or *what* of the personality. Okay, "she" emerges with intolerable situations, and from the note on the dream I knew there was capacity for violence. Now *where?* It was so hard not to push for deeper insight, but on the morning of each visit I had to remind myself to take my time. Go slowly. Do not cause resuppression.

As she wrote of suicide and her reasons for not having done this, one may have dismissed these threats as rubbish, saying she really didn't want to do it. I can assure the reader that Lia wanted to die, but she even lacked the ability to do that. She had made several attempts in the past and had failed. There was also the underlying factor that as much as she rejected her Catholic teachings, they were ingrained. It was for these reasons that I reinforced their teaching that it is a sin to harm oneself. After all, religion had been manipulated to create portions of her illness, so if I could manipulate it to help make her well, I'd use it in any way that I could. From Lia's journal:

During the past terrible eleven years when I was under the care of Dr. Ling, there were days when I was normal, and these days were as golden gifts, so beautiful that even now it is hard for me to describe them. It was as though I had been looking at the world, and life, through a sheet of waxed paper, and suddenly someone had removed the paper! Colors were there that I'd never seen before! Flowers bloomed and I could touch and smell again!

These few precious days kept a spark of hope alive in me. At these times I could reach out to Paul and beg his forgiveness for the horror I was putting us both through. Paul could be good to an extreme, forgive the unforgivable and be sympathetic to a fault, but even he, after eleven years of my illness, began to give way. He reached the point where, when I reached out for him, for his hand to support me, he could not easily respond. This rejection served only to push me back into my withdrawn, bleak, and hopeless (I felt) existence. There comes a time when a subtle change occurs within the mind/self, and somehow getting "well" seems so improbable that getting "out" seems to make more sense.

I have often heard persons of intelligence and training say that anyone who has thoughts of suicide is without a doubt insane. I repudiate this. There is really only one condition alone necessary to bring a normal, well-adjusted person to this point and insanity has nothing to do with it. All one must be is completely, irrefutably, profoundly deprived of hope.

Lia made repeated attempts to regain hope, above all hope in her marriage. There seemed to be no way for her to turn that offered peace and hope. On one distressing occasion she had seen Paul racked with back pain and she wanted to call his physician. He absolutely forbid this interference. She said that he seemed to react negatively to her suggestions for no apparent reason. "I only wanted to help him out of the pain and I'm confused about his not wanting my help. It only led to arguing and coldness."

About this time Lia learned that she was reacting more quickly and violently to his negative responses. She was feeling more and more stifled and this she could no longer accept, but as Lia she was always dominated. It was as though her life had to be patterned after Paul's, molding her "self" to fit his "self." In doing so she lost herself as a separate and unique individual.

No human being can operate successfully under these dictates. Lia had to develop a means of handling this suppression. It was not just his negative attitude, but the fact that he handed it down like a pontifical edict. When she told the priest of her plight, another edict had been handed to her, an edict that had caused her anguish and suffering. Both forms of "no" were handed down by the "authority." Lia was too well-trained in obedience to challenge either of these authorities. Only a nonentity would be able to defend her in the face of such power figures. When the altered personality was in charge, Lia was absolved of the responsibility and consequences. However, the absolution was not complete, since Lia always returned to face the results of the action of her altered selves.

The conflict flaming in her mind, to a degree, was keeping her alive. This feeling that there was an inner being that wanted to destroy her but who could accomplish this only by being destroyed also. And if she was to die, then there would be a release from this purgatory in which she was living. Living to fulfill the proclamation of a priest.

The Healing of Lia

Lia entered the office for her next visit with an air of confidence that I had not detected before. She walked down the hall with a kind of joy that, I suppose, I should have enjoyed seeing. However, I was disturbed without knowing why at the time. Laughing, talking with much animation, gesturing—by golly, she looked as if she were embarking on a Sunday picnic! Her attitude was so different that I suppose I was suspicious because the change was so profound. What I saw I found hard to believe. For a few moments I got on the ego roller coaster and climbed to new peaks. Wasn't this what I had hoped for? Perhaps, but I had to face the fact that I knew the personalities had not been integrated or resolved. The last dream Lia had given me showed this beyond a doubt.

After Lia entered the hypnotic state, she began to tell me in glowing terms how well things had been going for her, how she had been able to handle the rage. That was the most important thing: the rage. Since this had been her primary expectancy when she had first come to me, if she could handle the rage, then, in her eyes, she must be well on the road to recovery.

"You were there, Doctor Ward! Right there! I was able to control the rage because . . . you were there in my brain. I could hear . . . so plainly, so plainly . . . your voice helping me. . . ."

Instead of being pleased, I felt increasingly disturbed by what she was telling me. What she was saying and the apparent happiness she was experiencing did not rest easily in my mind. But why? Then it hit me—I was in control of a situation at which I was not even present. For the moment I set aside my decision about dealing with this problem and moved into the session and the current dream paper.

When Lia had arrived for this visit, she had, as usual, given my assistant her latest dream. There was still no mention of the dream brought by Paul that was written in the two different styles of script.

"Now, Lia, I am going to read this dream to you as you have written it and I want you to see it again in your mind as I read it":

> There is a large amphitheater and crowds are there watching and cheering. I appear at the top, and begin to hop and bounce and bounce and then I realize that I'm not really in the body at all, but rather am far off, observing. Then I look at the bouncing person but see that it is not a real person at all. It's only a rabbit, all dressed up very small and I don't know how I could ever have mistaken it for a person.

By damn, here it was, the splitting in symbolic form! It was right there! Now came the hard part: it was my responsibility to get her to work it through accurately. I began to lead her into the analysis.

"Lia, you can see in your mind the rabbit in the dream. Now, see in your mind's eye just what *meaning* the rabbit has for you."

When she replied, my heart sank. For the first time since we had undertaken the journey together she was trying to take me down a blind alley.

"I have to stand . . . off . . . just watch everyone else get the cheers? I try . . . I really try . . . but I can't. . . ."

Intellectualizing! She was intellectualizing all over the place! On and on. I believe if I had allowed her to continue at the rate she was going, we would still be sitting there! I had to cut it off; to allow her to continue would have only reinforced in her mind that her defenses could continue forever. Crossing my fingers, I injected as sternly as I could the first words that came to mind: "*Crap! That's a lot of crap, Lia!*"

If I had had access to the journal at that time, if she had expressed to me during this session what she later put into her entry for that day, we might have had a turnabout right then. As it was, she had me running down that alley at full speed, and her

The Healing of Lia

defenses were working beautifully. She seemingly had rejected the seed I attempted to plant, the seed only she could nurture. Much later I learned that the therapy suggestions did take effect and did lead to considerable reevaluation. But right now, I did not like the way things were going.

"All of that may be very true, Lia, but I want to read that dream again and I want you to look at it again, look with a deeper part of your subconscious. See what you do when you are in certain situations. See how you react."

My words elicited anger in her, anger she vented in her journal.

And when Dr. Ward asked me to tell him what the dream meant, he didn't understand and only said, "Crap! Bull!"

He does use unusual language at times.

But my words also bore the fruits I had desired, as I discovered later:

What the rabbit dream really meant was that whenever I found myself involved in a happy situation I immediately removed myself (self being the important word) and put myself over on the outskirts of life to only observe . . . not participate. His fault here was in not telling me why I might do this! If indeed the splitting of the "self" is an imposition of my own, then the reason must be found. Nobody leaves the party when he is having fun. So it follows that no one would leave life unless there was a damned good reason for doing so.

When I discovered this entry, written after our session, it was particularly interesting to me for two reasons. First, Lia had unconsciously paraphrased my meanings almost down to the last comma. Secondly, I felt it okay to go ahead and laugh because, by golly, I guess I might have been in her head after all!

Reading these and other of the journal entries later, I see clearly why I was so confused at this point in the therapy. Lia's "people" were running along just like her journal, only I didn't recognize the altered personalities as such. I found that each time I adjusted to her as a prissy prim enigma, I was faced with another alteration that used language reminiscent of navy shore leave after a long cruise. If this wasn't bad enough, the "person" who seemed hit the hardest of all was the one who sat in the chair and was frighteningly childlike and innocent. I was rattled by my own questions and growing more exhausted weekly, knowing that the only one who could explain this was the very sick figure who grew thinner and thinner each time I saw her.

I did not like the way things were going. At the onset of the session I was not really sure what the dream meant, but even if I did understand, it had to come from her. On and on she went, telling me how wonderful it was to have me in her brain, and giving me a lovely rationalization. I was trying to make a decision without realizing why I felt such discomfort. Then I knew what I must do, and felt an unreasoned urgency, a need to hurry. I can't say why I felt this, but I damned well did! I could not let this go on and on; I knew the dream was more involved, which bothered me, but I disliked something else even more—by latching on to me as her savior, she expected me to take up residence in her brain! As crowded as it was with personalities, she did not need mine! I had to make her see that I could not be with her in everyday life. She had to control her rage and her life, accept the responsibility for her own actions, good or bad. Everything else was an escape; I could not become another escape. But how was I to do it?

I made the decision with a prayer that it was the right one and interrupted her.

"Bull! That's bull and you know it, Lia!" Taken aback by my aggressiveness, suddenly she became very quiet and submissive.

"I feel . . . I have been living in an amphitheater . . . all jeering me. Jeering . . . not cheering me . . ."

"Lia, we can't ignore certain things any longer. You have got to face them! I am not in your head and I never have been. Understand that, Lia, once and for all. *I am not in your head, brain, or body.*"

This patient had long ago learned to grasp for straws in the wind. Dear God, I hoped I had not gone too far in pulling away the straws. As Lia recorded in her journal:

Dr. Ward made quite sure he removed my crutches, my supports. When I related how well I had pushed off my rage, the violence, by just listening to his voice tell me that it would "not matter," he derided me and said, "I'm not in your brain, and I never have been!" . . . But, God,

The Healing of Lia

I needed to feel that he was with me always, helping me when the pain was too great. He kept on and on . . . removing himself quite literally, until I knew that, of course, he was right . . . but it left such a void . . . a dark empty hole . . . and before, where I felt I had only to listen and hear his helping voice, there was only a terrible empty silence in my brain. I felt he had hammered off the cast and removed the crutches too soon . . . before the healing had begun.

I did not know of these thoughts at the time of therapy. If I had, I probably would have a lot more gray hair today. She had learned to separate herself and to deny that a problem existed. If I'd just known how she had felt at that time! When I retorted to her, I had cut off communication to a degree. I find it now very simple to understand the splitting, but on that day in August, it was not so easy to understand. In many cases it is found that the splitting will occur when there is the incapacity to handle situations, but why could she not handle her life? What was it that had created this inability?

I *had* to know more about her life, not just what had happened in the past, but what was going on *now*. What was it that was applying so much pressure that she had to bring about some form of denial?

The session was turning into a rather traumatic episode for Lia. I knew that she was not handling the fact that I was refusing to take up permanent residence in her brain. Now I was about to push her to deal with a very difficult part of her life: her life with Paul, and how to resolve some of the marriage problems. In the treatment chair, she looked so small and pale. Helpless. That is the way she had been most of her life, so this was not a new phenomenon. However, I knew that she was not helpless. She had withstood more during the past year than most people withstand in a lifetime. She had to recognize her own strength! She had to square off and take the offensive.

During the next half hour I tried to pursue several different tacks, mostly with no productive outcome. I almost pleaded with her to stop running and to discontinue her usual method of approach to life's perplexities. What became apparent was that she could not deal with the idea of her involvement, much less with the problems. She continued to tell me just how impossible her life with Paul was ("He has to change"), saying that she could not continue this existence with him. She felt if he would make major changes that she would get well.

Again I had to disarm her. I had to lead her to see that these were the games she had played for years, the self-deceiving games she had played with herself. She felt if she could just get Paul to make changes, then maybe, just maybe, she could avoid the painful process of making changes within herself.

I had seen Paul and had mixed emotions about his attitudes and beliefs. He had shown very little understanding of the problems that confronted Lia. She had gone through twelve years of psychotherapy. The two of them had gone to marriage counselors, they had participated in encounter groups, and each time he seemed unable to identify with what was being stressed or investigated. So why in hell's name did she think that now he was going to be suddenly hit by the immaculate light and become her salvation? Repeatedly we went around and around in a never-ending maze. All the walls seemed to have no doors.

At what seemed like prescribed intervals, Lia would suddenly begin to defend Paul, to accuse me of being unfair to him. And this defense would come right on the back of a tirade about his emotional cruelty. She would angrily say that I simply did not understand him. One moment she was the prosecuting attorney, and in the next she would be his staunchest defender. Was this just one of those situations in which, "It's okay if I knock him, but don't you do it or even agree with what I am saying"? I put a large question mark each time it happened. And the chart was soon a mass of question marks. I now made a move that came close to ending Lia's therapy. I told her bluntly that she could keep right on screaming for Paul to change until hell froze over, but she was going to have to face facts. The facts were that she could *not* bring about change in Paul, that she had no controls over or in Paul. Any alteration in his behavior would have to come from *his* desire and willingness to change. She could only change her own behavior and thereby indirectly affect his usual responses to her.

With finality I said, "Lia, very frankly I am tired of hearing what must happen to someone else in *your* therapy. I am not about to try to treat Paul in absentia! I am having enough trouble

The Healing of Lia

treating you! Don't tell me any more about what Paul must do. *Tell him!*"

There was silence, and I was very glad that she did not respond right away. I was thoroughly exhausted and aware that my exhaustion was due more to frustration than to the events that had occurred. When she spoke, it was in a resistant way and we were again off on our flip-flop, up-and-down dialogue.

"You just do not understand! I *have* told Paul! I have begged him! I have been down on my knees before him. I seem always to be feeding, diapering, walking, washing, soothing babies or tending to him . . . tending to him . . . but he has had his problems, too! He didn't count on all these problems! He never knew . . . I don't know how much is left inside Paul."

Feeling as if I would need therapy myself if things continued, I hammered a point to her. "Lia, first you sit there like a woman sounding as though she is on her last leg, then almost in the same breath you make excuses for Paul and surround yourself with another layer of guilt! Now—*which way is it going to be?*"

Anger came forth in very acid words. "I told you that you don't understand."

I think I understand more than you are really comfortable to admit! It's about time for you to give up some of your defense mechanisms, to really *face* the facts of your life and your therapy."

"But, I don't *know* which way I am going. I don't want to destroy what closeness we have . . . I'm afraid he will finally grow tired of me . . . and the problems."

Again my verbose little lady of the hour was off and running. I mean that literally. She was emotionally running with words. She wouldn't give and I wouldn't give, so, using the only defense she had, she regressed in the direction that I felt she probably would.

"*Paul has to change!* He has to! Don't you understand?"

I opened with both barrels. "Lia, you can accept Paul as he is and stop whining or you can leave him. These seem to be the only two alternatives open to you. We're at the same point at which we started hours ago. Any suggestions I have offered as a means of resolution are immediately negated by you. Any attempt to get you to seek alternatives for yourself is met with hopelessness on your part. Now, believe this, *statistics* say that Paul is *not going to change*, so the next move is up to you. Either accept him as he *is* by altering yourself or get out of his influence and life. These are your two choices."

Again there was silence. I really could not believe what I heard when she did start to speak again: we were again back at point one! I knew that we had reached a stalemate. Feeling that she had not *processed any material* at all, I got her back to a deeper state of relaxation and gave her suggestions that she would be more willing to drop her defenses and get on with her life. I felt that she had the ability to take definitive actions to solve her problems, and that she was now ready to do just that. My aggression did not come easily. Usually it is left up to the patient to decide when they are ready to move on to another phase, but I saw that this patient was deteriorating rapidly. She had tried over twelve years to make the decision to bring positive change into her life, and she was only getting worse. With these suggestions I ended the session.

The Healing of Lia

18

Lia sent a note to me before her next visit. It seemed that her life was one continuous upheaval after another, with little or no time for her to heal from one episode before she found herself facing another. Somehow she accepted this as her daily life, but I was busy enough trying to get her straightened out on her past forty-four years. The note read as follows:

> Dr. Ward:
> We have a terrible and heartbreaking situation at home. My oldest child ran away from home two days ago. She left a note of love and anguish, and took nothing with her. As she is over eighteen and left of her free will, the law cannot even help us find out in which direction she is headed. We feel she is headed for Canada. Her note indicated she is in distress (not "trouble").
> For this reason I may have difficulty in relaxing today in therapy.
> Lia

I had, on this particular day, wanted to work through a dream with Lia, but that would have to wait. The event at home would have to be dealt with before we could move on in therapy. Though understandably upset, Lia was able to drop into a good hypnotic trance, perhaps because of the complete exhaustion from the past few days, the type that just leaves one totally spent.

Beginning the session I found that again, there seemed little understanding or productive communication in the Farrelli household.

"All Paul keeps reminding me of is that Katie is over eighteen, and therefore has the 'right' to leave! How in God's name can he just glibly stand there and talk so damned pragmatically! I know how old Katie is! I gave birth to her! But knowing she's twenty only makes it worse. She's a woman, and she's out there alone on some street or road in this crazy world!"

What I was hearing was a mother in panic, and a husband who perhaps was no better off. There's more than one way to handle panic, and again Paul's way seemed to be one of resignation—or suppression. The biggest problem in Lia's mind obviously was Katie's safety, not her legal rights. Not enough days, months, millennia, had passed for her to heal and to forget what had happened to her—and right in her own neighborhood. Now here was her child, somewhere in this vast country, with very little money and even less in the way of clothing and necessities. What money Katie had, which Lia figured to be less than $200, would not last long on the road, not and have much left for food and subsistence. Therefore, in Lia's mind she feared that Katie might be hitchhiking and open to the wills and dangers of others.

Katie had always been the strong-minded, independent child of the family, though in their own way, each of her daughters has proven to be a self-thinker. And though obviously Lia would not want it to be otherwise, a little conformity probably would have been quite welcome in the home. After Katie's leaving, Lia could think back to so many things that had happened, but which at the time had made little impression.

"Lia, just let your mind drift back, back, back. Back to a recent event in your relationship with Katie. It will be a time of importance in light of what your present mind now knows."

Almost instantly she replied, "She became such a good housekeeper [laughing]. Weeks ago she began cleaning her room. All the things she has pack-ratted and collected, all her treasures, just hauled out in big bags and dumped in the cans! And then, about two weeks ago it was all done. Her room was suddenly not just neat, it was bare. As if nobody lived in it. I see that now . . . but I didn't then. I just saw it as clean, very clean."

"What does this say to you, Lia? What implications does your mind draw from this?"

"That she has cut all her ties to us in every way. But why? We love her! What have we done that Katie would hate us so?"

I interrupted Lia at this point to make her aware that she was making some very potent deductions here. "There is *no* indication that Katie hates you. As a matter of fact in the letter that she left for you, she expressed *love* for you, and wrote of her concern that you may not love her after this! Those are not the actions of a child who hates a parent.

"Katie does have some sort of problem, Lia, and we certainly can't deal with that in her absence, but somewhere, someday, perhaps she will reach a point of realization and work to solve that for herself."

This, I felt, was not a time for client-oriented therapy. If one was to have asked Lia what she felt *she* wanted to do about this situation, most assuredly she would have said to get her child back into the safe confines of the household. Maybe safe from physical harm, but certainly not from emotional harm. How Lia handled this situation was up to her; several courses of action were open, but she did not find the search for alternatives applicable to her at the time.

"I feel so helpless. Dear Lord, so helpless. There's nothing I can do—they all tell me that. The poor policeman probably thought I was acting like some wild lioness. And that's what I felt like. One of my babies is missing. My God, it was like battering my head on the closed door of bureaucracy. Can you imagine, they kept telling me all the 'rights' she has, all those permissive laws of righteous self-rule they present a child of eighteen with!

"And when he came out with the brilliant fact that since Katie was now her 'own woman'—I could have throttled him! Don't they know she is a woman . . . and what can happen to her. *She could be . . . raped . . .* OR KILLED!"

This last was accompanied by a long period of sobs, and I elected to just let her cry it out. Most of these tears were for Katie, and for the sorrow that she had lost her child. Many, however, were for herself at the hands of Oilcan Harry, and I felt it important to let her wash this wound.

Often I tell patients that I equate tears in my office with getting well or healing. It seemed that Lia was forever apologizing for crying, and today was no exception. After she had cried until her lacrimal duct ran dry, she seemed embarrassed and began asking my forgiveness. When I told her that she was only speeding herself to recovery, she wanly reminded me, "If tears would cure, Dr. Ward, I'd be the healthiest person on the eastern seaboard." A statement to which I gave a silent "Amen."

Basically, what Lia needed at this point, no one could provide. The police had given all the reasons why they could not participate in an intercession. All legally true, but not logical to this woman in distress. Paul had apparently responded, within his capacity at the time, and then withdrawn. There was no way I could provide her with comfort. All I could do was to allow her to ventilate, to use me for a sounding board, to scream at me without fear of reproach. No concrete support could be offered Lia that her daughter was safe, that she would ever return, or that she was even alive at that very moment! This is one of those times when I felt a double helplessness. It would have been ludicrous for me to say all the nice words of encouragement. I'm not sure what she had expected of me, probably not as much as I expected of myself. But when we had talked, or rambled, and I had attempted to get her to replace fear with faith, I sat there feeling very impotent.

When Lia felt the subject exhausted, that we had delved into enough of the past as to why Katie would have done such a thing, she said, "I think that's about it for today."

A discouraged lady headed back to her domain of despair.

19

Therapy was moving on. Each week I got into my car, drove the interstate toward Richmond and the brown stone complex, nervously wondering what awaited me at Dr. Ward's office. My feelings swung widely: warmth and comfort in the treatment room, being disliked by the man behind the voice, shattered defenseless. I clung to any softness in his voice and reached for any hint of warmth. Often the voice registering in my mind sounded cruel, without any trace of the things for which I longed. "Face it, he is no friend to you," I thought. "Why do you even come here?" But I went. Each week I went and hated it.

I was now functioning in an epiphytic way—completely rootless, baseless, "belonging" nowhere. Hanging on to whatever was handed me (a kindly spoken word could give me comfort for days), I absorbed verbal nuances and lived for them and on them. I needed "something" but was unaware of what that something was. At home I devoured self-help books and prayed repetitiously without knowing to whom. I now looked to Dr. Ward for the hand, the touch, the words to heal me. When they were withheld or spoken brutally (or so I felt)I absorbed that, too, and hated him for it.

Reach! (Why? To be hurt again?) *Reach again!* (Why should I?) And therapy became as my marriage, a deadly duel with still another man in control and with my life as the booty. As I looked to Paul for food, a home, love, and understanding, I looked to Dr. Ward for the map on which he might chart my course back to sanity. Each week became a grisly treasure hunt, with him ferreting for clues, with me grabbing for answers. In absolute frustration I saw only a piece of blank paper handed in return.

Who needs it? Who needs him? (You do, you do!) And not knowing that I *was* learning, *was* touching bases, I began listening to still another self, saying in seductive words, *run, run, run!*

One day as I reached the brown building and parked in the lot overlooking the lovely pond and gardens, I sat thinking of the past weeks, the pain of the words I had listened to in therapy like live electric wires: *"Tell Paul! Don't tell me! Crap! Ridiculous! Quit whining! Either get a divorce and move out or quit your whining! Bullshit, people don't just do things to you—you allow them to!"*

As the sun danced on little water rills, I sat counting the ways and reasons I hated the man on the fourth floor. Over and over he said, "Feel yourself breathing, your body living. You *are* living, you're *not* dead!"

Words. Each week becoming more painful, more cutting. *"Don't use me for a crutch! I am not in your head and I never have been!"*—this, when flung at me had very nearly destroyed me.

Sitting in my car I was aware of the throb of my right arm, blackened with bruises and stiffening so that even shifting the gears had been difficult. My hair was combed forward in a sweep of bangs to hide as much of my face as possible. I hoped this session would be an indirect one and that Dr. Ward would be unaware, not only of the bruising, but that it was barely possible the lump on my head might be worse than just a lump.

For some reason, today I welcomed pain. The night before I had sat on the edge of Paul's bed after a violent physical confrontation and asked tearfully if he could help me understand why I was not healing, why I was failing in my therapy. Paul's answer did not suit me then but it suited me now. Reiterating what I had been taught for a lifetime, he said, "Lia, all suffering is redemptive. It is given to us to expiate our sins." Our sins. But exactly which sins had I committed that called for such expiation? Paul was not the first to say these words to me, and he would not be the last.

I was not pleased with myself in therapy and was even less pleased with Dr. Ward, seeing myself becoming what I was not: more violent (I, who let out flies rather than kill them), riddled with hatred (I, always so ready to love), increasingly destructive

The Healing of Lia

(I, who longed to create), trusting no one after a lifetime of trusting everyone. (Perhaps this last was not so strange after all.) There had to be a turning-around sometime, someplace, but I needed a map, a plan, a hand. Knowing that the only person who could give these to me sat waiting on the fourth floor, I opened the door of the car, got out, and set my feet in the direction of the brown building and another session with Dr. Ward.

The weekly visits were becoming to me like entering the nether world must be for the damned: there simply was no other place for me to go. There was always kindness in everyone's manner when I went into the office, kindness that I never seemed to receive on the outside. Yet there is no way of ever feeling "at home" in a place of psychiatric treatment. Perhaps because no one, no matter how sick, really *wants* to be there. I had other reasons for not wanting to be there—I was beginning to *know* for a certainty what waited for me in the dim little therapy rooms.

". . . and I can't seem to eat. I've been throwing up every time I try to eat."

"So now you're going to starve yourself to death! If you can't do it any other way, you'll starve yourself?" And while I sat numbly in the reclining chair, my mind half in shadow, half in light, the derisive voice came and there seemed no way to shut it out. He scythed through whatever answers I tried to give in defense of myself with words as sharp as a honed blade. If my answers were not what he needed or wanted or if he detected a holding back, he used words like a cruel ankus, prodding, goading, piercing my deepest innermost self. In this game we played for my sanity there seemed to be no one on my side, no rules but his. And more often than not I felt he played unfairly, holding his cards tightly to himself, while mine were laid on the table for the world to see. Not fair, not fair! my mind cried as he took no notice whatever and plied me with yet another question.

Each week I was taken to the treatment room, settled comfortably in the recliner, and covered with a sheet (which made me feel safer, less in danger). After a greeting, which at times I found very formal, the induction was started. As the voice came, my determination to fight (I'll show him. He has made a fool of me for the last time!) ebbed, and my sharp, angry edges blurred, became hazy, faded away . . . awaay . . .aawaayy . . .

"Now, Lia, tell me about the bruises. Why did you hurt yourself?" So he had seen, he knew after all.

There seems nothing of which I am afraid now. Not of God, of His wrath, of pain, of dying. Only of being alone. How they try to frighten me! ("It's a sin against God to hurt yourself, Lia") and the penalty what? Damnation? I laugh to myself! To threaten me with such! I, who have traveled the length of hell ten times, a thousand times! But when the veil comes so softly and covers me, and I cry out for Someone, there is No One there. Perhaps I have just not hated properly. What I must hate is only the disease, the black, disgusting illness. Kill it, hate it, and kill it! I hate well, deeply and endlessly. But will Dr. Ward guide me, show me how?

Why did it have to hurt so if he really was helping me? Having no understanding of the whys of what he did to me each week, I felt him without feelings, without compassion, without mercy. Each time I left his office, my inner corridors papered with my own torn emotions, there were no words to tell how I despised him. The curious inequity of these weeks was that at this very time Dr. Ward's main concern was one that never occurred to me: my complete dependence on him. If anything, I would have said I had no dependence at all! Dependence on Dr. Ward! My voices were wheedling, Who needs him? Who needs him! all the while little parts of me were being left on his doorstep in tribute.

On and on the voice in therapy droned "Lia, picture yourself standing before a mirror. There are labels pasted all over your body. Bad labels saying bad things. Stupid. Sick. Undesirable. Ugly. All the terrible things you don't want to be. Now, begin peeling off those labels, one by one, and replacing them with good labels. Labels with attributes you have but don't know you have. Good. Healthy. Sexy. Beautiful. Everything good you want to be. . . ."

At the end of the session I was directed to have a dream that night, after which I would awaken, record it on paper (I slept always with a pad and pen at my bedside), and bring it with me the following week.

Following each session I would be taken into the small ap-

The Healing of Lia

pointments office to reserve my time for the next week in the large book on the desk. On my initial visit I noticed that unlike the book in Dr. Ling's office, or for that matter in any of my other doctors' offices, it had no last names recorded. All of us in the book were identified simply as "Robert," "Arliss," "Lia." Anyone entering Dr. Ward's office, for whatever reason, if he glanced at the book would never know that Robert was actually Robert Doe who was running for local alderman, that Arliss was the alcoholic wife of a prominent physician, and that Lia was Lia Farrelli who went around not knowing *who* she was. I was impressed by this protection, particularly since once, while waiting in Dr. Ling's office, I had glanced in the book to see the open dates available and recognized the name of an old friend. It dawned on me that anyone, anyone at all, could conceivably enter and examine such a record if they were unethical enough to do so.

Perhaps the hardest part of any therapy is going home after the session is over. If it went well and you would like to share it, you soon discover that no one can fully understand what you are saying; if it went badly, there are few who care to share that either. By now my family simply went on with their own lives on my therapy days. I would find them when I got home, sitting, laughing, enjoying themselves. After particularly bad sessions, when I felt as if I had been caught by the heels and dashed against a wall, I would go upstairs, knowing guiltily that I dampened and depressed everyone I touched.

There seemed nothing to assuage the influx of emotions. On one side, I had to live in the world of the normal, cope with it, with a marriage in deep trouble, with nearly grown children whom I could not understand, with negative influences a part of my daily diet. Like a goose that was being force-fed to produce foie gras, it was rather inevitable that I became distended, diseased. (But, whoever asks the goose how it feels?) On the other side, I had to absorb ideas in therapy, digest them, make choices, and enforce them—and to do all of this I was using a mind that blinked on and off like an incandescent bulb that is not screwed into place tightly enough. In mad random I blinked *on!* (Relax, you're all right!) *Off!* (How can I be when I don't even know who I am?) *On/off, on/off!*

It had been a bad session, and families being as they are, everyone carried his problems to the table that night. Dinnertime was becoming a ritual not unlike walking on hot coals, or running the mile with blistered feet. And it seemed that the longer I was in therapy, the worse it became at home. That night insults were served along with the chicken, barbed words barely disguised. The girls were in rare form and Paul, as usual, bolted his food and retreated with his coffee, leaving me with a half-eaten dinner and the relentless reminders that tuition was going up, somebody's organic chemistry book was costing $35, and nobody at all had a decent stitch to wear. I didn't blame Paul for running.

Feeling whatever benefits I gained in therapy slipping away, I left the house and walked out into the night alone. I am afraid of the dark and never walk alone, but I did this night, until streets became roads, and still I walked on. Far, far away from home and them. My family, my enemies. Right now they were my enemies, not because they meant to be or wanted to be; they simply were. Home was not a place of retreat, a place of warm company; it was a place to run from. They don't mean it, I told myself, they do love me! But I didn't believe it, and a part of me was outraged that I should lie about it so. This was no Yellow Brick Road that I walked, and there was no Oz in my future that I could see. "God, can't You help us? Don't You care?" I cried. And hearing nothing but silence, and since there was no other place to go, I turned for home.

Night. Sleep. A dream. Who is that screaming? I wrote in the journal:

I am standing on a sort of platform while all of them dance around me—Paul, Dr. Ward, Dr. Ling, everyone—and they begin to peel the labels off. But they are not peeling labels off at all! They are stripping me of my skin, pulling off long strips of my flesh and dancing about! And a trapdoor in my head opens and slowly poison is poured into the void. I'm no longer safe, there is danger in trusting anyone.

The dream was at night, and then another day came, another time, and morning was a thing to be met and conquered. Snowed under by the avalanches of daily happenings, each week in therapy found me clamoring for an opening to breathe. Paul's

The Healing of Lia

damage became more evident, showing perhaps in ways less obvious than mine, but showing. We could no longer talk. By his refusal to discuss any topics he considered painful or problematical (which included almost everything), our conversations were limited to the dull, the inane. The weather, when to paint the fence, did the dog need shots?—all safe. But his growing frustration with his job, the girls' changing moral standards, our pressing need for large sums for their education—all forbidden. *"No! Lia, I am not having any discussion about that now!"* he'd shout and walk away. And "now" being always, the problems stayed and multiplied in the septic sludge we lived in rather than face the unpleasant task of cleaning it out of our lives.

Looking exhausted and beaten, Paul came home from work one day and told me he had rented a cabin in the high country away from phones, business, family, worries, and that we were going to take a week to rest. Leaving instructions with the girls not to contact us except in a case of extreme emergency, we climbed into the old Jeep and headed toward the foothills and into the purple misted Blue Ridge. Leaving the interstate, we began to breathe easier, and on the twisting back roads we held hands, heading higher, higher.

Some hours later, as we waited for dinner to cook on an old woodburner, we sat bundled, warming ourselves with cognac and feeling our cares slipping away. As if the past years had never happened, we were finding in this place of quiet seclusion a togetherness we both had feared was lost. It was not. It might have been battered and bent, but it was not lost. And then we heard a sound, footsteps, and saw, to our surprise, an elderly woman in coveralls huffing the steep path to the cabin.

"Mr. Farrelli?" puff, puff. "Got a call down to the store," puff, puff. "Seems your mother's taken down and you are to call home soon's possible."

Paul blanched, and all the lines that the past few hours had erased were suddenly back in his face. We had had six hours exactly. The three of us got into the Jeep and drove back down the mountain.

Twenty minutes later, Paul and I were listening to Lori telling a confused story about getting a call from Aunt Mara saying that Gran had been taken to the hospital with what might be a stroke, but might not. Or might be a heart attack, or might not—but not to worry, that Gran was going to be all right. The confusion came because although Mara had promised to call and let the girls know the details to tell Paul, she had not. Doing what she could, Lori had called the hospital, got a favorable report, and called us.

"I didn't know what else to do, Mom. They say Gran's okay but that she needs rest. Don't worry, I'll call if we hear anything at all."

Gran might have been okay, but Paul wasn't. Despite Lori's promise, he became increasingly restive. Back at the cabin we ate a silent dinner, and I knew that my own reactions were the reverse of what I should have liked them to be.

I was angry beyond words that Mara had not had the common sense to wait a few hours, at least until she had something more concrete to tell. As it was, Paul was frantic, not knowing if his mother had suffered a stroke, a heart attack, or a simple case of vertigo. Wondering why she had not advised the girls in some way, I spoke with bare restraint in my voice.

"Paul, wait until light. We'll call first thing and find out the details. It may be good news! I know it's hard, but please don't do this to yourself, not until we know more."

I might have been speaking to a deaf, blind man. That night we spent lying awake, Paul agonizing, seeing his mother dead or paralyzed, feeling so far away from her. I agonized, too, but in a different way and for different reasons.

Without mercy I railed at myself. Dipping into whatever reservoir I had, I prayed for some feeling of pity for this woman who was mother to my husband. And the reservoir was empty of any feeling at all. Lying beside Paul in the darkness, listening to the night sounds on the mountain, I despised my own inability to forgive, to love her. I closed my eyes and saw clearly the lovely picture of Paul and me of only a few hours past, and it had again become a blasphemous triptych, with the three of us imprisoned forever. An icon of three where there should have been two. Shamed to feel such, I turned and held tightly to Paul's shoulder, which had grown cold from the mountain night air.

Morning found us heading not for a phone, but driving back to the city. It was a bad drive for both of us, Paul looking a

The Healing of Lia

hundred years older than he had the day before. What is the matter with me, I screamed silently at myself. Where is my humanity, my human decency? Am I so selfish that I can't let the past slide away? And reaching for some didactic philosophy, I realized that no judgment of me could have been harsher than mine of myself. But while one part of me felt this, some other part knew there was some justification for my anger. A subtle nuance over the phone told me the situation was in danger of being inflated into the sort of mini-hysteria that prevailed whenever anything at all happened to Paul's mother. *Now* is the time to change! I told myself. If I did as Dr. Ward directed, if I changed, perhaps it might cause an alteration in Paul's own attitude. Every drop of blood pounding in my head echoed the word I listened to weekly in therapy: *change! change!* But how? What would a "normal" person do at a time like this? What exactly was normal? I rolled the word around in my mind and had no understanding of what it meant. Normal? Change? They were words in a strange patois, some language of which I had no conception either consciously or subconsciously. It was like wanting desperately to set sail for Ireland and finding myself in a small, oarless boat with no map, no sextant, no chart of the currents. It was ninety-nine percent certain that without these I should miss the mark if I set off alone.

Trying to put my thoughts into rational sentences, I asked, "Paul, if your mother is in real danger, why wouldn't Mara have called the girls as she promised? She is bound to know that you'll worry, that we'll come back to the city. How could she do this?"

"Lia, please! Don't start! Whatever it is, I should be at home!"

"Whatever it is? If it's serious, yes, you should! But what if it's not? Do you realize that if we had been away in Bermuda or Hawaii—or *Europe!*—it would have been the same thing! A half-told, incomplete story and we're running back! Why not have made just one more phone call?"

"*I feel guilty not going back! I have to go!* They'll all think I cared more about my vacation than my mother!"

On and on the argument went, with Paul feeling that I was merely so jealous that I would keep him from his mother's deathbed. Horrible words were put into horrible sentences and hurled at each other with neither of us capable of saying what we were really feeling. Asking myself what exactly it was that bothered me, I found the answer rising from a dark corner saying, "Only that our time away together had meant something precious to him, too. If only he would say it. . . ."

We rode quietly until Paul brought up a subject I had dodged and sidestepped for years. When he said we would have to buy a family burial plot in case he needed a space to bury his mother, in a mad sanguineous fury I screamed that I would rather be thrown into the sea and eaten by sharks than be buried with his mother beside us. "Between us" is what I meant. With bestial pettiness and weapons forged in furnaces fired with pent-up anger, we waged a senseless war, until, victorious, we reached the city limits carrying each other's head on a pike. With careful deliberation, Paul drove straight for the hospital.

Not speaking, we rode the elevator, got off, and turned toward the room. I followed along beside Paul, knowing he did not really realize my presence as he moved like a compass needle, surely, unflaggingly, in the direction of his mother. All my senses warned me to stay silent, keep my counsel, and when we got to the door, I stepped aside to let Paul enter first. His mother was sitting in a large, comfortable chair beside her bed. Seeing Paul, she reached up and put her arms about his neck as he bent to kiss her. I stood for a minute or two just a step behind him, hoping for a sign, any sign, that I might reach out to her, too! But as his mother made no move to acknowledge me, I moved away to sit in a straight-backed chair along the wall. Paul knelt by her, and as I sat, feeling isolated and superfluous, I saw that she had good color and she was speaking slowly, distinctly, moving—her visible faculties seemed intact. Knowing I had no real place in the scene, I went to wait in the atrium until Paul was ready.

After the visit, Paul tried to calm himself, and realizing that our belongings were still at the cabin, we returned and tried to pick up the ends of our week together. It was just no good. Each day he worried what news he might be told when he called; each night he worried what the next day might bring. The day his mother was being electronically monitored, I could see his suffering and finally told him it would be quite all right if he wanted to go home.

More disappointed in myself than in him, because I felt that if I were more successful in therapy I should not have these feelings of inadequacy, I tried to be more supportive, more understanding. For days I would control my anger at being shut out, at feeling that he drew from what should have been reserved for me to give to his mother. Our life, through this time, was like living on opposite sides of an enormous tapestry: Paul on the finished side, seeing things in clear, vivid patterns, woven as he felt they should be; I on the underside, seeing things with the ragged, clipped edges and the patterns hazed, running in confusing, unbeautiful ways. He would tolerate no discussion, injecting always that his mother might die at any time, As usual, I finally broke completely.

"Yes, she might die! She is old and perhaps it is her time to die. But you're becoming a grave sitter, Paul. So caught up tending the dying you don't see the living! She's not dead yet, but something *is* dying before your eyes, and you're too blind to see it!"

And I removed myself from the arena, finding it easier than I thought to be silent. I shut myself off emotionally, and though we shared physical touching, there was no cerebral touching, none at all.

I was moving more and more into the life of an alien in the outside world. What did I need? Pity? Sympathy? Someone who would listen with love and concern? What I might have felt that I needed, and what Dr. Ward felt I needed, moved onerously on a collision course toward a denouement for which neither of us would be prepared.

One day, while cleaning out the drawers in my hall secretary, I came across batches of loose-leaf papers, bound notebooks, and odd scraps of torn papers. Sorting through with the intent to toss and burn—was someone playing jokes on me? Using my hand—but surely not—to write things about me? I found myself sitting on the floor reading and, when I began to digest the content, I felt at first numb fear, then a pragmatic erection of denial fortifications, defensive redoubts, fortresses against anyone ever seeing what I had put back into the drawer and shut away from conscious thought.

The pain is bad, so bad. I have called and made an appointment with Dr. Ling. More drugs? Shock treatments? Even that is preferable. I want to have the fight—the *need* to fight—taken from me. He can do that, and I will be quiet, forgetting all that has gone before. I have needed so much to be held, loved. It is my fault, I know this. I lack something. Perhaps I am unlovable."

Did I write this?

What I could not know, not in any of my "minds," was a simple fact: that even if it was given to me, I had lost the ability to feel any love directed to me. That the world could have knelt at my feet and I still would not have been able to believe, to trust, that I was indeed loved.

Paul came home that afternoon and found me sitting frozen on the floor where I must have been for hours. He wrapped me in his arms, telling me again and again that he loved me but could bear the way I was no longer. He looked as ill and old as I did. We were both so hurt; hurting each other had become a way of life with us because of this terrible, unfound sickness in my mind. He told me that he would go with me to see Dr. Ling, that there seemed to be no other answer.

During the week that I waited for my appointment with Dr. Ling, I tried to work at my job and live a normal life. I was losing time again, having periods of severe blackouts, but I did not tell this to Paul nor did I mention what I had found in the hall secretary. Paul was clearly more relaxed, pleased perhaps that I had made the decision alone to break my therapy with Dr. Ward. The changes that had come about in my attitude since I had been in hypnotherapy had frightened and dismayed him. The week was one of extreme anxiety for me, and judging from journal entries made at this time (which were found even later), I slept badly, having frequent and horrifying nightmares.

Dear God, I need someone to help me seal up whatever crack is in the woman who is "me." I get cold with fear at the thought of Dr. Ward ever reading the papers I found. I see myself screaming, chained in the dark place reserved for people who have lost themselves. I often think

The Healing of Lia

he must laugh at this ordinary middle-aged woman who slogs into his office each week. And I think I will never go back anymore.

Never! I would never go back. And from my desk at work one day I summoned the nerve to call Richmond and break the appointment still listed on the book in Dr. Ward's office. Why did I even do this? I could have simply not showed up for the appointment. Perhaps because I felt I owed him at least the courtesy of the words to be spoken: "Lia will not be in this week" (Or ever again. But no one would have known this until it was too late.) I knew very well the great effort Dr. Ward was putting forth to help me, but at this time I truly did not understand what I was expected to do. The failure was mine—but what did the word "change" mean? I wondered. I feared the word "divorce," which he had brought into my life. *"You have choices, Lia. Quit whining and make them."* Clearly iterated were two of these choices: Accept—or get out.

But he was wrong, as I wrote in the Journal.

Dr. Ward is quite mistaken. We all have another choice, but whether I take it remains a question. I feel such shame because I know that I am failing. The Church teaches that our suffering here is but a flicker compared to eternity—but never believe it—torment is torment, and hell is hell. And aloneness is aloneness. I don't sleep in anyone's arms anymore. Why fear the word "divorce"? I have always been alone. Is this the sense Dr. Ward wants me to understand—that I should not fear aloneness because I exist in it?

So the voice that sang *"run!"* had won, and my mind felt at once peaceful, quiet, strangely happy. At work I walked on air. The day I would have kept the broken appointment I remember feeling so wonderful, with no knot of pain in my stomach at all. There was one small moment at the hour I would have gone into the chair—a moment when I felt as one must when one is swimming and realizes that the shore is too far away. One moment to wonder, "Can I make it?", but then even that doubt was gone. I had awakened happy, had showered and stood looking at myself in the mirror. (Could that be me with my ribs showing, those tiny little breasts? Where is the fat lady who spilled over her bras only a few years ago?) Almost giddy, I dressed. (Cloak yourself,

Lia! No more Dr. Ward! No more fearing Thursdays on Monday and feeling ill until the next time! *No more!*)

Feeling crafty and superior that I had escaped such a fiend, I drove to work singing gaily, "Ho, ho! Up yours, Dr. Ward!" as other drivers looked at me and away again. In some mad, manic desperation that I mistook for happiness, I began the day in the perfect belief that all my troubles were over.

Until recently, Dr. Ward's thoughts of this broken appointment were a subject we never discussed. There are certain things that we do not speak of concerning my therapy, certain secrets he must keep that I would not presume on. He has good reasons for this, and for the other things still in the yellow folder with my name on it that he never talks about. These are the things that I am better off not knowing, and in this I accept his decision as infallible. When we did finally discuss it, an interesting incongruity occurred to me: that what may be a monumental incident in the life of one may be an incident of insignificance to another; that each of us is, indeed, at times very much a solitary island.

Seen from my point, the decision to run was brought about because the pain, physical, mental, and emotional, was unbearable, so unbearable that I was willing (one might say desirous) of relinquishing my mind to the machine. I knew that given half a chance, Dr. Ling, or someone else, could obliterate Lia from all conscious being. And it seemed a fitting way for her to depart.

If from some obscure recess a voice cried, "But I have gifts to give! Don't do this, not yet!" I answered, "Shusssh! No one wants your gifts! Go away. It's done."

Two days later Paul and I were shown into Dr. Ling's office.

An hour after we left Dr. Ling's office I realized that nothing at all had come of the visit, save perhaps that Paul was fifty dollars poorer in pocket and I was richer by way of three prescriptions for drugs. As Paul sat beside me in a large leather chair, I recounted everything to the inscrutable man who had known me for twelve years without knowing me at all. I told of the rages, the self-abuse, the periods of amnesia, the effects of the drugs. I told of my therapy efforts with Dr. Ward and my fears of not knowing what my illness really was. After a moment of repose, Dr. Ling said that if I would like he could arrange to hospitalize me immediately, but that for the most part he felt I

The Healing of Lia

was overreacting to a bad case of nerves. We left in thirty minutes with an appointment slip for the next week and three new
prescriptions: one for fifty sleeping pills, one for a hundred tranquilizers, and one for codeine against my abdominal pain. Stuff-
ing the papers into my purse I remember breathing deeply,
knowing for a certainty that if no new doors opened to improve
my life, I had just been handed my exit visas. It had been no
problem at all. I merely stretched out my hand. It seemed not at
all odd to have such things given to me.

At home again, it was not as easy as I had thought to cut
myself away from therapy with Dr. Ward. No matter that I had
faced the fact that he was "not and never had been" in my head,
he was most assuredly in my dreams at night. Sleep was for me
then a different thing than sleep must be for other people. I
seemed to waft in and out of partitions, feeling conscious but
not conscious, awake but not awake, numbed, unable to move,
feeling waves and currents of electric activity about me. I was
trapped on a gruesome canvas by Bosch, and each edge I approached to escape took me deeper into places I didn't want to
go. But all the while, a constant and soothing voice was behind
me. By day, as I went about my work, I heard the voice and tried
to shut it out. For some reason most of what I heard seemed to
be little homilies and stories from the Bible.

". . . remember Hagar the bondswoman. She begat in bondage and existed in bondage. Lia, I want to take you from your
bondage to live in freedom. Freedom from your illness."

Not this way you won't! Angrily, I would shake myself. He
had taken unfair advantage of me! He had put all this nonsense
into my head when I was in a defenseless condition! He droned
on and on as each day passed until I wanted to call him and
scream, "Cut out the poop, Dr. Ward! I wanted help from you—
not salvation!" But even this anger did not cut me off from the
voice. He had reached in and planted his words and told me they
would live forever in my mind. Damn him. Damn his words. If
he wanted to free me from anything, why didn't he just free me
from his own nagging voice?

I had dreams. Dreams of dark and swarthy Egyptians chisling
and hacking away to remove inscriptions from mighty monuments. I seemed to know what they were trying to do—trying to

remove certain names—obliterate them from the land and from the minds of the people. And I would shout up at them, "Fools! You can't take thoughts away from people that way!" And I knew that my mind was like the monuments. It had been incised deeply with words that were to have lasted forever. But each night he was in there—hacking, hammering, chisling away. *"Don't! Don't!,"* I shouted. But he did. Each day and each night he did. Until the time came when I had no strength left to fight. At the price of ten pounds of my body weight he accomplished what he had had to do. On the back of my eyelids I could see myself standing with the litter and rubble of my own life at my feet. And standing in front of me, there he was—a foolish, wicked little grin on his face—holding his mallet and chisel. And I said, "You can put it down now. I'm going to be okay." And when I got to my feet, I knew it was true.

Later, it was an easy thing to dial the number of the office on the fourth floor in the brown stone building in Richmond, and say, "Hi, this is Lia. Do you have anything open for, say, next Tuesday?"

And they did.

The Healing of Lia

20

There is a void for the next calendar week. Lia did not show at the office for her appointment. When I was told by my secretary that she was a "no-show," I think I just sighed and went about my day. I was tired of fighting to get her to work effectively. The last session had gone on for the better part of two hours, and I felt that we were at the same point when we finished as we were when we started.

It was not for several months that I found out what had transpired after the last visit. I knew that I had been somewhat authoritative and rough toward Lia, but I did not realize how close I had been to terminating the entire therapy. In my ignorance I just proceeded with my business in the usual manner. Her therapy had been rapid and very traumatic for her at times. Perhaps she just needed a week to rest. I certainly did. Then, as the days went by I became more and more concerned. Had I pushed too far? Would she return? At the end of two weeks, when I decided to have one of the receptionists call her, she called and made her next appointment. It was a relief to know that I was going to see her at least one more time.

When Lia did come for the next visit I could immediately see that there was something different about her. She looked like hell drawn through a knothole. There had been more weight loss, and at this point I began to wonder just how much more she could lose without collapsing. Her face was drawn and tired, but amazingly she related that she had felt better during the past few days. And how in God's name could you look like that and say you feel better?

She had written a note for me. Her message was that she had

had the enclosed dream and that she had felt much better after having it. This was difficult for her to understand because she had had the same theme in her dreams many times before, but this time it seemed to be so much more significant. There had been other problems during her absence from therapy and at that time I thought these accounted for her not coming the *previous weeks* to the office.

She and Paul had had another round, but there had been so many of these that I did not attach the importance to her statement that I should have. On top of all of this, one of her daughters had picked this time to tell Lia and Paul she was going to be leaving school.

For Lia, who had worked so hard to maintain a budget so that there could be money to send the children to school, this was the last straw. Her entire world seemed to be collapsing around her in a period of two weeks. There had been much concern and worry over the daughter, much consultation with school officials whom Lia had found to be uninterested and offering no help or direction. In looking back on this, I felt it probably was the best thing for her that no one actually could help with her feelings. She found that she could resolve the problem and accept the situation on her own.

The problem with the daughter really was not resolved, it was simply resolved within Lia. The renewed problem with Paul was within Lia also, but she had more difficulty accepting this. During the past two weeks she had had a recurrence of a problem which she had related to me during the original consultation.

"Doctor Ward, I'm having trouble again with my abdomen swelling. During the past week to ten days it's gotten worse. Worse this time I think than any time before . . . and it's hard on Paul, too . . . he's a normal man and has his needs. The doctors say that it's ovarian . . . a tumor, or something. When it swells I am just about incapacitated."

I did not find what Lia was telling me to be at all amusing, yet there was a slight smile within me. Thinking back to her last session, I had given her the suggestion that she would be able to find a way of dealing with her problem with Paul—there are many ways to solve the same problem. Was this Lia's way of handling a situation in a passive-aggressive manner?

The Healing of Lia

Hypnosis was introduced by Lia. It was still a neat experience to see her go into hypnosis. There was no longer the need for lengthy inductions. Within a very few moments she was in a profound state of relaxation. The therapy in hypnosis began.

"Lia, you have just told me that there have been several pains in your life, particularly during the past couple of weeks—pains concerning your daughter, pains with Paul, and a painful dream. We'll let the dream rest for a while and deal with the other pains. I want you to feel these pains. I want you to see the similarities between these pains—pains pertaining to your daughter and the pains with Paul. If you can and will, see the similarity between the two."

"No . . . no similarity! They are two different problems. I have no control . . . there is no control over my daughter any longer. She has to make her own decisions and abide by them. . . ."

"Right, Lia. She has to make her own decisions and abide by them. She is responsible for her own actions, is that right?"

"She is responsible for her own actions. . . . I can try to help her, but . . ."

"Now wait, Lia! If she is responsible for her own actions aren't you responsible for your own actions, also?"

"Don't do this! We spend so much time . . . I cannot control Paul . . . *he* must make his own changes!"

Suddenly I felt I was about to lose the round and it was going to be a repeat of the previous week's work.

"Now don't start that with me today, Lia! I have a great suspicion that you know exactly what I'm talking about! During the past few days, something has been happening within you. Tell me about the pain—and how it has been causing the problem with Paul."

"The tumor . . . swells . . . hard to have intercourse. . . ."

"That is exactly what you told me many weeks ago, when I first met you, lady. Here it is—on my chart—*verbatim*: You said, 'I swell so badly he can't penetrate.' When I asked you the frequency with which you had intercourse, you replied, 'Once or twice a week . . . except in the *bad times* when I swell so badly he can't penetrate me.' Now what did you mean by the bad times? What comes to mind, Lia, when I ask you what are the bad times?"

"There are so many bad times with Paul! After the last time . . . I went to Paul . . . tried to talk with him . . . tell him what had taken place here. He really doesn't want to hear . . . as if he is denying what is taking place. He just walks away . . . won't listen. . . .

"I pleaded for him to make some changes and to help me make others. There is no way for me to protect myself . . . I just had no way to go or to turn . . ."

"I don't accept that!" I was fairly well shouting at her now. "I believe that you did solve it! I believe you let your body be a means of protection for you!"

"I would not do that . . . I simply would not . . . are you suggesting that I made my body swell . . . so that Paul could not have intercourse?"

"Listen to your words! You said, 'so that *Paul* could not.' You didn't say so that *we* could not! As if you were not going to participate."

"That would be . . . wrong. So painful to deny him . . . as if I was denying my own marriage . . . our marriage . . ."

Before she could go further I interrupted.

"You have said that sex is a very natural part of marriage. Now, if within yourself you were trying to make some decisions about your *own* marriage . . . what action could you take?"

"It is ridiculous! I would not deny my marriage in that way. I don't want to cause Paul pain! I am not that type of person. He is so good to me in so many ways. . . ."

It was very necessary for me to get Lia to understand that nothing we were talking about was occurring on a conscious level. I believed that her subconscious mind had developed this defense to reject intercourse (or love, perhaps?). In a certain sense she needed to reject not just intercourse and sex, but Paul himself. She had felt so betrayed by him that it was becoming impossible for her to give herself completely to him.

Sex had had a great deal to do with so many of her problems in life, it would only seem logical to reject the causative agent. Even before she had experienced sex in any form, she had been accused by her mother of being a tramp. Sex had caused preg-

The Healing of Lia

nancies that had almost cost her her life. In order to preserve her life she had had the sterilization for which the church had told her she must do penance for the rest of her life. Is there any wonder she would want to eradicate it from her existence?

As I was talking with Lia about this problem and her relationship to Paul, we referred to the pain. Using this entrée of pain, I told Lia that I wanted her to see her latest dream in her mind as I read it back to her.

"This is an old dream . . . I've had it a hundred times . . . but it's so real this time that I awakened screaming and crying for my mother; I am a little girl, only four or so, and I'm sitting on the floor after a screaming temper tantrum. Mama is standing over me and she is shouting that I am exactly like Aunt Ava . . . crazy . . . crazy, and that I shall end up just like her.

"Aunt Ava has been locked away in Lofton State for over forty years for trying to kill my grandmother with a butcher knife while she slept.

". . . this horrible dream . . . I used to have it often but I have not had it in years. It was so real, so vivid. I was terrified but . . . I felt . . . better. For some strange reason I felt better and I don't know why. . . ."

"Now relax deeper and deeper, Lia. I want you to see a calendar, a big desk calendar." A slow, methodical age regression was done at this time. I had the feeling that Lia was ready to make a major step in her therapy, and I wanted her to get all the affect she possibly could.

"Now, on the count of three you are going to be right there again, seeing, hearing, feeling every emotion because you will be reliving it again . . . right there with Mama."

Shortly Lia's body began to jerk, and she was sobbing. She had the appearance of a child who has cried to the point where he cannot catch his next breath. The breathing is interrupted by hiccups. I asked her to relay what was now happening; at times it was difficult to understand what she was saying. She had the affectations and voice of a very small child.

Between the sobs and hics she kept crying, "Mama, Mama . . . don't Mama . . . don't . . . please don't be mad with me, Mama . . . all I wanted was to hug you, Mama. . . ."

"Now, Lia, you are going to go back just a little further in time. The clock is turning back, slowly, slowly, just a little back. Just at the beginning of your getting upset. Easy now. Take your time." I gave her time to orient herself and then asked her to look around and see where she was; I started to question again, "What is happening, Lia?"

In a childlike voice, Lia started, "Mama is standing there. She is so tall! I go up to her and put my arm around her leg. She tried to pull away, but I hold on good. No, Mama! Don't push me away! I want to hug . . . that's all I want is to hug you, Mama! No, Mama! . . . No . . . No . . ."

Now Lia starts to cry and within seconds she is crying out and banging her fists on the treatment chair arm. This goes on and on with her crying more and more. Gradually she begins to have the jerking respirations and intermixed crying.

"What is Mama doing now, Lia? Where is she?"

"She is standing right here, over me. Screaming. She is saying that Lia is crazy! I'm crazy! That I'm going to be sent away just like Aunt Ava. That I'm crazy just like Aunt Ava."

"Listen to her, Lia. Tell me exactly what she is saying."

Lia is almost hysterical by now. But she continued, "Mama says, 'You are crazy. You are just like your father's side of the family . . . there is nothing to do with you anymore. . . . You are the image of Ava. Crazy just like Ava. You know where she is, don't you? They carried her away and locked her up. That's just what they're going to do with you, 'cause you're just like her. Crazy.' Mama looks so mean, but it's my fault. I made her that way. I make her mad. But all I wanted to do was to hug her.

"I guess I am just . . ."

"You guess you are what, Lia? What is it that you are?"

"I am Ava. I mean I am just like Ava."

"As you are sitting there on the floor and looking up at your mother, just what are you feeling inside, Lia? You can use the grown-up part of you to help you describe what you feel if necessary."

"I feel so . . . alone . . . something . . . wrong with me. I want to show . . . to show Mama that I love her, but she pushes me away."

"When we want to love and someone will not accept that

love, and they push us away—what do we call that certain feeling?"

"We call it . . . rejection?"

"That's the feeling that you have had all right, Lia. Now I want you to feel that feeling of rejection and I want it to get stronger and stronger. I want you to take this feeling of being rejected to another time in your life when you had the same or a similar feeling. Right there on the count of three. One. Two. Three."

Lia sat, relaxed and easy, with a trace of a smile.

"Mama is going to be so happy with this! It does take a long time, but Mama is worth it." This was the way that Lia began. What was taking place in her subconscious mind I have since given the name the Valentine's Day Massacre.

Lia had gone to great lengths to make a very special valentine for her mother. There was lots of construction of paper and lace. And she decided there had to be a very special verse for the inside. She was obviously so proud of her creation.

After Lia was satisfied that the valentine for her mother was just right, she proceeded to give it to Mama and to show her the other valentines she had prepared. As Lia related giving the valentine to her mother, she started to withdraw, became very tense. Her face became set and seemed defiant.

"I did so! I made up those verses *myself*, Mama! All by myself! I *did!* I *did!*"

Seeing her dissolve before my eyes, I interjected, "Lia, what is Mama saying? What is happening?"

"She is . . . saying . . . *liar!* [here Lia is again sobbing, hiccuping] She is saying I *stole* my poems! She says she read them all in the newspaper!"

My memory of this episode is not pleasant. Watching a child (and at that moment Lia was very much back into her childhood) experience such a thing and having to remain apart and objective is a difficult thing. I sat and let her drift back to the scene in her mind. As she sniffled and cried she spoke brokenly, "I did so write them! I didn't . . . steal . . . I wrote . . . themmm. . . ."

The scene did not have to be described to me further. It was a simple case of a big person against a little person, and it ended with Lia, instead of delivering her valentine that year, being sent to bed to cry herself to sleep, wondering what she had ever done to her mother to make her act that way. The consequences of the event were that Lia never made—or gave—valentines again.

"Lia, that is all in the past now, I . . . ."

Before I could continue Lia interrupted me. "It is *not* all in the past! It still goes on! I am rejected and rejected! I remember running . . . panting, and crying through the woods . . . the path to the log lean-to. I'd hide for hours, sometimes all day, until the dark drove me home. I'd pour it all out on paper. . . . Stories . . . and she would ask, 'Good heavens, Lia! Whatever gave you the idea for such a sad, terrible story?' Home did. But I'd never say it to her."

"What else comes to mind, Lia? Weren't there good times?"

"I remember one evening after supper watching Mama sit and read the newspaper. I stood for such a long while . . . wanting to go to her . . . I always wanted to hug her . . . to touch and be touched . . . so badly that my heart almost beat its way out of my chest. Then I did it! I went to her chair, leaned down and kissed her cheek! She didn't move, not even enough to rustle the paper, but she did speak: 'What was that for? What have you done now?'

". . . that night was the first time I *killed her in my mind*. . . . Later, it became a ritual, carefully planned and executed, over and over. It still happens in my dreams; I waken screaming, crying . . . not because I kill her . . . but because she *won't die!* She stands there, laughing at me, and she simply won't die!"

Lia's mother probably had no understanding of what she was doing. I hope she did not understand! It makes it more digestible to my mind to say that, anyway. The power of the spoken word! Lia once said that it is inscribed forever on the subconscious mind, long after the conscious mind has forgotten it. Mama may not have lashed Lia with a leather strap; she lashed at her with words that almost destroyed her life.

"Stay with it Lia, get all of those memories moving! Let them just rise to the surface." She was going now and, I felt, was cleansing the crevices in her mind of years of muck and dirt.

The Healing of Lia

"Reach down deeper—tell me now what the memory is—where are you now?"

"So many years ago . . . I'm with my cousin, Joy . . . and I am sixteen years old . . . we're on the old paddle wheeler, the Mark Twain, going for a cruise. This night is so warm and lovely . . . we're double-dating—such a happy night . . . all set for a beautiful evening. But Joy just won't relax . . . she just stands at the rail so stiffly. My boyfriend Buddy and I stroll the deck with everyone . . . and we hug . . . and kiss. We're having a marvelous evening! Joy watched and watched . . . but I was so happy I never noticed. . . . Afterward at home I slept well. It was a wonderful time! I'm so happy!"

"You're happy. That's good, Lia. Now what happened?" Even I was not prepared for the anger in her voice.

"No! Not happy! Mama was waiting in the kitchen with the fires of hell in her face! Joy went home with a horrible story. She said, 'No wonder Lia has lots of boys to date! She puts out!' "

Deep humiliation was being shown by Lia now. It was painful for her to even repeat the story some thirty years later. I had to prod her to get her to finish it.

As the tears streamed down her face she started again.

"Joy went home and told lies about me! She told Aunt Addie, who phoned Mama. Mama wouldn't listen to me! She called me a disgusting whore! Joy tore away the last love Mama had for me with this lie! From that day until she died Mama always believed that lie! There was no doubt in her mind; Joy had spoken the truth and Lia the lie!"

"I know it hurts, Lia, but I want it to continue to hurt for the time being. I want you to take all that hurt and gather more as you go back in time. I want you to take all that hurt and all the information the deepest part of your subconscious mind has and go right back to the very first time that you felt rejected by your mother."

I had to encourage Lia to make this little trip. She was not sure that she wanted to remember any more of the bad things in her life right then. I assured her that she did not have to do it, but I felt she was ready to continue.

Silence predominated for a long while. I watched Lia, an

adult woman sitting in the treatment chair, as her facial features and expressions slowly became distorted. Her head then extended backward and started to rotate to the side. Her arms were brought up and lay across her chest; the knees were moderately flexed and I knew that Lia had regressed and was once again going through her birth experience.

The regression to the birth experience is not as unusual as may be thought. It happens very often in therapy; however, there are few who go through the head motions. There are very few laymen who even know how the head rotates and the neck extends.

The entire process took some seven or eight minutes. A couple of times when this was going on I tried to intervene and get some verbal feedback from Lia as to what she was feeling or experiencing. All of the questions were ignored or went unanswered.

When she was once again lying in the reclining chair, I asked, "Can you tell me what is happening now?" Again there was no response until I added, "You can use your ability to communicate in order to respond to me."

"I'm cold. It is now so cold. I am beside this other person, this warm, other person . . ."

"Lia, I have to assume that that is your mother. I would like for you to move just to the time when you can first look in your mother's eyes. Look at her eyes. What do you feel?"

"She is not smiling at all . . . just staring at me. I . . . don't know just what is happening. It is so strange to look at her! She is not happy. No, she is not happy. Anybody can see that." With this statement Lia began to cry, but it is a silent cry.

"She does not want me. She does not want me. She is talking to someone . . . and I know that I am not a pretty baby. She is not happy with me."

From this point there was a tremendous amount of discourse between us, and I could not determine how much of what was said fit into what I felt was happening. She continued to cry; she uttered long sentences that were so broken they didn't make sense to me. I could see Lia was pulling back from the woman who was holding her. She had gotten the message, spoken or unspoken, that she was an unwanted child.

The Healing of Lia

With this kind of beginning in life there is little wonder about the appearance of the child in the photograph Lia later showed me, the picture of herself with uncombed hair and unpolished shoes, looking so unhappy.

I calmed her down and assured her that she was going to be all right, that this episode in her life could be put into its proper perspective, and that we were going to do that right now, that she could take all these feelings, recognize them for their worth or lack of worth, and discard them.

"Rejection has been a big part of your life. It is a feeling that you have become conditioned to expect. But this expectation creates a need to find a way of handling it. You have handled it by withdrawing, by not allowing yourself to become involved. At times you have struck back. But you know it is not proper or acceptable to strike those who supposedly love you. So you had to develop a means of tolerating this rejection and loss of love—the feeling that maybe you never were loved at all.

"You have just said that you were an unwanted child. That you felt your mother did not want you and did not love you. You saw her as rejecting your love, and thereby rejecting you.

"Now is a wonderful moment in your life, Lia, a moment when you are about to discover something important for yourself! I feel that you're ready to do this, and I want you to feel that you're ready, also. Remember now the dream—the dream of you sitting on the floor with your mother standing over you. Screaming something at you. Remember now, the special feeling—the feeling that some change had come about in you. When you are ready and feel secure, I would like for you to go again to that time, that feeling. Take your time, relax, you are safe, you are secure, and you are going to be protected in every way."

During the next few moments I was filled with anticipation. I had worked so hard with Lia to bring her to this very moment, and I felt the time was right to proceed. I was not at all sure, however, that Lia was ready to make this step, and though I knew within myself where I hoped we were going, it was up to her to make the move or not. I hoped she would go back into the full emotional impact of that moment, but it is often found that when a patient has experienced the tremendous affect that

Lia had just experienced, the same emotional intensity cannot be recaptured. I did not have to wait very long because shortly, in a very calm, rational manner, Lia began to talk with her mother, not as the little girl Lia, but as an adult might. I admit it was somewhat of a letdown for me. But she had chosen to handle the situation in this way and that was her prerogative.

"Mama, why do you always reject me? Couldn't you have wanted me—even a little? Everybody loves a baby! But not Lia —nobody loved me at all. Mama! *Listen to me! Mama, you had better listen to me.*"

There seemed to be a change coming about at this point as she continued her soliloquy in a monotone. But then the conversation became much more heated, and suddenly she started talking, not in her adult voice, but in the childlike one she had used at the beginning of the session. She was, once again, literally crying, screaming at her mother.

"*All I wanted to do was hug you! All I wanted was for you to hug me!*"

Here I felt it important to intervene—I needed to know what was happening.

"Lia, the feeling—the feeling that something has changed— I want you to feel it again. Go back to the very moment when it happened—*you are there.* With your mother—she is screaming at you, and you at her. *Feel* the change that you know is happening. Touch it! Feel it! *Now!*"

And then I waited a moment until she relaxed deeper, her breathing easing a bit.

"Now. Before, when you were here before, you said something to me, something special, something different from any other time. Remember now, *now!*"

I looked at my notes, the jots of shorthand I had made when Lia had begun the session. One notation had seemed unique— and I must have felt it because I had underlined it. What she had said, and what she now repeated in the small voice of a child, were three small words, three words that had virtually destroyed her because she had believed them.

"Lia? Lia, listen to me now. Very carefully, listen. I want you to utilize your *adult* mind, to be able to utilize all the things that you have ever learned, all the education and experience, all the

The Healing of Lia

things you have learned here in therapy. Take them all now, and look, see this little child sitting on the rug looking up at the woman screaming at her. *See it now!* Tell me what you see."

". . . so helpless . . . there's nothing she can do to protect herself . . . if she just had someone to . . . care for her . . . protect."

"Lia, did she find a way to protect herself?"

"She could protect herself . . . she did . . . if she was really crazy? If she *really is* just like Ava . . . she could . . ."

"Is she really *just like* Ava, Lia? Go back now, see in your mind what you just said, the special thing you just told me . . . now!"

"I said . . . I—Oh, God! I said I *am* Ava! I said I *am Ava!*"

By damn, she found it!

We made it! All the weeks of work, all the hours of sitting with my backbone complaining, my bottom feeling flat and numb, pushing, pulling, pleading for her to take me to this minute! We had made it and I felt skyrockets going off in myself! She had done it; we had done it! Now, calm down! We might have reached the top of the mountain, but we still had a long way down. It was time to begin the trip home.

"That's *exactly* what you did say, Lia! Now it's important for you to understand that you incorporated the behavior of Aunt Ava into your inner self. What you have done is to take a portion of the personality and give it the name "Aunt Ava." The thing for you to know right now, as of this moment is you no longer have to be sick! You no longer need this illness as a means of protection. You can give it up. . . ."

". . . you mean . . . I don't have to be sick any more?"

"That's right, Lia! You don't have to be sick, not any longer! You can be well, happy, and live life to the fullest in every respect."

As I said this there was a flooding of tears, and she added, "I'm not crying because I'm hurting or unhappy! I'm crying because I'm so happy! I'm so happy that I don't have to be sick. I always believed that I had to be sick. It was the only life I knew."

"Lia, it was not the life you expected, but it was a life that became your only alternative. You accepted a suggestion in your subconscious mind and have lived to fulfill the prophecy. It's time to let Aunt Ava go. You don't need her; she only encumbered your life, caused you problems. Do you think that now you can safely allow that portion of your personality to just slide away, and get on with living a happy, normal life?"

"I want to! I really want to. Oh, I really do want to. Thank you for telling me that I do not have to be sick."

After the session had ended, I sat and pondered what had occurred. Her statement, "Thank you for telling me that I do not have to be sick," kept ringing through my head. She had been given final suggestions that day that she could accept a future of health and happiness. There could be a bright future for her if she could place the past in the past. Yet something was worrying me. "I don't have to be sick." Was it all that easy?

Too easy? Now that was a ridiculous thought. What in blue blazes had been easy about it? Lisa had suffered, lost weight, and, though she left with a smile, looked like an alcoholic on the morning after. There had been nothing easy about it. I could not accept that Ava was that easily disposed of, nor could I accept that all the bizarre activity was in a neat package now labeled "The Past." She had said she wanted to, not that she could, or would. The next few days or weeks would let me know.

The Healing of Lia

21

It had been a week since I had last seen Lia and we had identified the aberrant personality. I felt that the session had gone very well, and I'd been looking forward to her return, hoping that I might be able to see how she had integrated this new information into her life. When she did return, however, she began to talk of a problem which had not been discussed with me before. She stated this problem as some form of dyslexia or word amnesia. Apparently she had experienced it in the past, but it was becoming more and more visible with time. One problem she was encountering was with reading. She was having difficulty controlling her scan of words and retention of what she read. A second problem area was her inability to write entire words correctly. When writing she would leave off one or two letters, sometimes whole prefixes, and more often reverse the order of letters in the word.

In the past it had been a sometime thing, but in the past few days it was happening whenever she read or wrote anything. This had the effect of making her feel that she was losing her memory. More and more she felt an urgency to write everything down, feeling that otherwise she would lose it.

As Lia spoke, I pondered what she said and how it might fit in with what had been uncovered. I had the impression that while the dyslexia might not be a new event in her life, it had only intensified since her last session with me. Was this dyslexia related to the Ava personality? I wanted to know, but first I needed more information about the personality split and how it had worked in Lia's life. I soon found, when I began to question

Lia about this, that she definitely did not want to discuss it; she wanted to talk of her "new" difficulties.

It would have been easy not to raise questions here and to kid myself into thinking that one "easy" dueling session had solved all the problems! I knew better than to convince myself that this was true or possible.

I asked Lia if she would be willing to enter hypnosis and discuss the situation, and she was most agreeable. She was given the induction signal and allowed to drift quietly into her trance. Once this was accomplished, I asked her to allow her mind to go free and to come to rest at a time and place where she was most at peace and relaxed. Very rarely do I find it necessary for me to find where this place may be. This is the patient's very own "hideaway" and I do not need to intrude on that territory.

After she had properly relaxed herself, I asked her to allow a new visual effect to come into her mind. She would still remain in her comfortable domain but could visualize as I asked her to do.

"Lia, as you relax peacefully, let's now talk of the new problem. It may not be a new problem to you, but I have not been aware of it before. It is very important to you. It has to be important for you, since you have chosen this particular time to tell me of it. Does this new problem have anything to do with the work we did last week?"

And out came a simple little phrase: "It has nothing to do with her." Her? Assuming Lia meant the Ava personality, I missed the voice inflection and the meaning and just continued. But not for long.

"*Damnit!* You do not understand!" The angry, abrasive tone took me right off the seat of my chair. I understood that I surely did *not* understand!

"What? What is it, Lia? What don't I understand?"

When she spoke, the voice (whose voice, I was now wondering) was quiet, controlled, devoid of the anger that had just seconds before been flung at me. I knew that I was dealing with a shifting, but somehow the voice in the last reply seemed— different. Different in tone, timbre, in ways that caused the hairs to stand up on my arms. After a pause she continued.

The Healing of Lia

"It really has nothing to do with you. I realize that you're doing all that you can to help all of us." *All of us?* What was this "all of us?" Suddenly I was shocked into the realization that there well might be more than two sides to Lia's subconscious. I had a "definite" on Ava, but who was this calm mystery lady who reminded me of—what? Not sure if I should approach and force a confrontation or let it evolve on its own, I decided to do the latter.

"Lia," (by now I wasn't too sure it *was* Lia I was speaking to) "the Ava part of you has served many useful purposes in your life—she was there to protect you for the most part—would it be possible for Ava to come out, to speak with me now?"

"*Please*, Dr. Ward! Don't complicate things. Lia will tell you anything you want to know." There was that prim, ladylike voice again.

"*Lia* will tell me? If I am not to speak with Ava, may I ask who I am talking with now?" I have to admit I wasn't too sure I was ready to know.

"Well, of course! I try to keep Lia's life in . . . order . . . she has had so much to endure! So many conflicts . . . people . . . the Church . . . the Church has always been her friend! And how she stood out in school! She writes so . . . well . . . don't you agree?"

Well, whoever I was chatting with was friendly enough to ask my opinion. So, as casually as I could, I put a question to her: "Yes, definitely. But tell me something—about the writing of Lia's I have in my chart. It's interesting that she's never mentioned it to me, but I think she does know that I have the dream —the one written in two distinct scripts. Can you tell me about that?"

". . . better go. It is getting . . . so crowded, very crowded."

Crowded? I suppose I let some desperation slide into my voice. "No! Don't go, please! Stay, tell me about the dream, help me know what I need to know. . . ."

"What . . . do you need to know?"

Feeling like a punctured balloon, I knew from the wispy, questioning tone that it was Lia herself speaking—I had lost the other. It is difficult enough to carry on a conversation with three different people when you can see them and know who they are, but in this case I didn't even have a name for one of them! Feeling a bit silly I asked, "Lia, is that you?"

"Of course it's me!" This, followed by a mischievous laugh that—in the weeks to come—I would find was the true, main core of Lia. There was no time in the therapy situation to put my queries down fast enough. I knew I had lost someone who was quick and clever enough not to identify who she might be. Who? Why was she there? In time, before I had answers to any of my own questions, I was hard put to catch the voice-identities before they slipped away again. One (Ava) used curses; one (?) used her calm voice in a very familiar and controlled manner. Reminiscent of what? Shortly, when I did find out, I batted my head. Of course! I should have guessed! But for the minute here I was, sitting, watching Lia waiting in the chair for me to continue.

"Are you ready to tell me what is going on, Lia? Where is Ava? What part of you was just speaking with me? I was not aware there was another. . . ."

"Another? No other . . . there's no one. . . ."

I decided to let it go for the present. We'd move right into the dream.

"Okay, Lia. Now, a few weeks ago Paul brought me a dream you had written. In it you said you must tell me the truth. About 'her.' And written at the bottom of the page were words in a heavy script—not like your other writing. It said that if you did tell, she would kill you. Is the 'her' in the dream Ava?"

". . . not sure . . . she comes out . . . controls everything . . . felt threatened by you. Please . . . no more . . . no other in me . . . felt so much better last. . . ."

Trying to explain to Lia that I did not know if there were other personalities present was a very arduous task for me. At times it is very easy for the clinician to forget that he is talking with someone who may not understand all of the language and phraseology that he may use. I am quite sure at this point that I did not make myself completely clear to her, because there was tremendous apprehension and fear in her voice. Some months ago I heard an astute clinician make the statement that in handling a multiple personality, one must always be careful not to

The Healing of Lia

theatrically bring about more personalities than were already present. This clinician cited a case in which the physician had created such a rapport with the patient that the patient accommodated him each week by bringing in a new personality just to please him! I certainly wanted to avoid anything that could smack of this type of directive on my part.

My decision at this point was to work with Lia in generalities about her illness over a period of years and draw out more instances when the Ava personality was prominent. I hoped that at some time during this, if there were one or more other personalities present, they would emerge in some form and be dealt with at that time. If another personality did not emerge, it may be as satisfactory to ignore it. As to assessment of strength of one personality against another, I was sure that the Ava personality was the strongest in abhorrence of any that were present. If there were others, I had the feeling that they were relatively minor and/or very weak.

As I was sitting contemplating just what avenue to approach in Lia's treatment at this point, I suddenly had an escape for all my concerns. She had been lying in the chair completely quiet for some time, seemingly resting, and there had been no verbal interchange between us for many minutes. When she began to talk I recognized that this was not Lia Farrelli talking, but one of the alterations. It did not take very long for me to recognize that the Ava personality had emerged once again, though it was more an intonation in the voice than the usual display of marked hatred and anger.

"Safe! Always wanting safety! Her own Weakness—Sickness —that mushy attitude makes it easier and easier for me—she's so stupid . . . trying to keep me from doing what I have to do! I do it to *protect* her! And that Paul! What does he do for her? I hate him! . . . and she has to be punished, too . . . she does whatever he *wants* her to do and I *won't have it!*"

All this anger from Ava, in order to "protect" Lia? But before I had a chance to interject a word she took up her assault again.

". . . and he doesn't seem to be able to separate the two of us —why can't he *look* and *see* that I am quite different?"

I jumped in here with, "I thought that an agreement had been reached between Lia and me that you would not be necessary any longer—can you tell me why it is necessary for you to remain? Could we talk about that part for awhile?" I was ignored by the voice that was emanating from Lia. Angry, cursing, it was not about to let me gain control. Finally, putting as much aggression into my voice as I could, I told her in plain words that I was not going to recognize or respond to her unless she would answer my questions.

"Oh, yes, you will! You *will* hear what I have to say!" The voice was touched with anger, but underneath you could also hear desperation. The desperation became more prominent.

"*Damn you!* You are just like all men! A bunch of pious superior-thinking sons of bitches! All just alike! Her husband, the doctors, and *you!*"

Silently I sat listening to the bombardment until the content narrowed and became simply a repetition of unhinged words. Still I gave no response, and finally she ended with a matter-of-fact statement that seemed to end our relationship right there. "Well, sir! If you are not *there* then I am not *here.*"

I sat for a short interval watching the prone figure in the chair before I asked, "Can you hear me, Lia?"

". . . yes . . . I can hear . . . you. So uncomfortable. . . ."

Well, I thought, at least I know I have her back.

"Lia, I've been taking a few shots from the Ava side. I want you to be able now to come in contact with all the things that were said during that time—to hear exactly how this change took place and to be able to put it all in perspective."

". . . she does not like to be controlled . . . but what she . . . said . . . I have these thoughts sometimes but . . . could never say them . . . I'm so tired . . . explaining . . . feeling guilty . . . always explaining. Dr. Ling. . . ."

"Yes," I asked after a moment. "What about Dr. Ling, Lia?"

". . . could never tell him how it was . . . he kept saying how grand I looked . . . felt so guilty . . . humiliated. And then I would be out on the sidewalk . . . with nothing . . . nothing but the pills. . . ."

In a hazed, dreamy way Lia related how she began to take notebooks of questions with her to ask Dr. Ling. Her attention span had shortened so since the shock therapy that if diverted even for a moment she completely forgot what she had meant to

The Healing of Lia

ask him. I listened while she related how he always impressed upon her how "lucky" she was that Paul was so understanding and had not left her because of her illness. This evoked some small anger in her.

". . . lucky? I don't leave Paul when he gets sick! Why would Dr. Ling even say that to me?"

"All right, Lia. I know you are angry. Let's get back to Ava now. Relax and tell me more about Ava."

". . . Ava . . . is woven into my life . . . hurts . . . then *runs!* . . . she would go to Dr. Ling's office instead of me . . . he never did know . . . I didn't really know myself until . . . sometimes Dr. Ling would talk about our last visit and . . . I couldn't understand what he was even talking about. . . ."

"But you know now, don't you, Lia? You understand about Ava now?"

". . . yes, but . . . but I thought . . . she was gone . . . and now you say she just . . ."

I could understand Lia's fear, and admit that I would have been happier if Ava had just stayed "away." The important issue now was to calm Lia's fears and proceed with the therapy.

"Lia, you have made tremendous progress in dealing with the Ava side of your life. You recognize why she was there, why she was so useful to you in the past. It is only natural that some defenses would be thrown up around this personality—and great hesitation in totally eradicating her. Relax now, let these fears just slide away. You understand so much more than you did before. . . ." Here I waited a few moments to let her slip into a deeper state before we proceeded. In a short while the breathing deepened and we were ready, but before I could say anything, she began to speak in short, disjointed words.

". . . two . . . two women in . . . me. One is gentle . . . hopes . . . but other comes . . . on dark days . . . destroys all . . . hates . . . hates God! . . . curses . . . so much stronger than. . . ."

Here it was! This was the break that I had been hoping for! But could I get a true identification of this second aberration? Was Lia ready to give me the information? I was now very emotional and think I amused one of my assistants as my excitement mounted. "Now, Lia, you say there is a second woman within you. Fine. Now tell me about that woman. Just relax and let everything come flowing forth from you. You are able to handle this information, you have a keen interest in it, and the deepest part of your subconscious mind wants to identify once and for all just who this is."

". . . not sure . . . so much confusion . . . crowding. This calm . . . one . . . guides me. Sometimes when the strong . . . one fades I . . . have a sense of . . . calm . . . only want to be closer with my God again. . . ."

"Good, Lia. She guides you and helps you feel calm. When does she do this for you?"

". . . bad times. Last year . . . in the bad times when . . . people asked me what . . . what had happened to me . . . looked different . . . I felt so . . . humiliated but . . . then very calm . . . when Paul and I had bad . . . fights . . . bruises all over . . . my jaw hurt . . . didn't want to live. . . ."

Here she began to slip into the old hurts. She was most definitely in touch with the old times.

"Yes, that was one of the bad times. That was a hurtful time for you, Lia, but it is a time that has passed. It is all in the past. You are safe now. You are safe and not hurting. Tell me about the calm person who helps you."

". . . hurt so much but . . . then was protected by . . . very calm . . . protected like I was a little baby, a child . . . so nice . . . good . . . I wanted to be good . . . to do good things for . . . everyone."

"Is there a feeling within you, Lia, that you must always bear the brunt of what is taking place in life whether it's a problem situation or a service to be performed? Is there a part of you that feels that service and goodness come before all other things?"

The reply that came was a shock to me, and yet I knew this was what I had been waiting for for the last hour. A very calm, reassured, confident voice started, "I think I can answer that better than Lia can, Doctor Ward. When I became a part of Lia she was a very little girl. You see, there was no one who cared for her, no one who actually loved her. I saw her goodness. I felt that if I could mold her in some way, have some part in shaping this child, then I would have fulfilled certain—of my duties in life. She needed encouragement to do so many things to suc-

The Healing of Lia

ceed, and to enjoy some of the better things in life. But . . . she
. . . she was never able to understand the doctrine of the Church
and accept it for what it really is! Most of her problems were
really the doings of that other one! I was only here to help her! I
tried too hard to keep good and beauty within. . . ."

Somehow this lady rather depressed me instead of impressing
me. I felt affronted that her sense of "rightness" for Lia had been
decided when Lia had been "only a very little girl." So many
things had been decided in the mind of this little girl far before
she had the ability to make beneficial judgments for herself. And
I began to wonder if this calm, beneficent woman had not, in
her own way, been as destructive to the child as had angry,
violent Ava. I put a question to her.

"Is it just possible that by your insistence that she keep good
and beauty in her life, new pressures were applied? Pressures
which actually created problems for her rather than alleviating
problems for her?"

"I don't feel that that is a fair assessment of the situation at
all, doctor! You just do not understand how the Church works
—nor what it means to be a good Catholic!"

"Perhaps I do understand more than you know. But why
don't you just tell me how you feel about it? Was Lia ever a good
Catholic? Or Paul?" I had little nits of anger in me as I put the
question to her.

"Paul has always tried to be a good Catholic. This is one of
the things that Lia has never been able to understand! The fact
is that we do have to repent for our sins. . . ."

"It seems to me that you are actually setting up a situation in
which *you* have proclaimed Lia to be guilty! That *you* decided
she has to repent and be punished for her sins! Is this a fair
assessment of what has been transpiring? And before you answer
I would like to make it clear that I feel that this is exactly what
has happened, and what I have discussed with Lia in the past.
She did exactly this: found herself guilty, found the necessity for
repentance, and then proceeded to carry out the execution of
her own sentence! Were you the one who brought this about
and set it into motion?"

"Doctor, you simply do not understand and . . . it is better if
. . . I must go now. . . ."

Go? Decidedly angry at this person now, I let more of my feelings come into my voice than most likely was wise to do. "You have no right to pronounce guilt on Lia!" but too late, she was quiet.

There was no response at all from this personality. After a long period of silence, probably not as long as I felt it to be, I realized I was very frustrated, mainly at myself for not being able to draw out this personality, at least to encourage identification. But part of my frustration was due to the fact that I felt—knew —that I should have recognized and been able to identify her myself for some reason. She reminded me of, and here I was drawing a blank. Suddenly Lia began to speak, and my focus of attention moved again from introspection to the person in the chair.

What exuded from Lia's body was easily recognizable as Ava. The venomous tongue lashed out, "I can tell you exactly who it is, doctor, it's that goddamned nun!

Nun? Nun? And then the light turned on. Nun. Teacher. Of course! Prim, precise modulation of voice; all the qualities I had unconsciously noted in the voice were clearly reminiscent of some of my own teachers from grade-school days. Nun! And then I remembered the questions I had asked myself during the weeks of the word-association testing. Why would Lia, a married woman with three children and five pregnancies behind her, answer "I still am" in response to the word "virgin"? At the time I might have smiled, but I wasn't smiling now. I was beginning to know something. Not the why or the who, but at least something!

Before I could ask Ava anything at all, Lia sighed and breathed out, " . . . so tired . . . nobody knows how tired . . . Paul . . . he tried but . . . can't help me . . . doesn't mean to hurt . . ."

"Doesn't mean! How stupid can she be? He means it, all right! Just like the rest of his fucking family . . . their main joy in life is crushing other people. Imagine all those years!—*Praying* for me to get out of her head! I am the only strong thing in her head! He will pay for every miserable thing that he did to her. I don't have to touch him, but I will destroy her through him. That prissy, clean thing, I'll get her a taste of last year, and

The Healing of Lia

she won't be able to crawl back to her precious Paul! I am getting stronger all the time!"

I waited momentarily, seeing that still another shifting was taking place. Lia was obviously in great distress, great pain now.

". . . Lord, please help me, the drugs keep all of this away, at least for a time. Please, Lord, help me to keep everything calm, quiet, and under control and I will serve you."

There was a battle taking place here among all three personalities, and I felt that it was time for me to intercede and try to bring some reality into the situation.

"Ava, you are not getting stronger all the time! You are getting weaker! This is why you seem so very desperate now. You know that you are getting weaker! Your functioning, which has been so needed in the past, is now diminishing. Lia is able now to take care of herself. She had no need of you!"

Not waiting for a reply from Ava, I addressed Lia directly, hoping she could hear and understand me.

"Lia, do you see it? Do you see that Ava can go away now? That you can let her go?"

". . . Ava go? . . . Yes . . . bad . . . but other? Sister . . . Ann? . . ."

Sister Ann. Lia had once mentioned her to me as her only friend in grade school. The one who had treated her like a "real person." Sister Ann! In a journal entry, Lia had written:

I feel so safe on Mondays. It is so quiet. Running around in my head or brain are the words, "Neatness counts, Lia. Neatness! Nice round ovals!" I tried so hard to please them by holding the pen correctly and working very . . . Sister Ann used to always say, "Neatness and precision, Lia, your script is really you, you know! It tells them what kind of person you really are!" I loved her so very much. Why, now, is she so much in my memory? Lately whenever I pick up my pen I can almost feel her adjusting the angle on the paper to the proper slant.

She introduced me to the beautiful world of books (my only enduring friends), and to poetry! How proud she was, always, of what I wrote for her! It was for her, and she cared deeply. She reached out into that crowd of children and took my hand and told me I was very "special." Why, now, does she stand here beside me just as clear as a spring day? I can even smell the starch in her wimple, see her poor hand with the ringfinger missing, and feel the pride I felt when she gave me the religion prize in fifth grade. I knew it all by rote—all the answers—and it seemed beautiful, then. With her beside me it had been beautiful, but then I had to go home and I would lose it somehow.

I had a base now from which to work. But it was one thing for me to realize what had taken place in Lia's mind when she was a small child and another to get her not only to realize it but to feel secure enough to let it all go. Since she was remarkably open to suggestion (a prime cause for her problem in the first place), I began to deepen her trance state to increase this suggestibility.

"Lia, what life is really about is the capacity to take care of yourself and make your own decisions. Sister Ann has been your way of retreating into the past in order not to feel hurt and abandoned. She has been your way of returning into childhood, but instead of escaping hurt, she has actually caused hurt. Now, you are going to allow both of these personalities to fade. You can be responsible for yourself, stand up for yourself, and profess yourself to your God in your own way. Now I want your mind to be completely at rest. I want you to relax and accept all the suggestions about the control of your own life and your abilities to handle situations of the future."

What ensued from this point was a markedly cooperative Lia who seemed to absorb readily that she could put into the past her need to be a child and her need to allow the secondary personalities within her to take care of her. It was very hard to assess what lasting effects had taken place during this session, but somehow I felt that I had not heard the last of the alterations.

The Healing of Lia

Some six weeks after her departure, Katie **22** returned. At home it was a time of rejoicing and celebration. All the heartaches and pains were soon forgotten; the fact that she was safe and sound over-shadowed everything else.

As Lia looks back, Katie's return was the first time that either Paul or Lia had really listened to what their eldest daughter was saying in a long, long time.

Looking at Katie, I am immediately taken by her beauty. The olive dark of her Mediterranean ancestry could classify her as a gypsy beauty. Her eyes are large and deep. For her to be some-what the vagabond seems only natural. Escape had to come into Katie's life.

The necessity for this escape was taken to heart by Lia, and she immediately launched into another trip on the guilt express. Being the oldest, Katie was met with very high expectations and given the full reign of responsibilities. During the years when Lia was so very ill, much of the routine at home had to be supervised by Katie. All too often Lia felt the family was not responsive to her problems and the chronic nature of her illness. When she had "good days" and was functioning, the girls were so happy they willingly allowed her to fill the mother role completely. When Lia went through a very bad time in her therapy feeling all was lost again, she ran from her treatment with me. Katie ran also. Lia's latest regression seemed to tip the scales for Katie, and Katie had to remove herself from that atmosphere.

One of the plagues that had faced Katie all her years was of being a *normal* child. Being normal in such an abnormal envi-ronment gave her a feeling of being ephemeral. What was today may not be tomorrow. She had observed the pendular life of her mother, which had gone into another swing just prior to her "running away." Her father had remained steady but in an untouching, distant fashion. And to totally confuse her, both younger sisters were gifted children. In Katie's eyes, this was the norm. Lia had been functioning on a college level when she was in her high school, and so had each of the younger children. It would be a very delicate matter for her to keep everyone's perspective in equilibrium. Katie only knew that her position was equivocal at best.

Paul and Lia began to plan for the education of their children quite early in their married life. Education became something of a god to Lia. She could see how having to discontinue college had affected the course of Paul's life. A man who had such abilities in math and science was frequently reduced to doing manual labor. So much of what was no longer a part of Lia's life, she felt, was due to not being exposed to thinkers and artists.

Lia promised herself that her daughters would have complete educational opportunities, as she and Paul had not. There would be the funds, though she had no idea how. There was another surprise for this couple who were trying so desperately to simply hold their lives and minds together. The two youngest girls were placed in accelerated programs for gifted children.

Although funds were available for many of the programs, many hundreds of dollars would have to be provided for travel to and from summer schools, for advanced texts, for outside materials for experiments, and so forth. It seemed as though every time Paul moved he was asked for ten, twenty, a hundred dollars for this, for that. Being frustrated at not being able to always supply these funds led Paul to strike out in a misdirected fashion: fighting against Lia's homage to learning.

Slowly, over a period of time, Katie began to feel more and more like a stranger in this household. Conversations seemed to revolve around the latest need or accomplishment of her two siblings. Though she functioned as an above-average student, she gradually accepted the idea that she was far inadequate. Her parents seemed so occupied with the others, they accepted her accomplishments as normal. The fissure dividing normal from gifted grew into a chasm.

The Healing of Lia

Unable to function as she felt she should, Katie felt trapped and stifled. She felt she was making her frustrations and feelings known, but no one seemed to hear. Many weeks had gone into the planning of her escape. She was confused because she had no malice toward her parents and did not want to hurt them; she simply had a growing need to be out from under the competition. Playing in a ballgame is fine, but a little leaguer has scant chance against the pros.

Once Katie was away, the stark realization of her actions hit. She had managed to get to Chicago and find a close friend who had moved there years before. Almost immediately she was taken with how much her friend had changed, how difficult it would be to find a job that would provide just the necessities of life, how lonely it can be though surrounded by tens of thousands of human bodies.

This young woman grew mightily in a short six weeks. With that growth came the determination to return home and persist until she was able to show her family her needs, and discover what she wanted to do with her life. With this new fortitude and persistence, Lia was awakened and able to understand Katie's needs.

It had now been a little over three months **23** since Lia began therapy with me. She had reported during the past few weeks that she had noticed appreciable differences. Generally she was more relaxed and able to cope with day-to-day problems in a more confident manner. Still, there had been days when she was very fearful and nontrusting, yet she was just not sure what it was she was fearful of or about.

As Lia was leaving after her last visit, she had told me she was still anguished. I had given her the suggestion that she would have some thoughts about these feelings and would be prepared to discuss them with me on her next visit.

When she arrived this day, she was obviously very tired and had not been sleeping well. She related that she had been having more difficulty with the swelling of her abdomen and had increasing pain in the lower portions of her "stomach." She was noticeably paler. Though we had gone through a very hot summer, Lia had not gotten much in the way of a suntan. The puffiness about her eyes led me to feel not that she had just had a long bout of crying, but that physically she was quite unwell. Not wanting to fall into the error of treating only the "head" and of being unmindful of a real physical problem, I felt this possibility must be pursued. There was no question of there being a physical reaction within the body, just of whether that reaction had a psychological basis.

We met in the treatment room and she gave me a lovely smile, something she had been doing more and more. After a few minutes of idle chitchat, I asked how the week had gone for her. She replied that it had been very difficult for her, particularly the past couple of days. Quickly she added that she now knew that I had been right when I had told her I was sure we would have to do more work in relationship to the rape or to Oilcan Harry. During the week she had had recurrent thoughts about the rape, and with each episode she experienced accompanying rage and anger.

Evidence that the raging personality was still at work had been revealed by Lia in several instances. These rages were never as strong as in the past, but they were still there. Two weeks earlier, we had gotten the true identification of the Aunt Ava personality, and there had been a marked degree of release. This release had been associated with explosive emotion, but when asked if she could allow that segment of her subconscious to disappear, Lia had not been very convincing in her reply.

I informed her that it was now time to deal with this problem, once and for all. Her chair was reclined and I spoke with her for a few moments just to let her know that she was safe and that I was going to protect her throughout the session. She let the lines of tension ease from her face and I gave her the re-induction signal to enter into the hypnotic state. She quickly took herself to a very deep level of hypnosis, as I simply gave repetitive phraseology to aid her. It always amazes me that a patient can be so very tense and tied up with his emotions and when he goes into hypnosis, it all just seems to slide away. The muscles relax and the breathing smooths, and general peace takes over.

As soon as I felt Lia was deeply relaxed, I asked her to tell me about the thoughts or dreams she had been having during the past few days. Following these instructions to her, she began to have faster shallower respiration, and she said:

"I am kneeling in St. Boniface's Church early on this Monday morning and the rain outside is pounding on the roof. It's dark inside the church as only a dim candle is burning in the sanctuary. But there is no other light.

"I'm crying because I'm afraid, and I'm afraid because I know that he will be outside when I leave. And I don't know what to do. He has been turning up lately at many of the places where I make my weekly rounds; the grocery store on Thursday mornings at the square, and almost every time I am in church. I have begun to park a block away and around a corner, but still he finds me, and I am frightened by this.

"I sit down and begin to talk to my other person, my other self, who always seems to be calm, decisive, and less frightened than I. I say that I badly want the antique bronze sundial face but that I know he will not take money for it. My husband offered him money for it for my anniversary gift, but the offer was refused. 'Take it for a gift,' he insisted, but we both said we could not do that. He has made three unexpected visits to our home in the last few weeks, tinkering each time with the furnace and spending lots of time talking to Paul about fishing trips, the refinishing we do in our workshop on old furniture, and then having coffee or a lemonade in our kitchen before he goes on to other calls. He always uses the phone to call home and pick up his next call before going on. He is quite at home with us, as we are with him. It has been over fifteen years since he installed our first furnace, and he has made unquestioned emergency calls on days when no other service man would have come, Christmas and Thanksgiving included. I once referred to him to a neighbor as, 'Harry, the man who never lets you down,' and I can remember that he seemed strangely touched. But it was true, he never questioned the hour or day. He always seemed happy to get a call, even if it was a holiday for everyone else. And we liked him very much.

"I must have been in the church for an hour or more, and it is nine-thirty and I know that I must leave and run my errands. So I go to the door, and, not seeing any other cars, I put up my umbrella and leave. I walk in the driving rain around the corner, and there, standing beside my car, is Harry, smiling. He left the sundial the day before, and I found it on top of my washing machine when I came home from the market. Later he called and said that he would not take any money, but I might do him a favor and perhaps refinish an antique round oak table for him to square the deal. The table is not at his home, it is at his sister's home, and would I consider looking at it?

"Paul and I have been considering using the workshop refinishing to give me a little supplemental income, and so I thought that I might do this. But for some reason, I feel ill this morning.

The Healing of Lia

Ill, and frightened for no reason that I can explain. Except for a dim something in my head. I seem to feel that at some time . . . I don't remember when . . . Harry has tried to touch me, or kiss me, but no matter how I try to remember, it is just a dark spot in my mind. And I don't want anyone to know how frightened I am, or that I can't remember things. For two months I have been losing hours, and now often whole days, in my memory. I keep telling Paul that I don't remember things, and he is worried, but he doesn't know how much time I am losing. I really don't know, myself. But it is a lot."

At this point I interject, "All right, Lia, you are standing with Harry beside your car. Now what?"

"We stand by my car, and he asks if I have a few minutes to run by and take a look at the table. He is smiling, relaxed, and very natural. And I say, 'For a minute, Harry, but I have things to pick up at Southern Acres.' I don't have to pick up anything, and I don't know why I should tell such a lie.

"I have no memory of getting into my car or driving any-where, but in my dreams I am now standing on a porch of a strange house. I don't know where it is, but I remember a name, 'Mountaintop,' or 'Mountainside,' but I can't remember how I even got here. I feel wet, dripping from the rain and my own sweat, it's all running down my body because I feel so ill. And I try to remember just why I am here in the first place, and then I hear the calm one say, 'The oak table,' and I say, 'Oh, yes, of course.'

"The porch is empty because Harry has gone to open the back door of his sister's house. And then the door opens, and I can see in. It is a small sort of cottage, and separating the living room from the dining room and the hall is a sort of expandable baby-gate, behind which are two small dachshunds, yapping their little heads off.

"I do not step in but say to Harry, 'I am dripping wet, is there any place you can put my raincoat for me? It is soaking and I hate to stain the carpets.' And he answers, 'Yes, there is, we can put the coat over the rod in the bathroom and the umbrellas also, to let them drip.' In the dream it is so real that I can feel my clothes sticking to me, but I never go into the door because I feel that my head is splitting off, it hurts so badly."

Here was my lead and I felt I had to seize upon it, or again it would elude investigation.

"Now, Lia, you are standing on the porch. You are looking inside and you can see the interior of the house. You can see the two dachshunds, yelping behind their gate. You seem to have an inner fear, a fear that you can't really explain, because you trust Harry. He has been a family friend for years and a helper in your home. Yet you know that it is this man you fear. You are standing on the porch, and he has invited you in to hang up your coat, but you say you don't go in. What do you do now, Lia?"

Lia became very restless at this point, and her respiration rate increased. Evidently there was a great deal swirling through her mind. I repeated the final question over three times, and with exertion, she replied, "I don't do *anything*, I just *stand* there. I don't know! I don't know! I stand there. The whole thing is so bad, my head is splitting. My head is splitting off!"

I decided to join in here with her terminology and pry, "Your head is splitting off, Lia. What is splitting off? What is splitting? What is happening as this splitting is taking place?"

"It's the calm one who is now taking over. She says for me not to be silly, that it is perfectly all right to go in. After all, I have known Harry for years. It's just to go look at the table! What in the world could possibly happen just by looking at a *silly old table?* But I don't *want* to go in there . . . I don't want to go in there, *the pain is getting so bad. I don't want to go in there!*"

A secondary personality was becoming stronger and was beginning to take a more dominant role. I was pretty sure this was the Ava personality. It sure as hell did not seem logical that it would be Sister Ann. "Ava" was in a position to accomplish two things: she would be striking out at Paul, and, secondly, she could be a free-spirited self which Lia could never be.

Whichever personality I was dealing with, it was not about to provide me with too much information. Again I had the feeling we were about to reach a stalemate, so I decided to push harder to get some long awaited answers. I wanted to help her find out why the Ava side was still persisting.

"What are you feeling right at this moment, Lia? You can face it. You have become so much stronger during the past few weeks, you can face it. What are you doing now, Lia? Are you still on the porch?"

"I'm inside, but it is all so confusing." There was a very long pause here. My patience was getting pretty thin, and just as I was about to intervene again came a cry. "Oh! No! No! No! No, please, No . . . don't do that . . . don't look at me that way . . . don't get so close to me . . . What do you think you are doing . . . What are you doing . . . please . . . You should not do this to me . . . You are our friend . . . for God's sake . . . please . . . oh, my God . . . Please don't . . . You're hurting me . . . [there is pronounced fear in her voice and she is sobbing with every breath] . . . *You're hurting me* . . . [coughs and coughs, then finally a piercing scream] . . . I can't breathe . . . what is he doing? Oh, my God, no, not that . . . Oh, Mary, Mother of God, not that . . . No, that is so wrong . . . please!"

"What is happening, Lia? What is he doing to you?"

"He is sitting on my chest! It is so hard, so hard for me to breathe. His weight is crushing me. Oh no . . . Oh, my God, no . . . [Periodically I would intervene, and ask a question by repeating her last statement and then adding, "Now what?"] It's right there in front of me! He is sitting on my chest. It's right there in front of me. It's so horrible. It smells so horrible. Of oil. That horrible, sickening oily smell. I try to turn my head away. He is holding me . . . I can't move . . . *ugh.* . . . It's so horrible . . . my arms are held behind me . . . I can't move. . . . He is angry now . . . he says, 'You can take it in this end or in the other end! It don't make no difference to me.!' He tells me to shut up or he will shut me up . . . nobody will believe me anyway, he says. Now his hand is over my mouth. It is getting harder and harder to breathe. . . . Everything is fading in and out."

During all this, Lia exhibited a mass of contorted features. Her head was constantly twisting from side to side. At first the perspiration came in even beads over her forehead and gradually became more profuse, so that it was in continuous streams down her face. Horror was etched into her face; as her brow was tightly knit. When she was talking of having her arms held and saying she could not move, her arms were tight by her sides, and though she seemed to be struggling, the arms remained immobile.

Repeatedly now she was stating that things seemed to be fading in and out. It was getting more and more difficult for her to breathe. Whether or not she was having oxygen deprivation from the hand being held over her mouth, there is no way of knowing. If so, this may explain the fade in and out, but I felt this was a fading of one personality and the takeover of another.

"It hurts so badly . . . *aghhhhhhh* . . . *it's there* . . . so badly . . . my hands are asleep, they are not there . . . I want to go home . . . I want to go home. . . . Mother, please let me go . . . please let me go. . . . I'll be good if you will let me go. . . . *please let me go* [very high-pitched screams here] . . . *get off of me* . . . *get off of me* . . . *Paul, get off of me* . . . *you are hurting me* . . . Paul . . . please get off. . . ." Then there was sudden silence.

After the short period of silence, I was just about to intercede when Lia began again. This time, when she spoke, it was in the third person.

"He's on her . . . I'm okay. . . . He is sitting on her . . . he is telling her that she can take it in that end or the other. . . . He says that she has a choice . . . but she is fighting him. She is really fighting him. The bad things that she is saying. . . . They are not nice things that she is saying to him. Oh, my, he is pulling her legs apart. . . . Now he is doing it. . . . He is hurting her . . . she can't move anymore. . . ."

"What is she saying to him, Lia?" I interjected.

"It is hard to hear what is being said, that man is saying such vile things about her and her body. But he is talking about how she has changed, how she is a real little cat now, with lots of fight. She is screaming things at him, cursing at him. She's calling him a no-good bastard. He is like all men, they just want women for one reason. . . . They don't really care if they hurt or kill you, just so they get what they want. Nobody really cares if they hurt you or not. Even her mother hurt her all of her life. Now she is calling him by a different name. She is calling him Paul. She says that Paul has never paid any attention to what she has had to do or anything else. He just pays attention to her in bed. Now she is limp. It is all over. He is just dripping his oily sweat all over her. But she is at peace now. It is all over."

There was a very pronounced change in Lia, which came on

very suddenly, in less time than it took for me to scratch some notes and to look back at her. She had a horrible scowl on her face, but even more noticeable was that her profuse perspiration had stopped. It had stopped, but not before her clothes were completely drenched. When she spoke, it was in a very rapid, high-pitched voice, which I had heard before. It was the same voice that I had heard in short segments in the delivery room sequence and during the spontaneous abreaction to the rape in the third week of therapy.

"I'm in the car. . . . What am I doing in a car? . . . I can't drive. I have never driven a car . . . no I can't drive . . . I have never driven . . . walk and go to the telegraph office . . . have to walk to the telegraph office . . . have to open it . . . it is my job . . . not many men around any more . . . we only have to do our jobs . . . with this war . . . all the men are just about gone . . . we all have to do our jobs . . . have to walk to work . . . have to open up the telegraph office . . . just walk down the road a mile . . . that's all I have to walk, just about a mile down the road . . . then I am there . . . everything has to be ready . . . these days we have to have everything ready . . . lots of important messages might come any time . . . they might come in early today . . . have to get everything ready. . . .

"Well, I'm here at last. That didn't take so long to get here. Now just get the key out. [A sudden angry scream, and lots of hate showing on her face.] They have been here again! God-damn them! They have been here again! Why do they want to torment me? . . . got that horrible stuff all over my hands again . . . it smells so terrible. Why do they do this to me? . . . Got to get it off of me . . . so bad . . . I'd like to get them just one time, but no, they come in the night. I'd like to take each one of them that rub this cow shit on my doorknob, and rub their fucking faces in it! Who are they? I have to get the telegrams and messages in and out . . . I have to deliver the telegrams. . . . It is so much to do . . . have to get the addresses straight. . . . There are lots of messages and telegrams because of the war. . . . There are those bad ones about who has been killed, and they know that I have to deliver . . . deliver the death. . . . All the telegrams have to be sorted into the correct addresses. . . . It is so far to get some of them delivered . . . but they tell me I have to do it. . . . Can't stand here with the shit all over my hands. . . . It smells so bad . . . there is so much that has to be done! The war . . . so much death. . . . I'd like to kill those bastards who put this stuff on my doorknob . . . why are they doing this to me? I'll get even with them . . . I'll get even with the whole crowd.

"*I just can't do it all. I just can't do it all!* But there . . . there is something . . . it scares me, threatens me. Mama is always after me. Ava do this! Ava do that! She is always there to haunt me. Why does she push me so? What I have to do is to fight! That's what I have to do, I have to fight. Mama is always after me. She is just like the rest of them. She is just like the boys and their shit. Why can't she leave me alone . . . just alone? It is so much to have to do . . . have to get all the telegrams out.

"Mama, why won't you leave me alone? I have to do this, Mama! You just won't leave me alone. It won't hurt, Mama. It won't hurt you, not the way that you have hurt me all this time. The knife won't hurt you the way that you have hurt me. I know now that I destroy anything that threatens me . . . *can't trust anyone.* . . . No, can't trust anyone. Ava will destroy anyone who threatens me!

"Now they are coming to take me away. . . . Why are they taking me away? What did I do? It was they who did it, they did it all. Where are they going to take me? I am not sick. Why do they keep saying that I'm sick? It is them that is sick. *Not me!*"

Again, there seemed to be a transformation in both the appearance of Lia and in her voice. As she spoke now, it was in her usual tone but in the third person.

"Lia, what has happened? What year is it?"

"It is all so very confusing. She was there with Harry, and then everything is sort of jumbled after that. Aunt Ava got into the picture, and it was back in 1918, during the war. Aunt Ava worked for the telegraph company, and she seemed very happy. Everyone was sort of surprised that she could do the job, but she seemed to manage. They gave her more and more to do, and it got to the point that she had difficulty in keeping up with the job. There was a group of young boys who used to torment her all the time. They would call her names and taunt her . . . call her Crazy Ava, and things like that.

The Healing of Lia

"After a while, it seemed that Ava had more and more problems. Then came that horrible night when my grandmother awakened from a deep sleep to find Aunt Ava standing over her bed. Ava had a large butcher knife in her hand, which she was about to plunge into her mother. Grandmother managed to get away, but after that they sent Aunt Ava away to the state hospital and she has been locked away ever since."

It was my feeling that it was now time to help Lia integrate what was happening in her life.

"Now, Lia, I want you to look in your mind's eye. I want you to see just why Aunt Ava has not really been locked up all these years. I want you to see why she was there today and why she came there on the day of the rape with Harry. Why does she live in your mind still?"

Lia responded calmly, "She had to be there, she had to be here with me. Mama had said that I was just like her. Crazy, just like her! People have called me crazy all my life. Just like they called Aunt Ava crazy."

"No, Lia," I retorted. "Why does she still reside with you? Why can't you let her go?"

"Because. Because. Because she is my protector. She can do things that I can't do. She can protect me. She really is crazy, so she can strike back! She doesn't have to be always nice. She doesn't have to be quiet. She can do whatever she likes, and no one will dare do anything about it! If they do, she will take care of them. Oh, how I wish she had taken care of her mother, then she could have taken care of mine, also. Then I would not have been hurt so much."

It was very important that Lia understand just why Ava had played such a prominent role in the rape. I wanted her to realize that she was cross-connecting many things in her mind.

"Lia, do you recall, just shortly before now, that Ava was fighting off Harry and then she began to call him Paul? Is it not possible that this was a display of anger toward Paul? You have felt so many times that you would like to strike out at Paul, but did not dare do so. Paul, at times, you felt, only needed you sexually. Therefore, each time that Paul would 'take you' in such a way, did you perhaps see this as a form of rape?"

"There were many times when it was like a rape because I did not want it and there did not seem to be love coming from him. It was not making love."

"Was it easier for an Aunt Ava to strike out than for a Lia or a Sister Ann to do so?"

"Oh, my goodness! Sister Ann would never do a thing like that! She would never think of such a thing."

"Lia, you accepted the idea when you were only four years old that you were just like your Aunt Ava, and each time you heard it over the ensuing years, it became more and more of a reality for you. Now, I want you to see just how some other incidents in your life have been acted out just as Ava may have done them."

With this, I instructed Lia to consider several happenings in her life which were typical of a "crazy person."

This seemed to be producing very little reaction for Lia. Then, to my surprise, she shouted, "Oh, yes! The knife! The knife! Ava had tried to kill Grandmother with a *knife*, and that is how she got sent away to the hospital. And I tried to use a knife also! When Gina had been taunting me, and I was so very frustrated with her and with the feeling that I could not cope with the situation any longer. I picked up a knife and threw it at her and if that damned swinging door had not caught it, I would have stabbed her in the back."

"That's right, Lia. Now I want you to see another time when you had the same or a similar feeling."

"Mama, it was with Mama. We were at the kitchen table and she was constantly on me and would not stop. I picked up a butcher knife and lunged toward her."

What had occurred that day was almost a total re-enactment of Ava's reaction to her mother. When she had lunged at her mother with the knife it was the Ava self who was in control. Interestingly, Mama must have realized she had extended her luck just a shade too far. Unknown to Lia, she had made a very simple dress and placed it on Lia's bed without any comment. Apparently Mama did not have the capacity to vocalize, "I'm sorry."

"If you were Ava, then you could protect yourself. All of this became so twisted in your subconscious, it was as though you had built a fort of protection for yourself. Yet, there was also a

The Healing of Lia

counter-protection. Lia, as you continued to be Ava, with time it was almost like a prophecy. You were 'put away,' just as Ava was sent to the state hospital. Not once but twice.

"Being confined to the psychiatric wards did accomplish certain things for you. We have discussed your not wanting to grow up and accept responsibility for yourself. In the hospital you were not only protected from the outside world, which you found so threatening, but your every need was taken care of. If you continue to be Ava, and literally fulfill the 'crazies' image, you will have someone to take care of you all the rest of your days. However, right now you are going to begin to realize the joy that is within you. You begin to feel the urge to live. To live life to the fullest. You once told me you wanted so much to go about your life as others seemed to go about theirs. That is within your grasp now, Lia. The idea that you cannot take care of yourself seems to fade into the past. Each and every day a new confidence seems to well up in you and to multiply, growing stronger and stronger each and every day."

Positive suggestions had to be added now just as rapidly as I could put them together. Frequently I would repeat myself as I was doing this—the least of my worries. The suggestions must be repeated many times, so to go over the same material at this point was perfectly all right and served a useful purpose.

Once more I dropped back to the beginning of her problems. I wanted her to have continuity to her history. I spoke with as much *enthusiasm in my voice as I could muster.* As the past hour had gone on, it was more and more difficult for me to overcome my exhaustion, to sound enthusiastic.

"Lia, it is going to be all right! You are going to continue to heal and to grow emotionally each and every day. It is important for you to realize that your problem began many years ago, long before you could be expected to think for yourself, much less decipher what was happening in your life.

"When you were born, you felt as though you were not wanted and that you should not have come into this world. It was with this initial suggestion that you began your life of torment. The days of sadness and rejection started, and in your mind they never stopped. You may have been a difficult child, most children who have the feeling that they are unwanted are difficult people to live with. This probably compounded the neglect you sustained.

"The days before you started school were a continuation of crying to be seen and loved. The crying apparently was seen by your mother as only a further nuisance from a child she considered ugly. Finally, one day in a fit of anger toward you, she dealt the blow, 'This child is just like Ava!' That was the beginning of the true downfall of Lia. You were old enough to have heard and to have understood certain words that made you realize you were different. As a child, you may have interpreted aspects of this information incorrectly, but over the years it was repeated enough so that there is no doubt as to the origin of the suggestions.

"*To be like a crazy woman, you also must be crazy.* There had been so much anger in this house, it may well have been that you became the scapegoat for your mother's frustrations. If only you could have caught some nuance of love and latched onto this, it could have been a totally different Lia I met many years later.

"We knew that you tested highly in school. From what we know of education today, you were probably bored stiff. Within the rigid atmosphere of the parochial school, discipline became a problem. There was only one person who seemed to have faith in you and to be able to communicate love to you, and she was Sister Ann. She encouraged you and helped you through many of the daily tribulations.

"It is little wonder that you would want to incorporate Sister Ann into your life. She was all the things that you felt were good. She was a nun and therefore was holy. This meant that she was good, and you had been told that you needed to be good, *so you literally became Sister Ann!* You have related that, at times, it was as though she were guiding your hand as you wrote. I am sure at other times it was as though she were guiding your emotions. It was fine for her to be an inspiration for you. But for her to be intertwined into your own personality was detrimental to you. It was the Sister Ann in you who would step out and cause you to suppress rather than to defend yourself. You accepted the fact that you were a bad person, and from what you had been taught, bad people go to hell. Therefore, you subconsciously

The Healing of Lia

reasoned, if you are a nun, you don't go to hell. You are one chosen by God.

"A very simple but beautiful illustration of your thinking as Sister Ann was demonstrated on the word association test. When I gave you the word 'virgin,' you rapidly and without hesitation replied, 'I still am.' Naturally, as a nun you would be a virgin and would not participate in that 'sinful' and trouble-making act of intercourse. If sexuality were involved, it would be time for the good, calm Sister Ann to recede and the aggressive Ava to come forth. Ava could do these things, and Lia would not be responsible.

"Ann did cause other difficulties, as a nun must always be a good Catholic. Even in the face of adversity, when it was going to be a painful experience, you gave in to the strong teaching of the Church. If one is an obedient nun, there is no question of the right or supremacy of the Church.

"Lia, I have here one of the many notes you have written to me since you have been in therapy. I want to read this particular one to you now. I want you to listen and to realize just how powerful that obedience has been. This is what you wrote:

Dr. Ward,
I have discovered something in myself. It may not have any importance, but it is there and I find it interesting.

I always obey rules. Even when I do not have to. When no one else is looking or seeing or even caring. When it is ridiculous because the rule is ridiculous. When nobody else is obeying, I obey.

I follow *to the letter* each rule as it enters my life. Church rules. Driving rules. Household rules. Rules on boxes of detergents. Rules in cookbooks. Unwritten rules. Written rules.

I would never dream of disobeying or even deviating from a rule in the slightest degree. I have some sort of terrible belief (fear, really) that by breaking a rule, I have broken something sacred and that the punishment will be severe and immediate.

"Do you see now, Lia, for you as Sister Ann, there could be *no breaking of the rules*, and you recognized this? This undying belief was there, and it ruled certain periods of time that you have called life. But that really is not life. That is existence. God does not mean for anyone to live in constant fear. He teaches us love, and not fear. So now, I want you to let all of these fears go away. I want you to realize that no matter what you have done or have not done, you have suffered enough for a dozen lifetimes.

"I'm sure you learned many things from Sister Ann, many things that were good and useful to you at the time that she taught you. However, many of these things have outlived their usefulness to you, just as have many suggestions that you received from others. Also, it is so easy for a child's mind not to comprehend and therefore twist directions or instructions."

"Sister Ann was a person who loved you very much, Lia. But now is the time to let her go, along with Aunt Ava. It is time to let them both go and just be Lia, the Lia who is strong enough to take care of herself, the Lia who is good. You see, Lia, each of these personalities served a purpose for you. Now you can take the part of each personality that is necessary for you to feel secure and incorporate it as an integral part of the whole Lia.

"What I want you to do right now is to take from Sister Ann the general goodness of her as a nun and recognize that you can be worthy and good. I want you to give to her that portion of you that has felt unworthy and evil. Realize, Lia, that she can handle that evilness, she can deal with it, and give it up to her Lord. By accepting from her the good qualities that you have struggled so long to attain, you can begin to see yourself as deserving and reputable.

"There is also to be an exchange with Aunt Ava. You are to allow her to take with her the hostilities and angers that you have felt it necessary to hold within yourself for years. You can allow her to take them, and as you do you will absorb from her the abilities that you will use to protect yourself in so many circumstances of life. By doing this you will no longer need Aunt Ava to reside within Lia. In dealing with Paul you will champion your own cause. No longer will it be encumbent upon you to defend yourself by striking out at Paul, but you will be ever ready to do whatever may be vital at any moment to guard your own self-image.

"You have been so very good in your life that you were willing to punish yourself for the questionable sins you may have committed. That, Lia, was your only real sin. To take over the province of God, to play the part of God, to do His work. It is His job, and His job only to decide if we have sinned, and if we have, He decides the punishment. But above all, He is a forgiving God.

"It is time to send all remnants of Aunt Ava back to Lofton State Hospital. If you have feelings of anger, you will be able to express this anger in a calm and rational manner. If it is necessary to be more emphatic, then you will be able to be just that. You can stand alone. You can stand as a healthy woman, no longer Lia the little girl, but one who is mature and therefore able to control her life."

As I had been talking, Lia had been motionless, in a very deep state of hypnosis, except for the little jerks from her quiet sobs. It was as though she were hearing words that were almost foreign, as though she were hearing a new language for the first time. Presently, she slowly and softly spoke through her sobs.

"You mean, I can completely let both of them go? That they are ready to leave? That I am alone? That I am completely alone within my own body?"

"Yes, Lia, you can now be completely alone. The total integration of the personalities has taken place. You have seen why they developed originally, and you have worked to take the characteristics of each that will help you in your future life. You have expelled with them the traits of Lia that were no longer needed and those which you now find cumbersome and irritating."

With that statement, she broke into a big smile, which was rapidly followed by the first actual laughter that I had ever heard from Lia. I had heard laughter before, but it was always the high-pitched shrill of Ava.

There was one other factor I wanted to check out with Lia before I reinforced the dismissal of the two altered personalities. It was necessary for me to get permission from Lia for this to occur. When I inquired if it would be all right with her for Ava and Ann to leave, she responded with an emphatic, "*Yes!*" Then I reassured her over and over that she was now alone and that these two personalities were gone forever. When she had calmed down and after I had asked her if she was ready to be awakened, if there was any further work that she felt she needed to do, she was brought to the "waking state."

When this session was completed, I had to let Lia remain in the chair for a while. She was visibly shaken, but at the same time there was a new radiance about her. As she stood to check her "sea-legs," I was shocked by what I saw. On both of her wrists were large bruises, just as though someone had been tightly holding her wrists or as though they had been bound for a long period of time. When I pointed this out to Lia, she did not seem to be surprised. She told me she had noticed a similar occurrence on one occasion when she had had a dream about the rape. No matter how I examined the wrists, what I was witnessing was simply incredible! I almost wanted to doubt what I was seeing, but there was no denying that the bruises had not been there when the session had started, yet no one could deny seeing them now. They were there! I would not pretend to give Lia an explanation of what had occurred or how the bruises got there. I could not explain it then, and I do not feel any more capable of explaining it now.

It had been quite a day. Long. Straining. Laborious. I was very glad that I had arranged for Lia to come in for this visit during my lunch hour. In the back of my mind I felt it was going to be a loud and anguishing period of time, and I did not want any other patients to be present in the office. Lia has stated that she is a noisy lover. I had learned that she frequently was a noisy patient as well. Not only had it been hard for Lia and me, but one of my office assistants had heard all of the crying and screaming. She came to investigate and had heard a part of the regression involving Ava. She had become very upset to see Lia in such torment and was very much relieved when she saw Lia smiling so happily. It was a relief and a day of happiness for the entire office staff.

Before Lia left that day we talked for a while about just what all of this meant to her life now. She actually talked more confidently and continued to laugh. I did not and do not know what Lia's life holds for her, but I do know that she is now free to live that life. It would be necessary for me to reinforce her positive suggestions a couple of times; however, this could be done at her leisure. In fact, I felt that she could do this herself through self-hypnosis, which is exactly what she did do. She was seen just twice to renew the suggestions, and then she took over complete control of her life.

Her parting comment this day was, "I have looked thoroughly

The Healing of Lia

through my closet. All those long gowns, hostess dresses, long skirts. I, who never go anywhere, never go out to dress up really beautifully, I who count the pennies twice before I buy even the necessities. I have never been able to remember where they all came from, or when. They have been hanging there, neatly in the closet, waiting for what? Well, maybe they have been waiting for me. Instead of me finding a new wardrobe, the wardrobe will find a new me!"

The session was over. As I walked to the door with Lia that afternoon and said good-bye, I must admit to feeling a certain amount of trepidation. As I placed my arm about her tiny waist to escort her down the hall, I felt good, but she was still so frail that I wondered how she would fare "out there."

No one knows better than the physician that facing the world *outside* the door to the doctor's office is the hardest job for the patient. No matter how bad the pain of therapy (not only for Lia, but for me, too!), Lia had to return to her own world now, and it was the same world she had left just a few hours ago. The same problems awaited her, the same people, the same hurts. Only she had changed—not the world. Now, only time would tell if she had completely accepted the suggestions and could summon the strengths she would need to endure. My job—perhaps the *hardest* part of my job—would be to wait and see how she would react to her new life. In actuality, it is not a new life; her responses to the old life would be new.

I am not so rash as to believe that Lia, or any patient, is automatically "cured" just because I told her so! It would be great if this were true, but it is simply not the way it works. The patient is cured only when *he* believes it is so and even then empirical reality offers many painful stresses that test endurance to frightening limits.

The Lia who left my office that day was something every physician is happy, even proud to see; someone who had needed help and, though it had been a painful process, had found it in his office. I have a feeling I probably had a pretty silly grin on my face that day. My parting remark to Lia was to go out and treat herself to a new dress—which she did. Even though she had that closet full of clothes she could not remember ever wearing, a new dress is an item of importance for most women. Later

263

she told me she spent four hours walking her legs off shopping for it, proving one thing: obedience is still her hallmark!

Later, Lia recorded in her journal her reactions to this session. Without doubt, this reaffirms my feelings about the value and success of hypnotherapy. It is one thing to agree to everything the doctor says in his office, to nod and say, "Yes, I believe, I know," but what Lia recorded shows the depth of thought absorption, the value of rethinking when the glow is fading and there is no one there to support you and hold your hand. This, then, is what Lia told her journal—and that is the *important thing*—it is what *she* believed, not just what I *told* her was so:

I came home . . . floated, drifted! Home! And it was as if I was having one enormous orgasm in my soul. I can't ever, ever remember feeling so euphoric! Then I was so sleepy and so I napped for almost three hours and had the oddest dream.

I was seated at my desk at the office and a very handsome man came in . . . but I cannot recall any of his features, which is strange . . . he said, "Hello, Lia, I'm Dr. Ward," and of course he was because of the voice, and I replied, "Certainly you are . . . the man who never was there at all." "Perhaps I can now help you, may I?" He stared at me and I stared at him and then he just drifted away.

I have the strangest feeling of both loving him and despising him. For no particular reason at all! What do I know today that I didn't know before?

If one thinks of negative things it feeds and nourishes them, giving them life. As they grow stronger, you grow weaker.

Whatever we believe to be true about ourselves today, tomorrow we become. That much is certain.

People who take you down must be cut out of your life! Anyone who makes you feel less of a person is a danger to you. For with a knifelike tongue he can cut and wound a part of you which, being hidden, may never heal.

Doctors do not heal. Drugs do not heal. Hospitals do not heal. They aid, help, give rest and sometimes comfort, but they do not heal! Love heals. Only that. It's that simple.

Why do people turn their faces to the wall and die? (The world says, "There was no reason, no cause for the death.") They may have had food, drink, shelter, money, power . . . and more. But the person who

The Healing of Lia

feels loved, really loved, would *never* will away his life. They could not have felt loved. It's that simple. *They may have been loved . . . but they never felt loved.* Therein lies the difference.

Feelings count. This proves it. At the marriage encounter, Paul and I were taught, "Feelings are neither *right* nor *wrong* . . . they just are!"

I never really understood it then. But now I see the way we feel about ourselves, others, and our life in general, is the determining factor as to whether we live or just "put in time" here.

When others become our life, we will surely lose it. No matter how we love another, letting him become our whole reason for living will eventually destroy us.

Sickness of the mind or emotions, when not of a physical cause, comes invariably from the sickness of the soul, the "self," if you'd rather. That word is so damned important it should be tattooed on our chest. *Self!*

If love is the thing to heal the human condition and human love is withdrawn, held back, imperfectly given . . . then what do we do? Where do we go? To God? But how? We who have screamed curses and words of hate . . . who reject the "organized" way of communing with him? We who, for some unknown reason, carry our hurts, our wounds around in a sack, bound to our backs, with cords that cut and chafe but never loosen.

Was he right, the priest who told me, "Accept it, Lia. Stop running, stop fighting. Acceptance. Endurance. Meekness"? Will the karma be finished then? For I believe in that. A pattern; a planning for me. I was not just dumped here, given "free will" and left to fend for myself.

I knew none of this before. Did Dr. Ward do this for me? Then I just learned without knowing I was learning.

24

That last day in therapy was not my final good-bye to Lia. Some six months later I was called by a gynecological surgeon, Dr. Billdon. He asked in a very matter-of-fact tone, "Fred, sometime ago you saw a woman by the name of Lia Farrelli. Do you by any chance remember her?"

"*Remember her!* Oh, if you only knew how well I remember her."

As I sat listening for the next few minutes and Dr. Billdon was telling me of her most recent difficulty, my mind was racing back over Lia's weeks in my office. When he got to the final problem, so much of what Lia and I had talked about during our first visit together was recapped in one short moment.

"Fred, she's got a mass of some sort in her pelvis. I have been watching it for a few weeks, and it's definitely persistently getting larger. As a matter of fact it's reached the point now where it's making sexual intercourse next to impossible."

All the talk between Lia and me relative to the "bad times" when penetration was impossible had not served to stem the tide of growth for this mass. Yet Dr. Billdon had zeroed in on wording that duplicated Lia's language. Obviously, Paul was still being shut out. I'd hoped Lia's progress would lead to better communication in all realms, but it seems that was not the case.

Dr. Billdon relayed that he was not about to put the cold steel to this woman's abdomen until I saw her and gave the okay, even though he felt there was a chance the mass was cancerous. He added as he was signing off, "She certainly does have a long history. How are you going to handle her?" I fully admit I was

The Healing of Lia

not happy with the prospect of Lia facing another surgery, especially at this point in her life. She was just beginning to *live*. How in God's name was I to tell her now to accept that she might die?

Lia had been admitted to one of our local hospitals and had had all the preliminary work-up, including X rays, multiple blood studies, and so forth. Nothing was giving a definite answer as to what the mass could be. Not having had time enough to regain her normal weight since therapy, and with continued problems at home, she had an aura of chronic illness about her. Since she also had a large hard mass in her abdomen, I was not surprised when I saw on her chart, "Admitting Diagnosis: Probable carcinoma of the right ovary."

After going through the chart, which within a few days was quite voluminous, I got to the recorded history; it was all neatly (for a physician's writing, that is) on one and one-half pages. I had to laugh when I thought back to my chart with page after page of shorthand, squiggles, and swirls. There was one particular entry that focused my attention. "Though she has had a long history of mental illness, I feel there is no doubt that this is a real physical problem. . . ." Whenever there is a history of emotional problems, I'm afraid we tend to file all the complaints of such a patient under the heading of "psychosomatic."

When I went in to see Lia she was resting in a semi-private room with the privacy curtain drawn around her. It was about six-thirty on a wintery day, and the room was in total darkness. Even when I turned on the lights, the blue of the wall covering seemed to blend in with the mood of Lia. She was the pale, drawn woman I had met many months before.

When she had identified me in the darkness, she became emotional. With the light now on, I could see the tears well in her eyes and begin to flow over her thin cheeks. Rapidly she began to talk about ten different things at once. What Dr. Billdon had said, how she felt, and more painfully what Paul had said.

Attempting to bring a little levity into our meeting, I told her if she was going to bounce off the walls as she was doing, I would have to have her transferred to a rubber room.

She replied, "A few weeks ago I would have fought you over

those words, but now so much has come back. And if this really is cancer then. . . ."

"Look, Lia, we have not come this far for me to lose you to cancer, if that's what it is, so let's just take it one step at a time."

Lia was sitting up in bed Buddha fashion to allow room for her swollen abdomen. As she talked, Lia looked only at the bed. "Dr. Ward, Paul and I have discussed this thing over and over. He says that we must pray that it will be all right."

"That's fine, Lia. But praying alone is not going to solve this problem. You must have the surgery and get a proper diagnosis."

Lia added, "Oh, we agree about that. Paul has become quite resigned and, I believe, at peace over the situation. He says that if it is cancer, then it is just because of our sins."

With that I came out of my chair and was pacing the floor, angry words pouring from my mouth. I haven't the foggiest notion what I said. Lia has told me that some of it was not too nice. Knowing her as I do, if she puts it that way, I probably sounded more like I was at a men's smoker.

So it was all right back at square one as far as Lia and Paul were concerned. Lia had asked, "Paul, why must there be all this suffering?" And Paul told his wife the logic of suffering once again. There is suffering because it is a redemption for our sins. We all must suffer, but in this case it was suffering involving womanhood. All of this goes back to the original sin brought about by Eve in the Garden of Eden. Therefore, women must continue to suffer for that act. In Lia's case it was even more poignant because she had been so willing to accept the blame for their sexual guilt and for having had the hysterectomy.

Fortunately, I had finished my visit with Lia before Paul came to see her. I suppose he did come, though I did not see him until over a year after he visited my office at the time of Lia's therapy. Had he been there that night I probably would have been a heap on the floor by the time I spoke my mind and he had finished with me.

After I had expounded on and on, I wondered which of us needed a little hypnotic relaxation the most at this point. Reminding myself that Lia was going to have surgery in about twelve hours, I yielded to her. As always, she was able to drop into a very relaxed state in a few short minutes.

The Healing of Lia

Suggestions were given for her well being, faith, and reaction to surgery. More important, she was given the suggestion that she would accept the anesthesia with calm assurance and awaken refreshed and alert. Her recovery would be quick, and health would return as never before. We chatted pleasantly in a light vein after her trance was terminated. She was smiling and talking in a positive manner as I said good night.

On my way home from the hospital and on through the night I could not get Lia out of my mind. I wondered if what I had said to her was so much bullwash. The suggestions had been worded carefully so as not to rule out any possibility of carcinoma but to say we would take each problem as it arose. However, I was worried; several months had elapsed since she was first aware of a swelling in her abdomen, and now it was growing very rapidly. Tomorrow would tell.

Early the next morning, I was at the hospital and changed into a scrub suit even before Dr. Billdon and his assistant, Dr. King, arrived. When Dr. Billdon did appear, he said in his usual calm manner, "Okay, gentlemen, let's see what the hell we've got."

Standing at the head of the table looking down, I watched the surgically scarred abdomen being transformed into an abstract canvas of burnt umber as the Betadine sponges prepped the skin. In a very short time the four deft hands had the abdominal cavity open.

Although Dr. Billdon's face was covered by his surgical mask, I could sense his broad grin as his hand first entered the cavity.

"It's a cyst, Fred. By damn, it's a cyst."

Such music rang in my ear as Dr. Billdon was able to deliver the swollen cystic mass through the surgical incision. While doing this he commented it was just like a Caesarian section.

I added, "Well, maybe Lia figured if she had one more baby, God would finally forgive her." As I spoke all eyes turned toward me with a great question reflected in their expressions. This was not the place nor would it ever be the time to try to explain how deeply that sentence told the story of Lia's suffering. I left the operating room smiling.

That's the story. A story that Lia was concerned had no definite ending. To this comment I replied, "Lia, there is no ending

—that is the epilogue itself. Yesterday is history and is recorded in books, just as we are doing. Tomorrow is fantasy land, and there is nothing that we can do about it, nor is there value in trying to predict the future. There is only today. We must live each day as it comes. There is never a true ending to life . . . it goes on day by day."

For Lia, just as for the rest of us, it still does.

The Healing of Lia

Epilogue

Now that it is done, all the terrible writing, remembering, telling, I want to erase it and re-do it. I should like to tell the story of Lia, of her mother who loved her and who was all the lovely things a mother should be. And tell of a happy family, devoted, close, loving. But that would be a made-up story of a Lia who never existed.

In reading this many people may feel a faint unrest, wondering perhaps if they are this person or that person. Dr. Ward and I have worked very hard in disguising any description, any fact that might have been even faintly recognizable, while staying as close to the truth as possible. The people I want most to read this and understand why it happened and how badly it hurt will never recognize themselves because of our efforts to protect their privacy.

Where has my therapy brought me? What changes has it brought into my life? Many and few; some painful, some easy, some obscure, and some clear. And none at all that are perhaps obvious to anyone other than myself.

My new found wisdom, so diligently fought for, has given me the insight to realize, as do most of the newly wise, that I have a lot more to learn.

Change! This word which I absorbed from Dr. Ward in therapy, really meant learn—and I did. I have learned.

I have learned that what any of us take for empirical reality is, of course, our reality. What we see, what we feel, what we sense. Imagine walking to a street corner and seeing a man shot to death across the way. We have seen it, therefore it is true. But what we have not seen and have no way of knowing is that a movie camera is hidden behind a window and that it is all just a staged act, a sham, a piece of realistic playacting! How much of the World Out There is reality? And how far do I want to go into it to find the answer?

I am learning to conquer fear. I know this because recently when I drove out onto a main road I discovered that directly behind me was a truck—and the driver was Oilcan Harry. I was on my way to the bus stop to pick up Lori after her classes. Upon clearly seeing the face in my rearview mirror, I knew that if I let panic rule me then, it would be my master forever. I remember breathing, "God, please . . . " and no other words. Then I saw my Lori waving, smiling, and I pulled to the side and opened the door. When I next looked the truck was not in sight and the fear had gone. I knew that prayer had done what I could not have done alone.

Change! I have learned that I had prayed when I didn't know it was praying. When the words were curses screamed in unintelligible animal mewlings. That even then God understood and loved me when no one else did or could.

Change! I have learned that while there may not be perfect constancy in human love, it is enough to sustain us until we reach the place where we will find it. That it is enough to give love—but that strangely enough as we move out in a larger circle to make a life that is ours, the ones we love ask to join the circle.

Though I, as all women, was cloned from Adam's rib, I was meant to be a part but never a counterpart or duplicate of my husband. I must look deeply into my new self and discipline this self so that she won't make the mistakes the other did. I must trust again but not so rashly as to be blind to danger—to love, but not to worship any human.

Learn! I did, even to see beauty in the pain of sickness. I learned that the Potter often pounds and smashes the clay of an imperfect vessel to form a better one.

I learned to look at my face and see not the ugliness, not the lines and scars of the past, but the lights of joy. When I come into a room and others turn to look at me, I no longer want to break and run thinking, "They will see how unbeautiful I am." They won't for a good reason: it's not true anymore.

Learn! I have learned that anything, if repeated enough, can become a part of us. I am using this truism to practice forgive-

The Healing of Lia

ness. Of all my changes, learning to forgive is without doubt the hardest. But if now I find it an effort to say "I forgive" of certain people, I believe that in time it will come as naturally as the breath from my body.

Change! I have learned that if I must cut certain people from my life, it must be for the right reason. Fear is no longer an acceptable reason. Negativity is.

It is a mistake to think that since I now understand my illness, others will also. As any longstanding illness creates a certain indifference in others, the very people we feel will be most happy for our recovery often react with surprising indifference. Not long ago when faced with the necessity of finally explaining my illness to my sister Dorrie, I discovered the dangers of opening oneself, but even this lesson became a learning tool.

I had received a chafing letter from my sister telling me in plain words of her impatience with me for failing in what she felt was a social "duty," and Paul encouraged me to tell my family just why I had not always been able to perform my "duties" as they felt I should. I received Dorrie's answer on a day I was scheduled to work with Dr. Ward on our manuscript. I believe that even he, who is daily reminded of the unforgiving attitude of the world toward the mentally ill, was at a loss to understand this letter, which in part said:

> People grow tired of hearing about a sickness that never seems to mend. Whatever you are—schizo or whatever—I feel that if you can't function in society as others do, you should remove yourself from society until you can.

When he had finished reading the letter, Dr. Ward was quiet and very gentle in his advice. As we sat in his office that evening, it was hard not to feel bitter. The one small, tearful outburst I allowed myself only caused him to lean forward and say, "Don't, Lia. Don't let it take you down to that." Of course, he was right. I had a decision to make: stand up or fall again. Well, I did not fall. I used my sister's advice, but in a way that perhaps she did not intend. I did not remove myself from the whole of society, only from her society, and this, not as a surrender but as a tactical maneuver to avoid the negative input of someone who was (temporarily) better armed than I. The past, that time of trying always to please, of being a victim to the standards others set for me is over.

This small knowledge is a quantum jump for me. To know that all the ones I have so feared are only humans and that they can no longer hurt me. To see people with new eyes: Paul's mother as only an old, sick woman who never learned to release her son to his chosen mate, and to pity her for the love she lost that I might have given her; to see Paul sadly, because he is unable to see this too. To pity him, also, for the years this cost both of us.

My mental metamorphosis is not yet complete. Only part of my head and body is free; my wings are not fully formed, not dried and ready for flight. I still feel rather gauzy and insubstantial and unsure of myself. I have not completely lost my fear of failing, but even this is good. For now I have greater understanding of what is meant by the adage, "Only those who scale the mountain get to see the view." The view from here is beautiful!

The Healing of Lia